AF600613

CONTROL AND RESISTANCE

Food Discourse in Franco Spain

Control and Resistance

Food Discourse in Franco Spain

LARA ANDERSON

UNIVERSITY OF TORONTO PRESS
Toronto Buffalo London

Toronto Buffalo London
utorontopress.com

ISBN 978-1-4875-0669-8 (cloth)
ISBN 978-1-4875-3468-4 (EPUB)
ISBN 978-1-4875-3467-7 (PDF)

Library and Archives Canada Cataloguing in Publication

Title: Control and resistance : food discourse in Franco Spain / Lara Anderson.
Names: Anderson, Lara, Ph. D., author.
Series: Toronto Iberic ; 52.
Description: Series statement: Toronto Iberic ; 52 | Includes bibliographical references and index.
Identifiers: Canadiana (print) 20190222131 | Canadiana (ebook) 20190222255 | ISBN 9781487506698 (cloth) | ISBN 9781487534677 (PDF) | ISBN 9781487534684 (EPUB)
Subjects: LCSH: Food writing – Political aspects – Spain – History – 20th century. | LCSH: Cookbooks – Political aspects – Spain – History – 20th century. | LCSH: Food – Political aspects – Spain – History – 20th century. | LCSH: Food habits – Political aspects – Spain – History – 20th century.
Classification: LCC TX723.5.S7 A54 2020 | DDC 641.594609/045 – dc23

This book has been published with the assistance of the University of Melbourne.

University of Toronto Press acknowledges the financial assistance to its publishing program of the Canada Council for the Arts and the Ontario Arts Council, an agency of the Government of Ontario.

Funded by the Government of Canada
Financé par le gouvernement du Canada

Contents

Acknowledgments

This monograph was made possible by the strong institutional support that I received from the University of Melbourne. I would like to acknowledge the generous assistance of the Faculty of Arts in particular, in the form of both research funding and study leave. I am also grateful to my head of school, Professor Lesley Stirling, for her support and collegiality.

Dr Meribah Rose has been an invaluable help to me at all stages of this project. I wish to sincerely thank her for all her wonderful work both as an astute reader and as an excellent copy editor. I also thank her for the translations she has done of all the quotes in Spanish. She, Professor John Hajek, and I wrote a conference paper on food and fascism in Italy and Spain, and I am grateful to both of them for this intellectually enriching exchange.

I am obliged to Professor Bob Davidson, Mark Thompson, and the production team at the University of Toronto Press. It has been a pleasure to work with such a professional and highly skilled publication team.

I would like to express my appreciation to colleagues and friends from the School of Languages and Linguistics at the University of Melbourne – in particular to Heather Benbow, who has supported this project through her treasured friendship, good humour, and sharp intellect. Many members of the school have joined me in collaborative research and teaching in food-related subjects, and I thank them for their enthusiasm and commitment to the ever-growing area of food studies. In writing this book, I have also benefited greatly from very rewarding exchanges with undergraduate students. I thank the 2016, 2018, and 2019 students of "Cooking Up the Nation."

My international colleagues are a constant source of inspiration, and I am grateful for both their friendship and their outstanding scholarship in the area of Spanish cultural studies and Hispanic food studies. Particular mention goes to Eugenia Afinoguénova, Jo Labanyi, Rebecca Ingram, Suzanne Dunai, Sandie Holguin, Carolyn Nadeau, Rosi Song, Leigh Mercer, and Maria Paz Moreno. Thanks so much for being so welcoming of your colleague from the far-flung Antipodes!

I greatly appreciate Christine Arkinstall for being so supportive of my research over the last two decades. The undergraduate course I took with her on Spanish feminism at the University of Auckland, NZ, ignited my passion for scholarly research, and her research continues to inspire my work.

My most heartfelt thanks to Rosa Maria Martinez Conde and Miguel Angel Bernabe and their families and friends for welcoming me, and more recently Irene, into their homes on the countless occasions I have been to Spain since my undergraduate days. Spain presents an integration of food and culture so seamless that the majority of occasions in Spain involve a meal or the sharing of food, and I am immensely lucky to have been included in their family meals. Rosa and Miguel have been a great source of support for nearly three decades! When, during my post-graduate studies, my father died, it was their care and encouragement that gave me the strength to finish my master's thesis with the necessary grades to obtain a doctoral scholarship.

Bernice Anderson was also a great source of support during this time, and I am so pleased to have her as an aunt. As well as welcoming me into her house for some months when my father and her beloved brother died, she took it upon herself to make sure my thesis – which I was writing in the midst of intense grief – was up to scratch. This involved her going off on her own accord to study up on nineteenth-century Spain's notoriously complicated political system to make sure I hadn't made any errors. True to form, she made some much-needed corrections!

I also want to acknowledge my dear sister, Francene Anderson. She is such a beloved aunt for my children, and I thank her from the bottom of my heart for everything she does for all of us. Although Granddad Ted is not here with us in person, she does everything with them that he would have done.

Finally, my wonderful children – Irene, Vincent, and Jeremy – deserve a special mention for bringing me such happiness. I dedicate this book to them.

CONTROL AND RESISTANCE

Food Discourse in Franco Spain

Introduction

Food is a potent yet understudied site of control for authoritarian regimes. The analysis of food is important for the insights it provides not just into the material and everyday conditions of life under dictatorship, but also into subjectivity.[1] *Control and Resistance* investigates how food, through its connection to both everyday life and subjectivity, offers a site for the authoritarian state to introduce and enforce its hegemonic notions of citizens' participation in national life. These pages bring together and examine instructions and advice about food issued by political leaders, government officials, teachers, food writers, and medical professionals in Franco's Spain (1939–59), investigating how this body of instruction not only influenced ideas about food but also controlled other aspects of identity, such as gender and nationalism and, conversely, how disruptive food discourse and food practices allowed for the possibility of "not being governed quite so much" (Mayes 10).

Questions surrounding food's materiality come up a lot in research about food, so I want to clarify from the outset that I am not writing here about food as a material object, or about what people ate. Rather, I look at food discourse – or as one scholar describes it, "the talk of food" (Parkhurst Ferguson, *Word of Mouth* xxi). It is important not to lose sight of the fact that what people write and say about food is as significant as what they actually ingest.[2] As Priscilla Parkhurst Ferguson reminds us, food discourse is universal to all cultures, given that "in every culture people talk and write about food" (*Word of Mouth* xvii). Indeed, if the material object of food is valued for the way it becomes part of us, then food discourse should be seen as equally important for the role it plays in the "creation of [our] social worlds" (*Word of Mouth* xvii) or in the construction of our national culture (see Elias).

Although my focus is on food discourse produced during a period of authoritarian nationalism, there are myriad examples from the time of nineteenth-century nation building to present-day Spain that illustrate that food discourse more often than not transcends food; that is, that textual, visual, and media representations of food do not just instruct us in the right way to eat or think about food, they also teach us the right way to think about our identity. In the case of Spain, one of the most enduring and polemic features of Spanish food discourse has been the link between the "talk of food" and the question of what it means to be Spanish. Indeed, from the nineteenth century to the present day, Spain's centralist, authoritarian, and peripheral nationalist movements have all used food discourse to impose or construct their often-competing ideas of national identity.

A relatively recent example can be found in the food served at Felipe VI and Letizia Ortiz's wedding banquet in 2004. The then future monarchs' decision to serve a mix of wine and food from all of Spain's regions, described as typical of Spain's "gastronomía clásica española" (classical Spanish gastronomy; Hola),[3] evinces a clear appreciation of the symbolic value of food. In offering up food from every region of the country – presented under the umbrella term "Spanish gastronomy" – the newlyweds declared their intention to serve all these same regions. They also, significantly, used the occasion of their wedding to reinforce the belief inherent to centralist Spanish nationalism that the category of Spanishness – or in this case, Spanish gastronomy – is the greater whole in relation to Spain's different regional cuisines. The descriptions of the wedding menu in the press, social media, and television coverage are constitutive of food discourse, and this discourse does not just aim to create ways of viewing Spanish food culture; it also attempts to influence thinking about Spanish national identity.

A decade later, at the first banquet Felipe and Letizia hosted as incoming monarchs, they gave a special nod to Catalonia. In the lead-up to the polemic independence debate that has divided much of the country, the new monarchs requested not only a menu showcasing traditional Spanish cuisine but also one that gave pride of place to "cava catalana" (Catalan cava) instead of "el champán habitual de este tipo de ceremonias" (the champagne typical of this type of ceremony; Negre). The special place reserved for cava at this state ceremony was clearly meant to reassure Catalans of their influential position within the Spanish state compared to other, less visible regions of the Iberian Peninsula. A number of scholars have argued that cuisine is often more instrumental to the spread of politics or nationalism than political addresses or ratified documents (see Hiroko; Siegel; Vester). The importance placed on serving the right food and drink at the royal wedding and the later official banquet certainly evinces this, demonstrating an awareness amongst

Spain's ruling class of the power of food to influence support for the monarchy and centralist Spanish nationalism.

Harnessing the political potential of food or food discourse is of particular importance at times of social, political, and economic change (see Elias; Parkhurst Ferguson, *Accounting for Taste*; Vester). This monograph posits that food discourse was an integral part of the social order at the heart of Franco's "New Spain," a monumental transformation of the social and political fabric of Spanish society. Through food texts Spaniards were instructed in their place in a highly gendered, ultranationalist, and economically and culturally autarkic Spain.[4] Food instructions, preparation procedures, domestic manuals, descriptions of meals in literature and the media, images of dishes, accounts of national or regional food habits, and information about food in official reports and domestic magazines made explicit to Spaniards what was expected of them in a totalitarian and ultra-conservative Spain.

Although I write here primarily about official or hegemonic food discourse, I also provide examples of food discourse that was disruptive – either implicitly or explicitly – of official ideology. Food studies scholars argue that more attention needs to be paid to the multiple ways in which food functions as a form of resistance, with some going as far as to argue that hegemonic power and resistance go hand in hand (see Avieli; Vester). One aim of this book, then, is to contribute to this research via a focus on food discourse as a site of both control and resistance within Francoist Spain. Another aim of this work, given how peripheral Spain has been to food studies until recently, is to further solidify the place of Iberian Peninsula and Peninsularist voices in this field of inquiry.[5]

Since a number of my primary texts are cookbooks and gastronomic texts, this monograph – in addition to its primary aim of shedding light on the axis between food discourse, Francoist ideology, control, and resistance – also offers a history of Spanish food writing during two critical decades of the twentieth century. Because food writing has been marginal in the academy, there is still much to document in terms of Spain's corpus of cookbooks and gastronomic texts. One of the most comprehensive texts about Spanish food writing is María del Carmen Simón Palmer's *Bibliografía de la gastronomía y la alimentación en España* (Bibliography of gastronomy and food in Spain), which provides an inventory of all of the food texts published in Spain from the sixteenth to the twentieth century. This exhaustive bibliography proved to be an invaluable resource as I identified main themes or ideas in the food writing of the first two decades of the Franco regime. It enabled me to draw conclusions about the importance during this time not just of women's cookbooks, but also of texts that spoke to autarky and culinary regionalism/nationalism.

While Simón Palmer's bibliography helped enormously with my selection of texts, the nature of her study does not allow for any discursive history of Spanish food writing. Nor does it provide any analysis of the discourse defining Spanish culture that we can find in most of the food texts she lists. A number of scholars offer, to differing degrees, this sort of analysis. These include María Paz Moreno in *De la página al plato: El libro de cocina en España* (From the page to the plate: A book of Spanish cooking) and Manuel Martínez Llopis in *Historia de la gastronomía española* (A history of Spanish gastronomy). Moreno's monograph has been particularly useful for her assertion about the broader value of cookbooks: "La premisa fundamental de estas páginas es que un libro de cocina no es solo un libro de cocina. Más allá de su funcionalidad, toda receta nos habla del mundo cultural en que surge ... Un recetario es, como cualquier otro texto, hijo de su tiempo" (The fundamental premise of these pages is that a cookbook is not only a cookbook. Beyond its functionality, every recipe speaks to us of the cultural world from which it emerges ... A recipe book is, as is any other text, a child of its time; *De la página* 13). Moreno's statement about the need to treat cookbooks like any other cultural text informs the approach taken to cookbooks here. Yet her very broad coverage means that she is unable to draw conclusions about how the individual texts under consideration sit in relation to each other. By contrast, the narrower focus I adopt here allows me to draw conclusions about how themes or different types of food text "develop in reaction to [each] other" (Elias 5).

Writing about food texts is a relatively new trend in the academy, so it is useful to reflect on what such texts can and cannot tell us about the period under scrutiny. Because gastronomy has traditionally been gendered male, the relationship between the male-authored gastronomic texts or official treatises on nutrition and the broader political and economic context is arguably clear-cut. For while the binary opposition between feminine cookbooks and masculine gastronomic literature is sometimes too simplistic, gastronomy has long been seen as reflecting the public, and hence masculine, space (see Mennell). This enduring connection between gastronomy and the public sphere means that gastronomic-style food writing is more easily appreciated in terms of its contribution to public space.

Cookbooks, on the other hand, have traditionally been associated with domesticity and the feminine (Mennell). Although cookbooks are replete with recipes and instructions for how to cook, they tell us little about what people in fact ate. Instead cookbooks, or "words about food," Megan Elias contends, "for the most part serve other purposes – reinforcing class [and national] identities [and] establishing communal historical narratives" (239). Ken Albala writes, too, about cookbooks as historical documents, stating: "In examining food preferences found in purely prescriptive literature, we are, of course, one step removed from actual consumption. There is really no way to be sure if anyone consistently followed the advice offered in dietary regimes" (164). In a similar vein, Veit tells us that "we cannot assume that the recipes or cooking techniques that any single author suggested accurately reflect how… people actually cooked and ate" (27).[6]

Although cookbooks do not provide exact information regarding what people ate, what makes them particularly fruitful here as primary texts is their instructional nature; some argue that cooking is one of "the most instructed activities for the general populace in our society" (e.g., Tomlinson 203). Cookbooks are normally filled with prescriptive lists that communicate a strong of sense of normativity. Not only are the ingredients, procedures, and expected outcomes for each dish well defined; so too is advice on how to run a kitchen and feed one's family. The prescriptive nature of recipes makes cookbooks an important primary text in any analysis of authoritarianism and food. Looking for ways to control its citizenry, the authoritarian state can find that cookbooks offer a site to create compliant subjectivities.

My hope is that this analysis of food discourse published during early Francoism will contribute not just to Peninsular studies but also to food studies. In this introduction I outline some of the main concepts and theories from these two fields that inform my analysis. I situate my analysis of food discourse in terms of existing scholarship on the regime, especially that which looks at the broader use of discourse to indoctrinate the masses and maintain hegemony. Just as discourse acted as an important site of control during the Franco era, food discourse functioned similarly, and both play a role in the analysis that follows.

Food Discourse and Francoist Spain: The State of the Scholarship

In analysing the first two decades of the Francoist dictatorship, I address a gap in scholarship on the regime, given that research has tended to focus more on the 1960s and 1970s. Michael Richards – whose own study of repression and violence runs from 1936 to 1945 – argues that we must keep in mind the extent to which "the study of Francoism has tended to concentrate upon comprehensive definitions of the regime in the light of development" (1). Such a focus on the boom years of the 1960s and 1970s has produced, according to Richards, a skewed focus on narratives of development. Since Richards put out his call to scholars to write more about the post-war years, scholarly inquiry in this area has grown. I follow in the footsteps of scholars such as Peter Anderson and Miguel Ángel del Arco Blanco, who argue that if we are to have a more balanced understanding of Francoism, we must pay due attention to topics such as repression, hunger, and violence.

In terms of existing scholarship on Francoist Spanish food culture, the material object of food has been written about from the viewpoint of hunger and repression. As scholars argue, for example, food shortages were used to punish the losers of the Spanish Civil War (see del Arco Blanco, "Hunger"; Richards), while the promise of food encouraged Spaniards to act as informants, who were "rewarded with good jobs during a time of desperate hunger" (Sieburth 17). Researchers have looked at the supply of food in terms of state control or biopolitics (see Jiménez Aguilar; Pérez-Olivares) as well as offering fascinating historiographies of hunger that ask us to think not just about the state's impact on mothers' access to food but also the role of husbands, estranged or otherwise, in women's experience of hunger (see P. Anderson). Suzanne Dunai's work in this area is outstanding (see *Cooking for the Patria*). Another scholar to have written about food culture during these early years is Paz Moreno, whose work on Ignacio Doménech's *Cocina de recursos* (Resourceful cooking; 1941) offers an important analysis of the way in which this text offers a counterpoint to official accounts of hunger in post-war Spain (*De la página*).

There is also emerging research that provides a fascinating account of Spanish food culture and discourse in terms of narratives of development and modernization. This work traces how the unprecedented economic growth of the 1960s and 1970s required a different style of consumption than the model of austerity imposed by the state during the 1940s and 1950s. As Eugenia Afinoguénova has astutely demonstrated, it was both international tourists and Spain's middle class who would be cast as the consumers of Spanish cuisine in a top-down effort to support the restaurant and tourism industries ("De la carta"). Afinoguénova narrates the compelling story, neglected in scholarship on Spanish food studies, of how the *menú del día* (set lunch) evolved in conjunction with consumer culture of the 1960s and 1970s. Although the existing histories of the *menú del día* point to its connections with the tourist boom of the 1960s, they fail to take into account, she argues, the development at this time of a middle class in Spain, in which the national subject turned into a touristic subject and a consumer.

Existing histories of hunger and autarky tell us about food as a material object (both what people ate and the different factors – governmental or otherwise – that affected food supply). From the vantage point of cultural studies, we are learning more about the importance of previously ignored cultural texts, such as cookbooks, gastronomic treatises, and menus. All of the new research, I suggest, can be woven together as part of a broader narrative about the relationship between food culture, power, and resistance during the Franco regime, shedding light on the ways in which food – not just as material object but also as discursive entity – became both a mode of control and a space of resistance.

Franco and Fascism

When viewing food discourse as a control mechanism, it is particularly productive to focus on the earlier decades of the Franco regime, given the broad reliance of fascist or totalitarian regimes on discourse. Scholarship in the areas of critical discourse and twentieth-century European history increasingly points to the importance to fascism of persuasive rhetoric, or "text and talk." Indeed, in *Analyzing Fascist Discourse* Ruth Wodak and John Richardson go as far as to argue that "the entire field of language and politics in Europe was triggered by the urge to grasp the influence of persuasive rhetoric in … totalitarian regimes" (17). The centrality of discourse to fascism has also been noted to provide fascist regimes with a necessary form of symbolic violence. During times of fascist or authoritarian rule, according to some scholars, equally important as physical violence is the "violence" exerted by discourse as it imposes certain realities or truths on the citizenry (see Santiáñez-Tió).

Where Spain sits in any consideration of European fascism is polemic. Wodak and Richardson insist that it is important not "to blur [the] significant differences between [Europe's] different regimes" (4) and to remember that Spain has a less straightforward history of fascism than either Germany or Italy. As acknowledgement of this, they include a chapter on Francoist pedagogical discourse in a section they label "semi-fascist." However, some Spanish historians such as Juan Linz view the Franco dictatorship as in fact more repressive, more authoritarian, and more exclusionary than those of the other nations Wodak and Richardson describe as semi-fascist. Eminent historian Raymond Carr also draws comparisons between the Franco dictatorship and other European dictatorships, stating that in the early years "Franco's Spain took on a fascist colouring" (321). Although Spain was not, according to Carr, a totalitarian state, Franco's government was in fact "a more direct dictatorship than those of the Soviet Union, Italy or Germany" (321).

Although there is no consensus amongst scholars about where Franco Spain sits in relation to other fascist nations, the majority of historians of twentieth-century Spain agree that the regime had, at the very least, some fascist aspects. According to Ismael Saz, it is productive to think of the regime as a fascistized dictatorship, as the term "fascistization" "helps us to understand the ambiguities and the different grades of influence of the Falangist party at the core of the regime" (qtd. in Alares López 708). Many scholars also see "the first phase (1939–1945) as the most fascist [in the regime's] existence" (Núñez and Umbach 299), while others argue that "the regime underwent a clear process of de-fascistization between 1943 and 1957" (Iglesias 159).

For yet other scholars this tendency to divide the regime into different stages of fascism or totalitarianism is problematic because it can lead to "undue concentration on change at the expense of continuity" (Richards 13). Indeed, Richards asks us to not lose sight of the fact that "for many people, the dictatorship was experienced as a continuous repetition of loss, entrapment, fear and lack of control" (13). Sandie Holguín also emphasizes continuity over change, asking us to consider "the thousands of babies stolen from women between 1939 and 1950 and the continuation of that practice against 'social undesirables' until fifteen years after Franco's death" (1768). What is clear is that the experience of Francoism was not uniform. For some Spaniards, the regime would have been experienced as fascist only in these early years, but for many others the experience of repression and violence would have been a constant.[7]

Francoist Discourse and Control

The violence exercised by the regime occurred at many different levels, with the most apparent being the cleansing of Spain by way of "brutal incarcerations and executions" (del Arco Blanco, "Hunger" 459). Describing these killings, Stephanie Sieburth writes that at the end of the civil war the regime "extended the large-scale killings [carried out during the war] to all of Spain ... Unofficial executions by Falangist militiamen continued as well. Jails were emptied and refilled repeatedly as the killings continued" (17). Mass killings served, importantly, according to Sieburth, to instil terror in the defeated, which enabled the regime "to break the spirit of the defeated by humiliating them to abandon their most cherished values, and to replace those with Francoist beliefs" (18).

Discourse functioned, too, as a site of control and form of violence. As a number of scholars have shown, writers, journalists, politicians, teachers, and religious leaders all took part in the construction of an authoritative discourse that allowed Franco to maintain control of a divided citizenry. Derrin Pinto compellingly demonstrates how pedagogical discourse was used to "exert control over the conduct of young readers [and students]" ("Education and Etiquette" 10). Pinto's discursive analysis of school textbooks from the 1940s provides an excellent example of how pedagogues and writers created a totalitarian discourse that demanded an "unyielding adoration of the Caudillo" and total acceptance of the regime's "utopian vision of reality," especially as it related to autarky (10).

Francoist pedagogical discourse is an area of study that has attracted significant scholarly attention. This comes as little surprise given that the regime itself saw education as an ideal way to form the nation, as young people, it was believed, could be easily moulded. As one scholar writes, educational discourse "sought to recover the importance of the nation's traditions so as to promote a conceptual and symbolic imaginary that might lead to the re-Christianisation and Hispanisation of society" (Laudo and Vilanou 434). Other research provides an insightful account of how schoolbooks taught Spanish children the right way to feel and express emotions: "Children are asked to love and feel proud of their country, and at the same time taught to act in order to obtain love in return and constitute a source of pride" (Mahamud 668). Textbooks and educational discourse produced pupils, as these examples demonstrate, with a deep appreciation for those aspects of Spanish history that legitimized their leader's vision for Spain. Moreover, this discourse produced students who felt absolute adoration and respect for Franco.

The existing scholarship on Francoism highlights other forms of cultural production that the state used to create an all-controlling discourse about Spanish identity. For instance, historical commemorations were part of the regime's attempts "to impose a concrete national narrative in post-war Spain" (Alares López 707). In particular, "the celebrations of the Millennial of Castile (1943) attempted to stage a mythical Castilian past, bringing to life the historical images propagated by Falangist intellectuals and historians" (Alares López 711). If public celebrations constituted an important part of the regime's authoritative discourse, so too did press, radio, and film. Viewing Francoist films as a means of indoctrination, Fátima Gil writes how it was through this medium that the regime took part in the construction or imposition of moral attitudes and behaviours. This was particularly important for Spanish women, "who were the primary consumers of this art form and were also the leading characters – as wives, mothers, and sisters" (857).

Discourse directed at women was ubiquitous and unrelenting, found not just in films but in women's magazines, on the radio, and in domestic manuals. Such media converged to indoctrinate women in their subservient and compliant roles as mothers and wives. The regime's use of discourse to control women's behavior was unprecedented, according to Carbayo-Abengózar: "none of the previous Spanish political regimes had controlled the role of women in society in such a severe manner. Pilar Primo de Rivera and her Sección Femenina women, as they had promised in La Mota Castle, started to train the new Spanish women. Women were therefore going to become the controlling and the controlled" ("Shaping Women" 81). Carbayo-Abengózar's analysis of Francoist discourse draws on the Foucauldian notion of biopolitics, demonstrating the ways in which discourse was one of the regime's most effective weapons to control women's bodies. Sieburth also discusses the regime's control of women, stating that "it was women whose roles the new regime most needed to change to stay in power" (30).

The little that has been written about Francoist food discourse points to the importance of food texts and cookery instruction in teaching women how to manage their households, plan their days, and conduct their relationships (see Dunai, *Cooking for the Patria*). As I drafted and re-drafted this monograph, an unexpected yet important effect of my working through ideas on gender has been to position the gendering of food writing in Franco Spain alongside the hyper-vigilance of the female body. The control of bodies was a central part of the Francoist totalitarian biopolitics, and individuals were managed and disciplined for the well-being of the national body. It was the uniquely prescriptive and highly instructional nature of food texts directed solely at the female reader that allowed the regime to police and control her body to such an extent. Cookbooks and teaching manuals must be viewed as central to state biopolitics for the ways in which they do not just indoctrinate women in what is expected of them in the household, but also produce compliant subjectivities.

Francoist Biopolitics and Food

Foucault's writing on biopolitics sheds light, scholars argue, on how the Franco regime wielded unprecedented control of the population, "achiev[ing] institutional stability and political hegemony through strict physical and psychological repression" (see, for example, Iglesias 162). According to Foucault, Western governments since the late eighteenth century have attempted to administer and regulate human behaviour and control the mind and body in order to achieve the general acceptance of social and legal norms. Biopolitics, which assumes the responsibility and control of the vital processes and bodily discipline, is exerted by different official institutions (Foucault, *The Birth of Biopolitics*). In totalitarian states this control reaches unprecedented dimensions, as governments invade all aspects of daily life and subjectivity.

As Salvador Cayuela Sánchez has pointed out, 1939 marked the transition from an interventionist to a totalitarian biopolitics in Spain, as the regime embarked on an indoctrination process that was carried out by a number of key institutions. Indeed, as Cayuela Sánchez observes, through institutions such as La Sección Femenina (the Women's Section) and El Sindicato Español Universitario (the Spanish University Students' Union), individuals were corrected, guided, and submitted to strict discipline and correct behaviour (162). Such institutions took part in the creation of a discourse that "reached into the very grain of individuals, touched their bodies and inserted itself into their actions and attitudes, their discourses, learning process and everyday life" (Carbayo-Abengózar, "Shaping Women" 75). Although she doesn't mention biopolitics specifically, Sieburth's description of how the defeated played the roles "forced upon on them with little or no margin for individual variation" (27) certainly speaks to Foucault's view of discourse as inserting itself into individual bodies.

In the area of food studies, the term "biopolitics" has also been fruitful, providing us with a better understanding of how cultural representations of food and food discourses can push citizens and consumers into different subject positions. Foucault's original discussion of biopolitics looked at the way that modern political power managed individual bodies and populations. If government food policy is one of the ways in which people are regulated or controlled, another equally important yet less tangible area is cultural practices surrounding food, along with media and textual represents of food.

Food media comprises a multitude of circulating images and texts – cookbooks, food sections in newspapers, descriptions of food in official documents, and images of food in film and the press – telling us what to eat and how to think about food, and having an impact on subject formation. Existing scholarship argues that there is an absence of sustained engagement with such media and that we must further analyse "the biopolitical consequences of food media in the context of eating bodies and productive nature" (Goodman et al. 162). While biopower relies upon state efforts to measure and control populations, biopolitical interventions critically involve non-state actors such as food media.

Kathleen Vester's study of American food culture expands on Foucault's work by looking at how food advice in a democratic society functioned as a biopolitical tool: "Food advice … traditionally told readers not only how to eat well, but how to be Americans, how to be members of the middle class, and how to perform as heterosexual men and women" (3). Importantly, Vester's analysis makes the point that representations of food transcend food in as much as they direct readers or citizens in the uptake of class and gender. Another scholar who has looked at food discourses and the notion of biopolitics is Takeda Hiroko, who reflects on how "contemporary food discourse in Japan functions as a powerful biopolitical device by propagating the notion of 'delicious food in a beautiful country' on which Japanese people are expected to organize their everyday lives" (5). Eating, cooking, dieting, and thinking about food are things we do on a daily basis, and the discourses governing these processes contribute to shaping both individual everyday life and individual identity.

In prior research, I have applied the concept of biopolitics to official food discourse published during the Primo de Rivera early-twentieth-century dictatorship, showing how this discourse was part of the codification of patriotic eating subjects that were committed to Spain's modernization (L. Anderson, "A Recipe for a Modern Nation"). Food texts commissioned by this authoritarian government and other governing bodies attempted to manage the eating body, thus functioning as a biopolitical device that linked the Spanish citizenry to the nation. Vexed by Spain's economic *retraso* (stagnation), Primo de Rivera believed that one of the solutions to the problem lay in protectionism. A strong, protectionist National Economic Council was created in 1924 to oversee relevant governance and changes to legislation. Official food discourse – advertising campaigns encouraging the consumption of local products and foodstuffs, as well as cookbooks calling for greater consumption of Spanish oranges and rice – was also used to shape consumer and citizen behaviour in ways that supported the government's focus on modernization and economic protectionism. The daily act of eating or reading about a more modern diet was meant to give Spaniards experiences of themselves as modern subjects.

The Primo de Rivera dictatorship's use of food discourse to control consumer behaviour and shape the contours of Spanish food culture would influence the Franco regime's own recourse to such discourse. Primo de Rivera, though failing to realize many of his ambitions, "inaugurated policies that were to become corner-stones of the Spanish right and eventually of the Francoist state" (Ben-Ami x). This is certainly true for Spanish food culture. During the final stages of Primo de Rivera's dictatorship, official institutions commissioned food texts that would remain all-but-canonical throughout most of the Franco regime. Certainly, many food writers in Franco Spain treat Post-Thebussem[8] (the most well-known and prolific food writer from the Primo de Rivera era) as an absolute authority on Spanish cuisine, constantly invoking his patriotic codification of Spanish cuisine.

As we did of the Primo de Rivera dictatorship, we can view authoritarian food discourse during the Franco regime as a potent biopolitical tool. As part of the Francoist biopolitics, individuals were managed and submitted to strict discipline and appropriate behaviour, as the state promoted a stoic, patriotic, ultra-nationalist, gendered, and healthy body. Official discourse and food media converged to control the citizenry's behaviour and thinking about Spanish food culture and identity. Food discourse produced ways of eating and thinking about food that privileged patriotism and health over personal desire and disciplined the individual body into making sacrifices for the good of the nation. An aim of this monograph is to shed light on the disciplining mechanisms in food discourses and to situate them as central to identity formation.

Food Discourse and Resistance

Not just hegemony but also resistance sits well with biopolitics; Foucault writes about the possibilities for resistance, arguing that "we have to promote new forms of subjectivity" ("The Subject and Power" 785). Complete exit from social reality is not, according to Foucault, a possibility, yet he does mention the possibility of resistance. It is not only the food ingested that can challenge hegemonic practices; the ways food is represented also offer counterpoints to hegemonic discourse. I examine diverse food texts to interrogate the role of food under dictatorship, situating food knowledge and practices within their cultural, social, historical, and political context to understand the intimate, daily ways subjects resisted the culinary hegemony of authoritarian regimes.

The everydayness of food offers unique possibilities for resistance. According to Henri Lefebvre, "everyday life is profoundly related to *all* activities, and encompasses them with all their differences and their conflicts; it is their meeting place, their bond, their common ground" (97). Though related to all activities, everyday life is not separate from the broader cultural, social, and political context, yet according to Mark Gardiner's critique of theories of the everyday, "daily life evinces a 'slippery,' elusory quality that evinces a not insignificant degree of resistance to the technologies of power, largely because its very presence is often not registered by the panoptic sweep of bureaucratic surveillance, indexing and control. The everyday remains an inchoate and heterodox mix of fluid, multiple and symbolically dense practices and ways of feeling and knowing" (230). It is the elusory quality of the everyday that underpins investigation of the possibilities that food, intricately connected to daily life, offers for resistance.

A number of food studies scholars consider that those possibilities require more attention (see Elias; Vester 7–8). In their seminal study of American food trends, Kathleen Lebesco and Peter Naccarato analyse "the value of culinary capital in promoting resistance to privileged food practices," describing culinary resistance as a type of food discourse that "celebrate[s] eating practices that run contrary to privileged culinary trends and expectations" (86). As their study demonstrates, there are lots of ways for consumers to resist dominant food practices. Importantly, these sites of resistance "do not just contest dominant culture but ultimately effect change in the criteria for culinary capital" (Lebesco and Naccarato 86).

In her study of American food culture, Vester explains how power or hegemony works bidirectionally, sometimes being upheld and at other times subverted. Drawing on Foucault, she writes: "the power relations implicated in discourses that he defined as paradigmatic for modern, democratic, Western societies are not stable but constantly changing … hegemonic discourses are constantly challenged by marginalized ones struggling for access or counter-hegemony" (4). Another scholar writing about instances of culinary resistance is Nir Avieli, who in his *Food and Power* states emphatically that it is not possible to think about culinary hegemony without discussing culinary resistance. With resistance being "an immediate and inevitable consequence of hegemonic power" (226), for every case or setting involving culinary hegemony Avieli analyses culinary resistance. He describes his approach as Foucauldian, writing that "every application of food system's power is met with resistance as some seek to define the food systems of all and others fight that definition" (14).

Scholars of the early Franco regime have also written about the place of resistance in Franco Spain. In her outstanding study of the use of *coplas* (folk songs) during the Franco regime, Sieburth writes, for instance, that "for the defeated, the coplas were one of the very few ways that they could raise their voices and tell a painful story in the first person without putting themselves in danger" (9). Another scholar writes how resistance in cultural production was significant for the way it allowed for the "creation of alternative realities" (Núñez Puente 226). Importantly, these alternative realities made room for experiences of gender, sexuality, and nationality that differed from those imposed by the regime.

In the area of Francoist food culture or food politics, there are various examples of discontent or resistance to official Francoist ideology. Richards's and del Arco Blanco's social histories of autarky and hunger provide a number of instances of small-scale protests and public discontent about the regime's corrupt and nepotistic distribution of food. These demonstrate that the citizenry did not just accept official food provisioning. Del Arco Blanco writes of dissident behaviour that took place in public spaces, with small groups of people refusing to accept the unfair distribution of food. Chalked signs began to appear in some places asking for better food, he writes, and "discontent with food supplies was also shown through jokes made at the expense of the regime and authorities" ("Hunger" 475–6). Alejandro Pérez-Olivares also examines examples of resistance in post-war Madrid, analysing the spaces of resistance that emerged in response to official rationing and distribution of food. He writes of "una serie de 'contraespacios,' lugares donde los vecinos podían organizarse al margen del orden establecido aprovechando la interconexión de ciertas infraestructuras" (a series of "counterspaces," places where neighbours could organise themselves at the margins of the established order to take advantage of the interconnection of certain infrastructure; 10).

These examples of alternative spaces and civic resistance point to the importance of considering resistance in any study of hegemony and power. Such spaces allowed citizens to bypass state control in some circumstances, creating alternative realities or ways of accessing food. While these historians provide examples of civic resistance to the Franco regime in matters relating to autarky and the corrupt handling of food, I consider the way in which food discourse provided alternative realities to those created discursively by the state. In some other national contexts, it has been shown that "food discourses have been defined by their resistance" (Avieli 12). This book shows how culinary resistance, or resistance to official food discourse, was important for the way it provided the Spanish citizenry with a discursive space where both food culture and identity were experienced as something other than exclusively monolithic, gendered, and autarkic.

Censorship in Franco's Spain: Resistance, Oversight, and Food Texts

Although censorship is not discussed in detail in this monograph, here I provide a framework for thinking about the censoring and likely self-censoring of food texts. One of my main conclusions regarding the censoring of food texts is that censors were not at all alert to the potentially subversive nature of food discourse. The view censors likely had of food writing as inherently apolitical makes the study of culinary resistance all the more important, because it meant that writing about food was a place where critique – implicit or otherwise – could be directed to the regime.

Describing Franco Spain's censorship mechanism, Raquel Merino and Rosa Rabadán write: "The fascist State used legislation to enforce official censorship, overtly controlling all types of information [and ensuring that] cultural manifestations were closely monitored and controlled by the military authority and the Roman Catholic Church" (125). All published works were censored for even the slightest criticism of official discourse. The fear of persecution for the most trivial of offences contributed to an atmosphere in which most citizens engaged in some degree of self-censorship. Aware of censors' broad mandate to root out attacks on national unity, morality, or the key institutions of the regime, many writers and or publishers censored, consciously or otherwise, their own works.

In the existing scholarship on censorship in Francoist Spain, there are only a few references to food. According to del Arco Blanco, for instance, the censoring of references to hunger and deprivation was so extreme in post-war Spain that the only reliable accounts of the food situation were found in foreign texts: "Sin estar sometidos a la censura y parcialidad de la documentación franquista, informaron al Foreign Office sobre la penosa España que existía fuera de los muros de embajadas y consulados" (without being subject to the censorship and bias of Francoist documentation, they informed the Foreign Office of the pitiful Spain that existed beyond embassy and consulate walls; "Morir de hambre" 247).[9] In his study of how the press became one of the state's main instruments of propaganda, Justino Sinova touches on the topic of the censoring of food, writing that just as hunger or images of hungry bodies were censored, so too were words that suggested culinary abundance or luxury: "con la misma severa intención, determinadas palabras que sugerían lujo y abundancia estaban desterradas del lenguaje de los periódicos" (with the same strict approach, certain words that suggested luxury and abundance were banished from newspaper vocabulary; 36). The function of censorship, especially in relation to the press, was therefore to hide the very uneven access to food in post-war Spain.

From research at the Archivo General de la Administración (General council archives) Alcalá de Henares, I ascertained that there is a censorship file and/or report for most of the food texts scrutinized in these pages. Interestingly, all of the food texts considered here passed easily and without criticism. The fact that subversive food texts were not censored needs to be considered in broader terms against the backdrop of the body of disruptive cultural texts that were published during this period, notwithstanding their subversion. Indeed, as a number of scholars have shown, many writers, artists, and filmmakers found ways of critiquing Francoist ideology in spite of state control and censorship. In relation to film, for example, Raúl Cancio Fernández writes: "La audacia de esos cineastas junto con la parquedad de miras de los censores, permiteron que obras maestras del cine no se quedaran para siempre en los estantes oscuros de un almacén o definativamente destruidas" (The audacity of these filmmakers, together with the censors' limited review, meant that cinematic masterpieces would not remain forever on the dark shelves of a warehouse or be definitively destroyed; 141). About poetry, Eleanor Wright explains that some "poets used allegory, elegy and document to veil criticisms under the clothing of metaphors comprehended by adept readers" (180). Playwright Antonio Buero Vallejo similarly engaged in a "realidad posibilista que le permitía publicar sus trabajos a la vez que criticar aspectos del régimen franquista" (possibilist reality that allowed him to publish his works, even while they critiqued aspects of the Francoist regime; Favoretto and Anderson 1). For her part, Loren Chuse writes about the resistance to Francoist tropes of flamenco found in music from the period (107).

While this broader context of subversive cultural production highlights the possibilities for critique of the regime despite extensive censorship, it is important to note the added advantages that food writing would have had. Although it is increasingly common for feminist scholars to remark on the political potential of women's cooking and collections of recipes, cookbooks have historically been seen as belonging exclusively to the domain of domesticity and the feminine.[10] The rigid gender divide at the heart of Franco's New Spain would only have intensified the traditional belief that cookery instruction did not in any way transcend the kitchen. This view of cookbooks as existing in opposition to the masculine sphere of politics and issues of national concern would likely have meant censors were not in any way on the lookout for political or social critique. The connection between cookbooks and domesticity can be seen, therefore, as advantageous in the context of censorship, as such texts were subject to less scrutiny.

While cookbooks had the advantage of their connection with the private realm of the home, some disruptive gastronomic writing also went unnoticed, in spite of gastronomy's being gendered as male and of the public domain. The view that subversive gastronomic writing was devoid of political content in spite of its relevance to public matters can be traced back to early-nineteenth-century France, where it was argued that gastronomic writing should deal exclusively with matters of taste rather than being a place for social and political critique. Describing a separation of food and politics at this time, Rebecca Spang writes that "the new gastronomies and guides of the Empire and the Restoration demarcated the table as an autonomous realm, one structured by rules distinct from those that governed other aspects of social life. Within this newly circumscribed context, authors might interpret meals without reference to overtly political concerns, either aristocratic or republican" (151). Given the hegemony in Spain and beyond of French gastronomy until well into the twentieth century, this nineteenth-century view of gastronomy as apolitical would have likely still had currency in Spain, thus affecting reader/censor expectations about the content of gastronomic texts.

Overview of This Book: Autarky, Gender, and Centralist Nationalism

Each of this monograph's three sections deals with one of the main pillars of Francoist ideology. Economic and cultural isolation are the focus of chapter 1, which looks at the interrelation between food discourse and the Francoist political economy of autarky. While existing scholarship on the autarkic policies of Franco Spain has dealt compellingly with a number of connections between food and autarky, I consider how this ideology was sustained or disrupted in food discourse.

Another way in which official discourse sustained autarky was through what I call "culinary patriotism," or "culinary xenophobia." Given that autarky was part of a broader wish to seal Spain off from outside influence (see Richards), it follows that official food discourse produced a culinary or gastronomic map of Spain that was proudly free from external influence. This notion of Spanish food culture as pure or closed off from "corrupting" foreign influence shaped not just the contours of Spanish gastronomy but also individual subjectivity, as Spaniards came to define themselves in these terms too.

To understand the connections between food discourse and the political economy of autarky, it is imperative also to turn our eyes to food shortages. Economic autarky was responsible for the devastating hunger so many Spaniards suffered during "los años de hambre" (the years of hunger), yet Francoist officials downplayed enormously its impact on Spain's foodscape. Official food discourse, including cookbooks, upheld this approach not just by minimizing hunger, but also by excluding the hungry body from the public sphere. In erasing such deprivation, officials upheld Francoist biopolitics by directing Spaniards to embrace stoicism and ignore suffering in the name of patriotism and national well-being. Official discourse also sought to erase any mention of culinary abundance, so as to convince the Spanish citizenry that everyone had access to the same modest amounts of food.

Chapter 1 also analyses the ways in which cookbooks responded to these trends in official discourse. Cookbooks, while reflective of official ideology, do not always uphold all aspects of hegemonic food discourse. In a way, cookbook authors create a new type of food discourse as they attempt to uphold dominant discourse while writing cookery texts that will be commercially viable and of interest to their readers. An even more clear-cut example of culinary subversion can be seen in those cookbooks that take issue with the official discourse's exclusion from public view of both the hungry body and hunger. The examples of culinary resistance discussed challenge the Francoist biopolitics because they allow Spaniards to read about the experience of hunger. Rather than discipline readers into stoicism or denial of hunger, such texts provide a space for them to experience the physical and emotional toll of insufficient access to food.

One of the other main pillars of Francoist ideology, gender – or the rigid divide between the two sexes – is the focus of chapter 2. Scholars have certainly between alive to the "conexión entre la configuración del 'Nuevo Estado' y la política de género, es decir la construcción de asimetrías entre hombres y mujeres" (connection between the configuration of the 'New State' and gender politics, namely the assymetries constructed between men and women; di Febo 19). As part of Franco's National Catholic ideal, Spanish women found themselves once again relegated to the home. The government, in a move reminiscent of the nineteenth century that undid all of the progressive gender legislation of the Second Republic, made clear its expectation that Spanish women would dedicate themselves solely to the private domain and to the care of their husbands and families. Scholars have drawn attention to the fundamental role in the transmission of Francoist ideology to Spanish women played by the Sección Femenina (SF; Women's Section; see Dunai, *Cooking for the Patria*; Enders; Ofer, *Señoritas in Blue*); with the growing interest in food studies, some scholars have even turned their attention to the cookbooks written or commissioned by the SF (see Dunai, *Cooking for the Patria*). As with each of the topics addressed by the chapters that follow, there are food texts that create an alternative reality or disrupt official discourse. While the SF cookbooks produced female readers who were acutely aware of gender difference, there were non-official cookbooks that produced a social and cultural world in which female and male realities were less polarized.

Two aspects of my analysis are worth mentioning here. First, previous research has not considered the SF's cookbooks or food texts within the broader context of gender and food discourse during the Franco regime, and accordingly we could not know how authoritative these official food texts were, compared to other women's cookbooks published contemporaneously. Moreover, that the SF food texts were studied in isolation has meant that it was not possible to appreciate just how resistant some non-official food texts were, not simply of the highly instructional nature of the SF food texts but also of the immutable gender divide they upheld.

The second important point of difference with existing scholarship is my analysis of how these official cookbooks produced readers who were acutely aware not only of gender difference but also of hierarchy. Cooking is one of the most instructed activities in which we take part; it is thus not surprising, I argue, that official Francoist cooking instruction has the secondary function of producing readers who unquestioningly follow orders. Existing scholarship on the Franco regime illustrates the ways in which school textbooks taught children "unyielding adoration of the Caudillo (military leader)" (Pinto, "Indoctrinating the Youth" 649). Just as Spain's education system had the function of creating subjectivities who adored and obeyed their country's leader, I suggest that official cookbooks did not just teach women how to cook and perform as wives and mothers, but also produced compliant subjectivities who followed instruction and showed an absolute respect for male authority.

In chapter 2, I identify what it is about the form and content of the SF cookbooks that allows us to read these texts for their attempt to produce obedient cooks and wives. The complete absence of narrative in these official texts represents a genuine point of difference with other women's cookbooks, rendering them highly instructional. For one of the main functions of the narrative that we often find in cookbooks is, as a number of scholars have shown (Parkhurst Ferguson, *Word of Mouth*), to make recipes less about instruction and more about relationships and storytelling.

The SF's ideal of a compliant cook does not, however, go unchallenged. Chapter 2 concludes by showing how some non-official food writers attempted to create more autonomous and less obedient subjectivities; they provided readers and cooks with opportunities to make their own decisions rather than just follow orders. This focus on creating less obedient subjectivities represented a challenge to Francoist biopolitics.

Another important function of the SF's food texts, as chapter 3 shows, is to produce readers who were acutely aware of the important, yet incomparably smaller, role of regional cuisines in the greater whole that was Spain's national cuisine. Notwithstanding the apparent promotion of regional cuisines in most of the food texts I analyse in chapter 3 – a mix of cookbooks, gastronomic texts, and official food periodicals – these texts in fact function to assert a monolithic centralist Spanish food culture whereby regional cuisines are either subsumed into the greater whole of Spanish cuisine or co-opted for the purpose of nation building. The notion of a shared cuisine, as numerous scholars have shown, is a key component of any national identity, which "projects order on chaotic transnational and regional foodscapes and simulates stability and tradition, while manifesting the cultural dominance of certain populations" (Vester 18; see also Parkhurst Ferguson, *Accounting for Taste*; Elias). In constructing a New Spain, Francoist officials clearly understood the importance of unifying a very divided citizenry through allusion to a shared cuisine, with the phrase "a la española" (Spanish style) being used on some of Franco's earliest official menus to refer to a standard or common Spanish food culture.

Nor was the official use, as early as 1939, of "a la española" merely descriptive of Spanish food culture. As I show in this chapter, it was also aspirational, foreshadowing the regime's decades-long discursive production of a monolithic national food culture. Some very astute but perfunctory observations have been made about the Francoist discursive codification of a homogeneous culinary code for Spain (see Medina; Roser i Puig). Yet there has been no analysis of the very food discourse that produced this monolithic culinary identity. Chapter 3 provides an in-depth analysis of the way in which both official and non-official food texts produced readers, cooks, and citizens who saw regional cuisines as integral, yet insignificant, components of the greater entity of "Spanish cuisine."

My analysis in this chapter of the discursive codification of a monolithic culinary code for Franco's New Spain in both gastronomy and recipes also enables me to consider the different ways in which gastronomic texts and cookbooks engage with the question of Spain's national culinary code. As I show below, male-authored gastronomic texts produced during the first two decades of the Franco regime are similarly concerned with defining the limits of Spanish food culture or gastronomy, while women are tasked with domestic food writing and food preparation. Undeniably, not only do male-authored texts sustain the regime's centralizing agenda through their codification of a monolithic food culture, but they also uphold conservative gender ideology in the way they relegate women to the margins of gastronomy. By polarizing feminine and masculine appetites, as well as gendering gastronomic authority as male, Franco Spain's gastronomic writers exclude female food writers from the realm of gastronomy.

The gendered divide I identify in this chapter between male gastronomy and female cookbooks can also be thought about in relation to chapter 2's identification of the SF's highly prescriptive food texts for women. Indeed, as I show throughout this monograph, during the first two decades of the regime food writing evolved differently for female and male readers. Food texts written with men in mind – generally well supplied with discussion of Spain's national culinary code in the light of history, politics, and high culture – produced male subjectivities who were part not just of Spanish gastronomy but also of the national project. By way of contrast, food texts written with female readers in mind were on the whole highly prescriptive, reinforcing not just women's role in the domestic sphere but also female compliance, both in relation to the SF (as mouthpiece for the state) and to their husbands. Because food texts aimed at the female reader were uniquely prescriptive, Spanish food discourse can be looked to also for the way in which it partook in the regime's hyper-vigilance of the female body.

This chapter also considers resistance. While most of the food discourse under scrutiny upheld Francoist biopolitics in its production of a gastronomic sphere or space that was both unified and gendered as masculine, there were food writers who offered an alternative way of experiencing national identity. Disruptive food discourse reminded readers of the importance of viewing or experiencing regional cuisines as entities in their own right, rather than as small elements of Spanish national cuisine. Not until much later on in the regime would cookbooks dedicated exclusively to a single regional cuisine be published again, yet as early as 1942 readers were reminded of the importance of such cookbooks.

To summarize some of the key concepts of this monograph: My focus here is food discourse, or "talk of food" (Parkhurst Ferguson, *Word of Mouth*), and I aim to show the ways in which official food discourse was part of the regime's broader use of discourse to indoctrinate the masses. An important function of this food discourse was not just to teach Spaniards the right approach to food, but to produce subjects who understood what was expected of them in terms of autarky, gender, and nationalism. This type of food discourse is particularly potent as a site of control for the way it links not just to subjectivity but to everyday life. Food discourse was also at times oppositional, providing Spaniards with different realities from those imposed by the state. The traditional view of food writing as connected to domesticity or concerned solely with matters of the palate perhaps meant that censors were not as alert to the politically subversive nature of some of the food writing looked at here. Anything but apolitical, food discourse was a place where identities were imposed and contested.

1 Food Discourse and the Production of Autarkic Subjectivities

This chapter looks at the nexus between the political economy of autarky and food discourse during the first two decades of the regime. From the outset of its rebellion against the Second Republic, "the New State had begun to develop its economic policy of 'autarky,' or self-sufficiency" (del Arco Blanco, "Hunger" 3). Influenced by fascist Italy and Nazi Germany, Franco believed that total self-sufficiency would not only make Spain economically strong again, but would also provide the necessary protection from foreign contagion. Autarky, as one official publication explains as early as 1940, "equivale a poder, plenitud de soberanía e independencia respecto de toda otra facultad directiva exterior" (equated to power, full sovereignty, and independence from all other external executive authorities; Ferrer Calbeto 5). Autarky's connections to food are numerous. First, food self-sufficiency was considered a prerequisite of economic independence, and the regime was steadfast in its determination that Spain would not be dependent on external supplies. In turn, as is commonly accepted, the political economy of autarky had a disastrous impact on food supply, and although it was never recognized in official discourse, hunger and food shortages are considered by most to be a direct result of such policies.

In terms of scholarship on hunger and autarky, there are two standout scholars. The first is Michael Richards, who has provided us with a brilliant and compelling cultural and social history of autarky during the totalitarian years of the dictatorship. As Richards maintains, the notion of autarky was about so much more than simply the economy and could be viewed as "a broader desire to seal off society, to enclose Spain" (2). Miguel Ángel del Arco Blanco insightfully adds to Richards's study through a detailed account of the daily mechanisms of autarky, or the "reality of autarky on the ground" ("Hunger" 460). Unlike Richards, del Arco Blanco looks at people's lives and daily experience of autarky and food supply, but the two concur that food shortages and the black market allowed the New State to repress its civil war opponents on a daily basis. On this point, del Arco Blanco writes of how "hunger formed the ballast of the new ship of state because the regime was able to force some into starvation while allowing others to profit through the control of much-needed resources" ("Hunger" 458).

This chapter adds to this body of scholarship by considering how the political economy of autarky as it related to food was sustained and/or disrupted in food discourse. Official food discourse played an important role in imposing autarky on account of how it taught readers the "right" approach to food in Spain's post-war autarkic economy. Just as the principles of self-sacrifice and culinary self-sufficiency were central to autarky, so too was a "taste" for indigenous foodstuffs. Official food discourse hence sought to produce citizens with these preferences and beliefs. Such was the influence of official attempts to increase consumption of rice and oranges that a number of cookbooks dedicated solely to either rice or oranges were published. Cookbooks and official food discourse upheld the Francoist biopolitics in the way that they managed the individual body's taste and food choices, creating an eating subject that put national well-being before individual preferences.

Male-authored gastronomic writing also sustained the Francoist biopolitics through the codification of culinary patriotism and culinary xenophobia. This gastronomic writing produced readers and citizens with views of Spanish cuisine as existing separate from other national cuisines, thereby upholding the notion inherent to autarky of Spain as both economically and culturally isolated from most other countries. While culinary patriotism is the trademark of male gastronomic texts from the 1940s, the only female-authored gastronomic text studied here takes issue with this steadfast rejection of foreign cuisines: the Marquesa de Parabere's writing challenges official discourse by encouraging her readers to think about Spanish gastronomy as inherently connected to other world cuisines. This sort of food discourse allows for an experience of a cosmopolitan openness to other cultures.

Another way food discourse upheld Francoist biopolitics was through the erasure of hunger. Despite widespread suffering, Spaniards were encouraged to remain stoic in the name of patriotism and national well-being. In this context, it is important to note the challenge to the Francoist biopolitics that one prolific author and culinary luminary posed by allowing his readers to experience the physical and emotional trauma of hunger. Official food discourse also sustained autarky by rendering invisible not just hunger but culinary abundance. Retrospectively, we know that officials and well-connected families wanted for very little during the years of hunger, even as most Spaniards suffered extreme food shortages. Yet, as we will see, official food discourse spoke very little of abundance. Other tomes inadvertently reveal, however, just how much food some Spaniards had. In this regard, these sorts of cookbooks fulfil an important function in post-war Spain, for they are able to reveal – inadvertently or otherwise – what official discourse refused to acknowledge.

Eat More Oranges

An important function of food discourse from the first two decades of the regime was to create a taste amongst readers for autochthonous foodstuffs suited to Spain's autarkic political economy, such as oranges. In producing readers or subjects with a taste for local rather than foreign foodstuffs, official food discourse sustained the Francoist biopolitics, as individual taste was managed for the well-being of the collective body. Significant, too, was the way in which this discourse produced in readers a belief in Spain's capacity to feed her own people while remaining closed off to food imports. The official food discourse looked at here comes primarily from the publication *Alimentación nacional* (The national diet), which was published bimonthly between 1941 and 1953 by the Comisaría General de Abastecimientos y Transportes (General commission for provisions and transport) and in 1943 published an article calling for Spaniards to consume more oranges. The ideas contained in *Alimentación nacional* found their way into the weekly newsreels of the time called *No-Do*s as well as into cookbooks dedicated exclusively to oranges.

Through a biopolitical lens, it is possible to view these texts about and images of oranges as playing a critical role in upholding Francoist governance. A range of experts, including government authorities, speak authoritatively about oranges, thereby putting into circulation a truth discourse about this Spanish-grown fruit. While biopower relies on state efforts to monitor populations, biopolitical interventions critically also require non-state actors, such as food media. Together, these different government agencies and the food media promote a discourse about food consumption that targets individual behaviour as the solution to Spain's food problems. According to this all-encompassing discourse about food, if Spaniards put patriotism before their own individual preferences, the country will be able to remain economically and culturally "free" from outside forces.

Official food writing during the Primo de Rivera regime operated similarly, for during that period oranges were linked both symbolically and literally to the regime's politics. In the early 1930s, orange consumption was used as a way to create citizens with a belief in regeneration and modernization; just some ten years later oranges would be drawn on in an attempt to produce autarkic subjectivities. The Franco regime cast the orange as the ideal produce of autarky in its attempts to create an increased appetite amongst Spaniards for this locally grown fruit. The shift in the symbolism of oranges is an important example of the ways in which officials appropriated Spanish food culture for broader political and cultural purposes. In both regimes, an oversupply of oranges was a driver of the eat-more-oranges campaigns, yet the meaning attached to orange consumption varied considerably.

Until the 1960s, especially during the post-war period, the Spanish economy depended on oranges, and "durante el periodo de reconstrucción europea [la naranja] se convirtio, gracias a las divisas, en la tabla de la salvación de la España de la autarquía" (during the period of European reconstruction, [the orange] became, thanks to foreign currency, a saving grace of autarkic Spain; Alberola 95). Indeed, the centrality of oranges to the Spanish economy has led scholars and journalists to conclude that it was "una helada en 1956 [que] forzó a Franco a autorizar los planes de estabilización que cambiaron el país" (a frost in 1956 [that] forced Franco to authorize the stabilization plans that changed the country; Alberola 95). Vicente Abad provides a short history of oranges during the Franco regime in his "Naranjas y autarquía (1939–1960)" ("Oranges and autarky"), describing the official and centralized control of orange consumption and production during the early part of the regime. Abad writes in great detail about El Sindicato Nacional de la Naranja (the national orange trade union), which was officially opened on 11 July 1940 in Madrid. According to Abad, this Sindicato was the product of Falangist ideology:

> El predominio del grupo falangista sería determinante a la hora de configurar la estructura interna y las funciones del Sindicato de la Naranja, pensando para ejercer un control absoluto sobre el conjunto de la economía citrícola y adoptando una actitud intervencionista que abarcaba todos los aspectos de la misma. (183)
>
> (The dominance of the Falangist group would be decisive when it came to configuring the internal structure and functions of the orange trade union, which was intended to exercise total control over the entire citric economy and adopted an interventionist attitude that affected all aspects of the same.)

The fascist and interventionist control of the citrus economy rendered the orange an ideal foodstuff of autarky, for this fruit could be cast not just as indigenous to Spain, but also as the product of the political economy of autarky itself. Indeed, the unique place of the orange in post-war Spain's autarkic economy drew comment from El Sindicato de Frutos (the fruit trade union), which in 1949 described oranges as one of the "frutas más disciplinadas dentro del conjunto económico nacional" (most controlled fruits within the entire national economy; qtd. in Abad 194). The political relevance of oranges to fascism was due also to the fact that during the immediate post-war period, oranges were exported to Germany as part of Spain's war debt with the Germans:

> La firma del tratado hispano-alemán a primeros de octubre de 1940 contemplaba la exportación de 300.000 Tm de naranjas, y un nuevo signo de debilidad de las autoridades españolas, convertía los Nazis en distribuidores exclusivos de la fruta. (Abad 182)
>
> (The signing of the Hispano-German treaty at the beginning of October 1940 provided for the export of 300,000 tons of oranges, and a new marker of the Spanish authorities' weakness, with the Nazis taking on exclusive distribution of the fruit.)

The oranges sent to Germany in the immediate post-war period represented, according to Abad, half of Spain's orange supply, so it was also necessary for the Spanish state to ensure local consumption of oranges in the later years of the dictatorship.

According to figures provided by the Ministerio de Agricultura (see A.G. Pérez et al.), as well as statistics cited in Abad's study, exports of oranges went down between 1944 and 1947. Given this drop, it made sense that *Alimentación nacional* embarked on a campaign to increase the consumption of oranges within Spain. Certainly, according to one of the early articles in this periodical, exports of Spanish oranges "sufren las naturales limitaciones que el momento bélico impone" (suffer the usual limitations imposed by wartime), which means that "el levante español conoce horas de angustia" (the Spanish east experiences hours of anguish; Issue 15, 5). According to the article, the Spanish government would do everything possible "para que el preciado fruto llegue a todos los rincones de nuestra patria" (to ensure the precious fruit reaches all corners of our homeland; Issue 15, 5). Accompanying the article is a map of Spain replete with drawings of Spaniards patriotically consuming Spanish oranges. Such an image produces readers or citizens who see their own Spanishness or national identity as dependent on orange consumption. The function of this is twofold: the government seeks to both support local orange growers and produce a citizenry who understands food culture in terms of what is locally produced.

Of interest in this context is *Alimentación nacional*'s report on a short film titled *La naranja* (The orange). The cartoon-style film tells "la historia de la naranja hasta su aparación en España, señalando incluso las cifras totales de producción" (the history of the orange up to its appearance in Spain, even noting the aggregate production figures; Issue 10, 4). Relevant to the regime's autarkist view is the way in which the article deals with the film's account of the orange's introduction to Spain at the time of Arab rule: once in Spain the orange sheds "su exotismo, y agradecida a nuestra tierra y nuestro sol, que le dieron nueva vida" (its exoticism and, thanks to our soil and our sun, which give it new life), is quickly embraced as a national treasure (Issue 10, 4). As a fruit that grows prolifically in Spain, the orange symbolizes Spain's capacity to feed her own people. However, in order to maintain the notion – inherent also to autarky – of Spain as culturally shut off from the corrupting forces of foreign influence, the article must first free the orange of its exotic and foreign origins.

Spain's oranges are also rendered 100 percent Spanish through references to their ubiquity in Spanish art and literature. *Alimentación nacional* reminds readers of the important place of oranges in the literature of Azorín, which sought, as critics have shown, to define an eternal notion of Spanishness. Also mentioned are Joaquín Sorolla's depiction of orange gardens in his typically Spanish landscapes, such as *Entre naranjos* (Amongst the orange trees), which he painted in 1903 for the well-known Argentine medical doctor José R. Semprún. Sorralla's painting – described as "un cuadro alegre de asunto valenciano" (a cheerful picture of a Valencian theme; Issue 10, 4) – is important not only for what it says about the bonds of Hispanidad, but also for its idyllic depiction of the culture or lifestyle associated with Spanish oranges. With Azorín and Sorolla regarded as canonically Spanish in the style and content of their work, *Alimentación nacional* casts oranges as iconic for their place in the cultural production of two such Spanish greats.

The idyllic or iconically Spanish image of oranges, as depicted in *Alimentación nacional*, was also an important feature of the advertising material and labels used for both internal and external supplies of oranges. The Biblioteca Nacional de España (Spanish national library) has a collection of labels that use iconic images and values associated with Spain, such as sunshine, the beach, health, vitality, and beautiful women often in typical Spanish dress to sell or promote oranges. As the descriptions of some of these labels highlight:

> Las etiquetas están ilustradas con figuras y retratos femeninos representadas con la presencia de la naranja de una forma más o menos manifesta. En una escena la figura pletórica de una joven bañándose en el mar con una naranja en la mano transmite la imagen de salud unida a la fruta. (Generalitat Valenciana 180)
>
> (The labels are illustrated with feminine figures and portraits, together with more or less obvious representations of oranges. In one scene, the corpulent figure of a young woman bathing in the ocean with an orange in her hand projects the image of health associated with the fruit.)

Both domestic and international consumers are encouraged to view the consumption of oranges in terms of the promise of a happier, healthier lifestyle.

The Spanish orange also features in *No-Do*, the weekly Francoist newsreel obligatorily shown in all Spanish cinemas and the only newsreel permitted in the country. On 1 January 1951, *La Naranja y su Riqueza* (Oranges and their wealth) was shown as part of "Imágenes, Revista Cinematográfica" (Images, cinematographic journal). A ten-minute short film opens with images of an idyllic Spanish country side replete with orange-laden trees. Workers are depicted happily picking this locally grown fruit, which is then sent to factories where women pack and prepare the produce for export to neighbuoring European countries, such as Sweden, England, Denmark, and France. The images used on the packing boxes include a radiant-looking child, as plump and healthy as the orange that is being traded. As well as highlighting the health benefits of citrus fruit, the short film reassures readers that the citrus industry will bolster the Spanish economy.

The health benefits of oranges are discussed as well in *Alimentación nacional*. Oranges are cast as the ideal food of autarky, not only because they are grown in Spain but also, according to this official publication, on account of their superior nutritional value. Unsurprisingly, the Primo de Rivera dictatorship's efforts to increase the consumption of Spanish oranges also included touting the orange's medical and health benefits. However, if during the Primo de Rivera era healthy eating was linked to national regeneration and modernization, in the immediate post-war years what oranges could offer was somewhat different. In the context of those bleak years, greater orange consumption offered the promise of "alegría, salud y vida" (happiness, health and life; Issue 10, 4), implicit in which is the belief that even during the harsh post-war years, Spain's naturally abundant foodscape would keep the nation alive, healthy, and happy to boot.

This health discourse is top-down, but also involves a process of subjectification as Spaniards are directed to produce themselves as healthy, happy, and patriotic citizens. Attention to subjectification is crucial to understanding the relationship between biopower, food, and structural inequalities. While some Spaniards in the post-war era would have been able to make healthy food choices, due to their privileged access to food, most were not. In similar fashion to other examples of food biopolitics, vulnerable populations are disciplined to work on themselves in the name of their own health as well as the collective well-being. This discourse about oranges creates a reality whereby Spaniards are made responsible for keeping the nation healthy, as well as supporting its economy through the consumption of locally grown produce.

Written just after this official attempt to increase orange consumption is a book by Manuel de Torres Higinio Paris Equilar, *La naranja en la economía española* (The orange in the Spanish economy), published by the national publishing house Editorial Nacional. In his discussion of the place of oranges in the Spanish economy, de Torres Higinio Paris Equilar writes that "se notó a partir de 1940 el notable aumento de la demanda interior" (from 1940, there was a notable increase in domestic demand; 277). That this increased demand within Spain coincided with the campaign described in *Alimentación nacional* to encourage greater orange consumption points to the influence of official discourse. Beyond affecting consumer behaviour, the discursive codification of oranges in *Alimentación nacional* also influenced other food writers. Not only, therefore, does food discourse shape consumer behaviour; it also influences subsequent codifications of food culture.

An example of the influence *Alimentación nacional* exerted on subsequent food writers can be found in Sandoval Amorós's 1953 cookbook *Comed naranjas: La naranja, alimento, la naranja, medicamiento* (Eat oranges: Oranges as food, oranges as medicine), which draws on the combined fields of nutrition and cuisine to give weight to the argument for greater orange consumption. Sandoval Amorós's text includes a fascinating discussion of the role of the orange in the Spanish Civil War. He writes of lower mortality rates of Republican prisoners compared to those of citizens of major urban centres, stating that

> el secreto no estaba en otra cosa que en la excesiva cantidad de naranjas y albaricoques que se comían ya que eran los únicos alimentos que se podían adquirir comprados en las cantinas de los establecimientos penitenciarios. (10)

> (the secret was none other than the excessive quantity of oranges and apricots that were eaten, given that these were the only foodstuffs that could be acquired through purchase in prison canteens.)

The image of well-fed prisoners in Sandoval Amorós's cookbook highlights the potential of an autarkic economy in the most extreme of circumstances. By claiming that the fruits of autarky can keep prisoners alive even during the devastation of the civil war, Sandoval Amorós was probably trying to reassure his readers of Spain's capacity – during the relative calm of the post-war period – to feed her own people without having recourse to external food supplies.

Interestingly, this image of Republican prisoners being fed oranges can be found in the Nationalist propagandistic film *Prisioneros de Guerra* (Prisoners of war), produced during the civil war. This "documentary," which shows several scenes of prisoners of war eating or being fed in the Nationalist prisoner camps, includes at one point an image of a character consuming an orange. The prisoner looks well fed and content as he slowly peels the orange, preparing to eat it. Of interest is how interwoven all of these images and texts are, constituting a discourse about food that in this instance creates in viewers a belief that even Republican prisoners of war are in robust health thanks to the generosity of the Nationalist troops and Spain's abundant foodscape.

At the end of his prologue, Sandoval Amorós writes of how he hopes his cookbook will make a modest contribution "a la obra ingente que realiza el estado español en pro de la salud pública" (to the colossal efforts of the Spanish state in favour of public health; 12). Linking his medical and culinary arguments for greater orange consumption to state efforts to lift per capita consumption of Spanish oranges, Sandoval Amorós ties his food-writing explicitly to official discourse. It is, according to his prologue, in the name of public health or hygiene that he puts out his call to Spaniards to eat more oranges. Managing the eating body involves asking it not just to consume more locally grown produce, but also to make decisions about food consumption that prioritize the collective health of the citizenry. This food text also functions to produce readers who are convinced of Spain's capacity for alimentary self-sufficiency. The recipes that constitute its pages can be seen, therefore, to symbolize the desired national virtues of autarky, frugality, and self-denial. Urging citizens to consume more oranges is ultimately a call to incorporate these post-war values.

A Taste for Rice

As Tiago Saraiva explains, "every fascist regime of the interwar period became obsessed with projects for making the national soil feed the national body" (3). Saraiva gives examples from different fascist regimes, writing in the case of Mussolini that the Italian dictator was obsessed with freeing Italy from the "slavery of foreign grain" (65), while the Nazis insisted on food independence as a "necessary condition for both the biological survival of the race and its political independence" (71). In her study of fascism and food in Mussolini's Italy, Carol Helstosky notes that the only foods officially endorsed during such times "were those that could be produced within Italy" and that beginning in 1928, "ordinary Italians were bombarded with propaganda that stressed the political utility and health benefits of consuming only domestically produced foods" (5).

That Francoist officials had Mussolini's own program of reform in mind is supported by the many references in *Alimentación nacional* to Italy's stoic embrace of autarky. For instance, in one of its first issues, from 1941, there is an article titled "Pan y Guerra" (Bread and war), which describes how

> el pueblo italiano ha acogido con disciplina firme y serena la nueva medida de racionamiento del pan. Prueba de su magnífico espíritu de resistencia y patriotismo. El pueblo italiano puede hoy apreciar los beneficios del trigo y la autarquía económica que Mussolini ha llevado a cabo. (Issue 2, 24)
>
> (the Italian people have welcomed the new bread rationing measures with discipline and serenity. This is evidence of their magnificent spirit of resistance and patriotism. Today, the Italian populace can appreciate the benefits of wheat and of the economic self-sufficiency that Mussolini has achieved.)

This description not only links Francoist food culture with that of Mussolini's Italy, but also makes clear to Spaniards the fortitude of character that is similarly required of them for the greater good of autarky.

Mussolini encouraged the consumption of locally grown produce, such as rice and vegetables, so as to conserve wheat stocks and end Italy's "vexatious" dependence on foreign supplies of wheat.[1] In similar fashion, the Franco regime also encouraged the consumption of locally grown produce, and in *Alimentacion nacional* references to Spanish rice are ubiquitous. However, in the case of Francoist food discourse officials do not just attempt to shape consumer behaviour and demarcate the borders of Spanish cuisine; they also codify food culture in such a way that readers have the utmost faith in Spain's capacity to feed her own people while remaining closed off to foreign imports of food.

There were a number of different reasons Spanish officials chose to focus on rice in their attempts to convince Spaniards of the merit of autarky. First, rice production in the immediate post-war period was greater than during the civil war years. While rice production in 1939 dropped by around 30 percent from rates in 1931–34, it rose again to almost 1934 levels in 1940, and also increased in the early to middle 1950s (see the Instituto Nacional de Estadística's yearly reports on rice). This increase reflects a number of successful state efforts in the post-war period to support rice production. As Camprubí explains: "In order to ensure enough rice to meet demand while avoiding expensive imports – that is, in order to assure rice self-sufficiency – the authorities took over control of the cereal's production and distribution" (506). Increases in rice production could be claimed to result not just from state intervention, but also from the mechanisms of autarky itself, since the production and distribution of rice, as well as being centralized, was also managed according to the principles of extreme economic nationalism. Not only, therefore, did the increase in rice consumption prove Spain's capacity to feed her own people, it is also spoke to the merits of the very political economy of autarky that the regime was attempting to promote as viable and sound.

Rice was also cast as an ideal fascist foodstuff or a culinary symbol of Franco's autarkic political economy because official rice producers had, since the outset of the regime, insisted on the unsuitability of growing foreign rice varieties in Spain. Advantageous, too, was the fact that since the outset of the regime, rice had been fashioned as a political tool at the service of the victors. The federation of rice growers offered Franco a victorious rice chest and presented him with a published account of the heroic efforts of those who risked their lives planting rice on the fields of Valencia at the end of the war during Republican bombing: "Hizo la federación cuanto pudo para conseguir un precio excepcional para aquella cosecha que tanto había costado – se tuvo que plantar, escardar y segar muchas veces bajo el fuego de las ametralladoras del enemigo, produciéndose heridos y muertos entre los que realizaban aquellas faenas agricolas" (The federation did what it could to obtain an exceptional price for this harvest that had cost too much – which had to be planted, weeded, and sown many times under fire of the enemy's machine guns, resulting in wounded and dead amongst those carrying out those agricultural tasks; Rodríguez-Roda 18; see also Camprubí 505–6).

This same publication, published in 1940 by the Federación Sindical de Agricultores de España, gives thanks to state efforts to increase rice production:

> Sin la generosa ayuda del Gobierno del Caudillo, representado por el excelentísimo señor Ministro de Agricultura, hubiera sido imposible

> la reconstrucción de la economía arrocera que este año acabamos de iniciar... Sirvamos lealmente las consignas del Caudillo y al aumentar nuestra producción pensamos que con ello colaboramos directamente en la magna impresa de hacer mas grande, libre y poderosa nuestra Patria. ARRIBA España. (122)
>
> (Without the generous support of the Caudillo government, represented by his excellency the minister for agriculture, the reconstruction of the rice economy which we have begun this year would have been impossible ... Let us loyally obey the orders of the Caudillo and, by increasing our production, we consider that we are collaborating directly in the great enterprise of making our homeland greater, freer and more powerful. UP WITH Spain.)

This book also contains lots of images of rice growers and rice plantations, including reproductions of prints depicting Spanish rice production by well-known Spanish artists, such as Genaro Lehuerta's *Plantando el arroz* (Planting rice). Lehuerta's print depicts four workers harvesting rice in unison with almost dance-like movements. A romantic depiction of rice production, this image does not in any way show the hard physical labour involved in bending down to harvest rice. All aspects of rice are thus glorified in this publication, from its Spanishness to the way it is harvested and produced.

With Spanish rice being an apt culinary symbol for the political economy of autarky, as well as proof of Spain's capacity to feed the nation, it is no surprise that *Alimentación nacional* writes of its many virtues. Within the context of the devastation of Spain's post-war foodscape, blamed repeatedly on the Republicans, rice is held up as a beacon of hope for its capacity to feed the citizenry. *Alimentación nacional* reassures its readers that thanks to state efforts in certain areas of the country, "la producción de arroz camina a equiparse con la de antes de la guerra" (the rice production is heading towards pre-war levels; Issue 2, 2). It is also quick to point out that this increase in rice production has created "un cambio del mapa físico de la patria. Un convertir las tierras pobres, exhaustas, escasamente productivas en otras ricas, productivas y generosas" (a change in the physical map of the country. Land that was poor, exhausted, scarcely productive has become rich, productive, and generous; Issue 2, 2). If readers are to believe official claims about the viability of autarky, they must first be convinced that Spain will be able to keep the country's citizenry healthy and strong. The discourse about rice in this official publication certainly achieves this aim, as it creates the sense that there is an abundance of this foodstuff in Spain.

Alimentación nacional also emphasizes rice's superior nutritional value, going as far as to describe it as "la base de la alimentación humana" (the base of the human diet; Issue 4, 6). This highly nutritious and 100 percent Spanish foodstuff is also discussed for the "personalidad productora [que] ha dado [el] país" (productive character it has given the country; Issue 9, 1). Equally important are the ways in which discussions of improved rice production serve to generate gratitude amongst the citizenry. Reminded on numerous occasions of state efforts to improve rice production after the devastation wreaked by Republicans during the civil war, readers are encouraged to feel grateful to the state for its duty of care in matters of nutrition and food. *Alimentación nacional*'s discursive codification of rice produces readers/citizens who do not just believe in Spain's capacity to feed its citizenry on the fruits of autarky, but are also united in the gratitude they feel towards their country's leaders.

Spanish rice production also features in *No-Do*, the weekly Francoist newsreel. On 1 January 1955 *El Arroz y la Paella* (Rice and paella) was shown as part of "Imágenes, Revista Cinemotagráfica." The short documentary starts off with an image of a paella pan positioned against the backdrop of the Valencian landscape. For most of the documentary, the viewer sees images of rice production, from its plantation to its packing and distribution to other countries. Much of the information given is of a technical nature and serves to highlight the rigorous approach taken to rice production, which Francoist authorities took over. *El Arroz y la Paella* reminds viewers of the successful state intervention in, and centralization of, rice production. We are shown paella cooked in both domestic and professional settings, yet the actual consumption of rice is not discussed. Rather, the grain – loaded with symbolic meaning that can be harnessed by the regime – positions Spain as an important rice-producing nation thanks to state intervention and autarkic policies.

While *Alimentación nacional* provides a lot of information about the increased levels of rice production across the Iberian Peninsula, it does not discuss issues relating to rice consumption. As one important part of the ration system, "the state became the supplier of rice for consumers through the General Commission of Provisions and Transportation (Comisaría General de Abastecimientos y Transportes)" (Camprubí 428). Radcliff estimates that rations in the mid-1940s covered 73 percent of bread needs but only 25–30 percent of daily rice needs (233). Pointing also to a less clear-cut story regarding Spain's abundant supply of rice are official reports such as the following, from the Comisaria General de Abastecimientos y Transportes:

Por el Ministerio de Industria y Comercio se autorizó, en el mes de marzo de 1940, a la Federación citada para efectuar compras de arroz en el extranjero a cuyo efecto se dieron órdenes al Instituto Español de Moneda Extranjera para situar los oportunos créditos. ("Asuntos varios")

(The Minister of Industry and Commerce authorized, in the month of March 1940, the aforementioned federation to effectuate purchases of rice abroad, with the effect that orders have been given to the Spanish Institute of Foreign Currency to make the necessary appropriations.)

Although, according to Radcliff, most of the population did not have access to enough rice and Spain was reliant – as this report indicates, for the early years at the very least – on imports of rice, *Alimentación nacional* excludes mention of this fact. Indeed, by describing only improved levels of rice production and failing to discuss the actual levels of rice consumption or the country's intermittent dependence on imports, *Alimentación nacional* creates the impression that Spain had a surplus of the grain.

The views about rice found in *Alimentación nacional* have an impact on that foodstuff's textual construction. Although rice is codified as highly nutritious in these cookbooks, there is no mention of the limited amount of rice that most Spaniards had access to at this time. Yet these texts create readers or citizens who believe that thanks to state efforts to improve production, there is now an abundance of rice. With little rice to eat, most Spaniards would probably have not used the recipes in the ensuing cookbooks. The cookbooks therefore may have had little impact on cooking habits, but can nevertheless be seen to take part in the production of readers with a belief in autarky and Spain's capacity to keep the nation healthy and well fed.

The first cookbook I will consider was commissioned by a state entity. A relatively modest book of some eighty pages, *Fórmulas variadas para guisar el arroz* (Various ways to cook rice), produced by Valencia's Cooperativa Nacional del Arroz (National rice cooperative) in 1947, is made up of three sections: an introduction to "el arte culinario arrocero" (the art of rice-based cuisine) by F.A Gómez, president of the national rice federation; a few pages on the health benefits of rice consumption penned by Dr Gimeno Márquez; and a section containing an array of predominantly Spanish rice recipes.[2] An example of the recipes he includes in his book is *arroz con leche de almendras* (rice with almond milk):

Para cada libra de arroz prepárese otra de almendras, otra de azúcar, seis huevos, dos onzas de piñones y un cuarterón de canela. Póngase al fuego un cazo lleno de agua, y tan pronto hierva échense las almendras, que así se mondan, y se las echa después en agua fría. Luego hay que picarlas en union de los piñones, y se hace leche desliendo la masa en agua fria y colandola a traves de un lienzo. Lavado el arroz con agua tibia, extiéndase en un tablero para que se seque. La leche anteriormente hecha ha de ser puesta al fuego en una cacerola nueva, y allí se añade el arroz, después de medio cocido por seperado con agua y sal. La canela ha debido tenerse en infusión en un puchero, y esta infusión va derramándose dentro del arroz, al cual se añadirá leche hasta que esté bien cocido. Entonces se aparta del fuego y se le echan por encima unas yemas desleídas en leche fría, espolvorenado después con azucar y canela. Por si se enduriciera, conviene reservar algo de leche a fin de ablandarlo a punto de servirlo. (84)

(For every pound of rice, prepare one of almonds, one of sugar, six eggs, two ounces of pine nuts, and a quarter pound of cinnamon. Put a saucepan full of water on the stove, and once boiling add the almonds, so that they can be peeled. Then place them in cold water. Afterwards, the almonds must be ground together with the pine nuts. Milk is made by dissolving the mixture in cold water and straining it through canvas. Wash the rice in warm water, and spread on a board to dry. Put the previously made milk on the stove in a fresh saucepan. Add the rice, after half cooking it separately with water and salt. Infuse the cinnamon in a pot. Pour this infusion into the rice, and then add the milk until it is well cooked. Take it off the stove. Over the top, place some egg yolks dissolved in cold milk, powdering with sugar and cinnamon. Reserve some of the milk in case it becomes hard in order to soften it when serving.)

As well as providing relatively simple recipes, such as this one, which makes use of typically Spanish ingredients and cooking methods, this cookbook codifies rice as an autochthonous foodstuff, glorified for being perfectly suited to the needs of the Spanish physiology. The importance of rice resides, too, in fact that it is the main ingredient of a number of iconic national dishes, including paella, which according to Gómez has taken on the status of national dish amongst foreign visitors to Spain.

Aside from this mention of the popularity of paella amongst foreigners, the rest of the cookbook is all but free from foreign influence. Interestingly, the only foreign recipe included in this book is *Arroz argentino* (Argentine rice), most likely reflective of the warm relations between Argentina and Spain at this stage, or as a sign of gratitude to the Perón government for the assistance it rendered to Spain during the first decade or so of the Franco regime. Certainly, *Alimentación nacional* lauds the trade agreement between Spain and Argentina for the way "nos permitará recibir un millón de toneladas de trigo, tabaco y maíz a cambio de treinta mil toneladas de hierro y otros productos" (it will permit us to receive a million tons of wheat, tobacco and corn in exchange for thirty thousand tons of iron and other products; Issue 12, 25). According to the author, the importance of this trade agreement cannot be underestimated, as "tiene inmensa importancia para nuestro equilibrio económico y un hondo sentido espiritual que no cabe desconocer" (it has immense importance for our economic balance sheet and a deep spiritual meaning that cannot be overlooked; Issue 12, 25). The importance of both this trade agreement and the notion of *Hispanidad* to the Franco regime means that the author of *Fórmulas variadas para guisar el arroz* produces readers or citizens who see their national identity and food culture as open to Argentine influence.

Hispanidad was a crucial aspect of Francoist ideology, especially in the early years of the dictatorship. The concept was intended to strengthen ties between Spain and Latin America, emphasizing shared past, language, culture, race, and especially religion – but all in Spain's interest. *Hispanidad* functioned as a "triple metaphor" that conjured and linked the ideas of a national Spanish essence or soul, its crusading role for the Roman Catholic Church, and the "Golden Age" of colonial power that connected Spain with its former colonies in "Hispanoamérica" (Großmann 756). Through the inclusion of this Argentinian recipe, the author gives readers permission to think about their national identity as consisting in small part of this notion of *Hispanidad* that was so central to the regime.

Fórmulas variadas para guisar el arroz also upholds official discourse in the way it codifies Spanish rice as nutritious and easy to digest. According to the medical introduction to the book, "no existe ningún alimento mejor y más sabroso que el arroz" (there is no foodstuff better or tastier than rice; 4). Moreover, unlike other foodstuffs such as meat, fish, and eggs, "el arroz alimenta, pero no envenena, ni carga la sangre de toxinas ni ácido úrico" (rice feeds, but does not poison, nor does it load the blood with toxins or uric acid; 6). The daily diet, according to del Arco Blanco, was scarce in proteins ("Hunger" 468). At a time when most of the animal proteins mentioned here were still very hard to come by for most of the population, casting rice – a product of Spain's autarkic political economy – as a superior foodstuff is an excellent example of how this cookbook sustains official discourse. Implicit in these comments about the advantages of Spanish rice is the belief that the even scarcer protein-rich foods mentioned are somehow superfluous and that a diet rich in the fruits of autarky is more than sufficient.

Such cookbooks contribute to a hegemonic nutrition discourse. Their focus on the health benefits of rice links healthy eating to ideas of citizenship. The good Spaniard pursues a healthy lifestyle, because good health is a key requirement for being able to carry out one's civic duties. In line with Foucault's biopolitics, these cookbooks frame nutrition as a personal choice, masking the fact that the Franco regime's political economy of autarky was responsible for the food insecurity faced by most of the country. These texts uphold the Francoist biopolitics because they discipline the individual body to the extent that eating becomes about civil duty and collective well-being, rather than individual desire.[3]

Of interest also are the differences between this 1947 food text and ones published in the middle to late 1950s. A comparison of these different cookbooks provides an excellent example of how discursive codifications of rice changed according to broader economic dictates. During the 1940s, when official discourse highlighted Spain's increased rice production, Spaniards were encouraged to view rice as an ideal foodstuff, yet as Spain entered a period of modernization and economic growth, rice ceased to be codified as a nutritionally superior ingredient. For instance, in the 1956 cookbook *El arroz y el bacalao: Formas tradicionales de prepararlos en España e Hispanoamérica* (Rice and cod: Traditional Spanish and Hispanic-American recipes), we see a shift away from food discourse that directs readers to eat only rice, with the text encouraging the incorporation of other ingredients into meal plans.[4] Indeed, the value of rice, according to these authors, lies primarily in how easily it mixes with other foodstuffs: "El arroz es uno de los cereales más socorridos, y que puede guisarse con casi todo lo cocinable" (rice is one of the most commonly used cereals, and it can be cooked with almost everything that can be cooked; 5).

Another cookbook evincing such a change is Asunta Podesan's 1959 *El Arroz: Como base de alimentación* (The rice-based diet). At the time of its publication, Spaniards had access to a great deal more food than in 1947, when they were directed to embrace rice as a superfood of sorts. In line with the greater availability of other foodstuffs, Podesan describes rice as "un alimento muy incompleto" (a highly incomplete food; 7) and encourages Spain's housewives to treat rice as an entrée: "Pretendo con el presente librito, incorporar a la mujer española a la primera fila del saber cocinar con el arroz, en una serie de platos de esos primeros platos" (With this little book, I intend to incorporate Spanish women into the first ranks of knowing how to cook rice, with a series of first course dishes; 10). By asking readers to see rice as an ingredient that mixes well with more expensive proteins or vegetables, Podesan's text attempts to produce subjects or citizens who support Spain's growing economy. Significantly, to be a compliant eating subject at the dawn of Spain's period of modernization and economic growth requires citizens to view rice as just one of many ingredients available to them, a stark contrast with cookbooks that had since the post-war treated rice as a mono-ingredient.

What is similar, however, about 1940 cookbooks and Podesan's 1959 text is the way she positions rice as an ideal foodstuff "como base de la alimentación infantil" (as the base of a childhood diet; 11). Food writers uphold Francoist biopolitics by emphasizing child nutrition. According to scholars of food biopolitics, "because children are subjects who are socially constructed as both future citizens and at risk they are thereby seen as valid sites of political intervention in the name of public good" (Gibson and Dempsey 44–5). Writing about the importance of keeping children well fed, food writers in Franco Spain make clear that the child's body is a shared responsibility and must be safeguarded for the well-bring of the nation. It is significant that the unique and superior benefits of Spanish rice feature alongside recipes and images of portly, cherubic infants. At times of hunger and deprivation, the suffering of children takes on a particularly chilling dimension. Readers of these sorts of cookbooks are reassured, however, of the power of the Spanish state and its autarkic political economy to provide food that is not just "free" from foreign contagion, but also nutritious enough to keep children looking so well fed.

An Appetite for Culinary Patriotism

Often, in times of national trauma, "threats to healthiness and purity of the body politic are identified with the 'foreign'" (Brinker-Gabler and Smith 15), and in Franco Spain there was a full-scale attempt to isolate the Spanish body from foreign influence. Carbayo-Abengózar explains how nationhood in post-war Spain referred also to "the exclusivity of a self-sufficient, self-controlled and autarkic vision of the state" ("Shaping Women" 78). This connection between nationhood and exclusivity, which would subsequently be discussed in terms or purity, saw an emphasis on maintaining Spain's traditions "as opposed to being open to new ideas" ("Shaping Women" 77).

Food discourse played an important function in upholding this notion of Spanish nationhood as closed off to foreign contagion in that it took part in the production of a culinary sphere that existed in isolation from other national cuisines. Texts such as Alberto León's *La cocina clásica española* (Classical Spanish cuisine) and Bosch Bierge's *Cocina regional española* (Regional Spanish cuisine) codified Spanish cuisine as proudly free from the influence of other national cuisines. Through their own gastronomic patriotism or culinary xenophobia, the authors of these texts make explicit to readers the right way to think about Spanish cuisine in the context of autarky and self-sufficiency. This food discourse produces subjectivities who are themselves patriotic/xenophobic, therefore upholding Francoist biopolitics.

León's *La cocina clásica española* was published in either 1940 or 1941. The copy held at the Biblioteca Nacional has the censors' stamp on it, although the censors' report at the Archivo Nacional in Alcalá de Henares does not note anything of interest about this text. León's history of gastronomy starts with a trenchant critique of the negative impact that foreign cuisines have had on the state of Spanish food culture: "La vieja y tradicional cocina española, tan sana y rica en delicados condimentos como deliciosa en el gusto de sus platos sabrosísimos y exquisitos, va sufriendo el empuje avasallador de las corrientes extranjeras" (The old and traditional Spanish cooking, as healthy and rich in delicate condiments as it is delicious in the flavor of its tasty and exquisite dishes, is suffering from the overwhelming push of foreign trends; 7). Citing Emilia Pardo Bazán, León writes:

> La ilustre Condesa de Pardo Bazán dice al frente de su libro *La cocina antigua española* las siguientes atinadísima palabras "Hay muchos platos de nuesta cocina regional y nacional de justísima fama ... que cada nación tiene el deber de conservar." (7–8)
>
> (The illustrious Condesa de Pardo Bazán states at the front of her book *La cocina española antigua y moderna* [Ancient and modern Spanish cooking] the following well-known words: "There are many dishes of our regional and national cuisine of well-deserved fame ... which every nation has the duty to preserve.")

Pardo Bazán made this comment about food heritage in the context of late-nineteenth-century Spanish nation building; León positions his call to Spaniards to conserve their culinary heritage against the backdrop of autarky. His comments about Spaniards needing to protect their food heritage become part of the broader argument of autarky that each nation needs to conserve its unique national character and spirit.

La cocina clásica española discusses the unsuitability of "las reglas extranjeras" (foreign rules) to Spain's foodscape. Foreign cooking, León writes, is unsuited to the Spanish palate and is not "en consonancia con nuestro clima ni con nuestras circunstancias geográficas" (in harmony with our climate or our geographic situation; 9). His book of gastronomy – which includes "una serie de recetas españolas – olvidadas en su mayoría" (a series of Spanish recipes – for the most part forgotten; 9) – proposes a month-by-month plan for the economical and organized housewife. León's emphasis on seasonal cooking and using the fruits of the Spanish soil reinforces the notion inherent to the political economy of autarky that Spain requires very little foreign food aid. Finally, León positions his own gastronomic book of recipes against that of Ángel Muro (1839–97), who was condemned by many Spanish food writers for penning a bestselling collection of Francophile recipes rather than taking up his patriotic duty to conserve Spanish cuisine (see L. Anderson, *Cooking Up the Nation*).[5] In the context of autarky, León's culinary patriotism produces citizens who understand not only their duty to support local production and consumption but also to protect Spanish cuisine against the negative influence of vexatious foreign cuisines.

Bosch Bierge's *Cocina regional española* (Regional Spanish cuisine) – also published at the outset of the dictatorship – is as patriotic and protective of Spain's culinary heritage as León's text. For Bosch Bierge, given the richness of Spanish food culture, it made no sense that French cuisine was so hegemonic in Spain throughout most of the nineteenth century. "Estas consideraciones," he writes, "nos han incitado a editar este tomo para cantar alabanzas de la Cocina Regional Española, de la que damos una sencilla muestra, que podríamos duplicar tan rica es la variedad del contenido del culinario del hogar español" (These considerations have prompted us to edit this volume in order to sing the praises of Spanish regional cuisine. We offer here only a small sample, but could multiply this tenfold, so rich is the variety of Spanish home cooking; 4). So supportive of official discourse is his culinary patriotism in relation to French cuisine that it borders on xenophobic. The language he uses is reminiscent of the discourse of autarky, in that he talks about the need to protect Spanish cuisine from other cuisines and make sure they do not penetrate the homeland. Bosch Bierge's call to protect Spain's culinary borders is replete with references to autarky's broader aim of sealing Spain off from the outside world, not just economically but culturally. His food text produces, therefore, readers and citizens who are not only patriotic about their cuisine but also committed to the desire for isolation inherent in Franco's political economy.

Disrupting this culinary patriotism is the Marquesa de Parabere, born María Mestayer de Echagüe, who published her *Historia de la gastronomía* (A history of gastronomy) in the early 1940s. It is of great interest to see how the Marquesa, a renowned Francophile, deals with the official codification of Spanish cuisine as separate and closed off to other cuisines. This food writer and restaurateur, who used the name "Marquesa de Parabere" both for the culinary texts she wrote and the two restaurants she opened in Madrid, made a unique contribution to Spain's epicurean scene. She was born in Bilbao in 1878 to the city's French consul and his wife, and her upbringing and personal connections with France meant that she moved seamlessly between French and Spanish cultures. The impact of this mixed cultural heritage is evident in her various culinary activities. Author of one of Spain's best-selling cookbooks, *La cocina completa* (The complete kitchen; 1933) and owner of the iconic Madrid high-end eatery El Parabere, first opened in 1936 and then again in 1941 after the Spanish Civil War, the Marquesa attained commercial success without a doubt due to her adherence to the dominant French culinary trends of the time.

On account of the resounding commercial success of *La cocina completa*, much more has been written about de Parabere as an author of cookbooks. However, *Historia de la gastronomía* is unusual in that, aside from being her only gastronomic text, it is one of the few texts of hers to be published for the first time during the first two decades of the dictatorship. The tendency in official discourse to equate Spanishness with cultural and political isolation from the outside world saw some food writers take a highly patriotic view of Spanish cuisine in relation to other national cuisines, especially French. The genealogy of overzealous culinary patriotism can be traced back to the Primo de Rivera dictatorship, when the Patronato Nacional de Turismo (National tourism board) commissioned Post-Thebussem to write a gastronomic survey of Spain's regional cuisines. Writing from a position intended to vindicate Spanish cuisine, Post-Thebussem launches missive after missive against French cuisine. Thereafter, as a way perhaps of showing adherence to official ideology on cultural isolation and autarky, a number of food writers from the first two decades of the Franco regime make either implicit or explicit reference to Post-Thebussem's ardently patriotic codification of Spanish cuisine. In marked contrast is the overtly pro-French and anti–Post-Thebussem stance that de Parabere takes in her *Historia de gastronomía*.

The Marquesa was a bit of a rebel on several fronts. As owner of a high-end restaurant at the height of post-war Spain's deprivation, de Parabere was subversive to say the least in her approach to rationing and food shortages. Her restaurant El Parabere opened for the second time in Calle Villanueva and was

> un local de lujo, que rápidamente se pone de moda, muy concurrido por políticos, aristócratas, artistas, toreros, comerciantes y hombres de negocio.

> Al ambiente distinguido hay que añadir una buena cocina, basada en alimentos que recibe de Francia gracias a su prima. (Garzón Sáez 3)

> (a luxury venue, which quickly became fashionable, well frequented by politicians, aristocrats, artists, bullfighters, merchants, and businessmen. On top of the distinguished atmosphere, one has to mention the fine cuisine, based on foodstuffs she receives from France thanks to her cousin.)

In addition to the restaurant's provision of French-inspired cuisine, other visible signs of Frenchness included the French consul's decision to put a French flag at the entry, which signified France's protection of de Parabere. In spite of the rationing of food, common during the post-war period, she maintained a sense of luxury in her restaurant, having expensive foodstuffs sent to her from France and overcoming the "plato único" (single course) restriction placed on restaurants by serving different courses on the same plate at the same time.

Given the evident Francophile feel of de Parabere's restaurant, it comes as little surprise that she also takes a pro-French stance in *Historia de la gastronomía*. What is perhaps surprising is that in such a totalitarian, insular phase of the dictatorship, de Parabere is not censored for writing insistently about the superiority of France in matters of taste and gastronomy. Clearly cognizant of the omnipresence of censorship at this time, in her prologue to *Historia de la gastronomía* de Parabere brings up the issue in relation to her "promotion" of French cuisine:

> Tal vez me censuren porque abundan las anécdotas francesas. De ello no tengo la culpa. Los franceses, siendo la nación que se ha preocupado más del yantar y beber, nada de extraño tiene que su historia coquinaria sea más extensa que la nuestra. (15)

> (Perhaps they will censure me because French anecdotes abound. I am not to blame for this. There is nothing strange about French culinary history being more extensive than ours, given that France is the nation that has paid the most attention to eating and drinking.)

It is likely, as with many of the "disruptive" food voices I consider in these pages, that de Parabere's *Historia de la gastronomía* was seen as posing less of a threat to official discourse than "masculine" texts or cultural products typically associated with the public sphere, primarily because it was written by a woman.

It is de Parabere's trenchant critique of Post-Thebussem's Spanish culinary patriotism that represents the most important disruption of official discourse. De Parabere takes issue with Post-Thebussem on multiple occasions, especially in relation to his discussion of the genealogy of Spanish and French foodstuffs. According to Post-Thebussem's rewriting of the gastronomic relations or rivalry between Spain and France, archetypal French dishes, such as truffles and alioli, were in fact originally from Spain (see L. Anderson, *Cooking Up the Nation*). If such claims go unchallenged by subsequent generations of Spanish food writers, de Parabere is not so complaisant in her treatment of the earlier gastronome, whom she evidently finds highly vexatious: "¡Post-Thebussem! ¡Post-Thebussem! Deje en paz a la trufa. La *verdadera* trufa es la francesa" (Post-Thebussem! Post-Thebussem! Leave the truffle alone. The *real* truffle is French; 114). She is more moderate in her culinary patriotism than other, less transgressive food writers, and de Parabere's openness to foreign (especially French) cuisine fits well with her preference – as evidenced in her other food endeavours – for culinary cosmopolitanism.

Food Shortages and Culinary Abundance

As noted above, economic autarky was responsible for the devastating hunger suffered by so many Spaniards during "los años de hambre" (the years of hunger). Official discourse all but ignored the effects of autarky on Spain's food supply by either rendering invisible or trivializing hunger. Many food texts – such as José Sarrau's cookbook *Nuestra cocina* (Our cuisine; 1946) – supported official discourse by ignoring the devastating hunger caused by the regime's political and economic policies. Other texts, by way of contrast, are disruptive and make clear the devastating food shortages suffered by many. Such texts challenge the Francoist biopolitics by allowing individuals to experience hunger in all its horrific dimensions, rather than enjoining them to be stoic and patriotic in the face of such suffering.

Describing the decade or so after the civil war, del Arco Blanco writes: "los largos años cuarenta han quedado grabados en la memoria colectiva como momentos de escasez, de penuria y, en definitiva, de miseria generalizada" (the long 1940s have been engraved into the collective memory as moments of scarcity, hardship, and, ultimately, widespread misery; "Morir de hambre" 241).[6] It has been estimated that in addition to the deprivation suffered by most of the citizenry throughout the 1940s, a staggering two hundred thousand Spaniards died of starvation during the post-war years. In spite of the undeniable gravity of the situation, official discourse underplayed the issue of the country's starving or dying citizens. From chirpy instructions to tighten one's belt for the good of the nation to infamous suggestions to let the people eat "carne de delfín" (dolphin meat; qtd. in Preston 411), officials either ignored or trivialized hunger. Moreover, citizens were instructed to prioritize national pride or the principles of autarky. This can be seen for instance, in Suñer's infamous claim that Spaniards would be happier eating no bread at all than foreign imports (see Preston 411).

Most studies of Franco Spain concur that autarkic policies were the main cause of hunger and economic stagnation during the first decades of the regime. As one pair of scholars explain:

> The resounding failure of nationalist policies was apparent in the economic stagnation of the 1940s … The recovery of Italy, France and Germany after the Second World War was swift, whereas in Spain the per capita levels of 1935 (the last year before the Civil War) were not reached again until the mid-1950s. (Tortella and Houpt 145–6)

Food supply was negatively affected as "efforts [were] made to prevent the importation of a range of foodstuffs, some of the staple dietary necessities of the population" (Richards 91). Estimates for the 1940s indicate that consumption of food decreased enormously. By the second half of the decade, officials found themselves forced to accept some food from other countries given the gravity of the situation.

The way in which hunger and food shortages were dealt with in official discourse was not straightforward, given that there were a number of conflicting issues at stake. First, Spaniards were asked, as is evident from Suñer's comments about bread, to make stoic sacrifices for the principles of autarky. While the citizenry was asked to cut back here and there, the extent of hunger and suffering was never fully acknowledged in official discourse, as that would have been paramount to admitting the failings of the regime's approach. What's more, official discourse remained silent about luxury and abundance in order to cover up the inequities of post-war Spain's foodscape and the fact that Francoist officials and well-connected families had ample access to food.

Alimentación nacional certainly creates an impression of a foodscape devoid of luxury foods and culinary abundance. The recipes provided are described, for instance, as "completamente caseras y económicas" (completely home-made and economical; Issue 9, 21), producing in readers a belief that the country's post-war foodscape required economizing moderation on the part of all Spaniards. Moreover, *Alimentación nacional* contains a number of references to cheap restaurants, thereby reassuring readers that for the time being luxury restaurants have ceased to exist: "En el diario "Pueblo" se ha hecho un reportaje de los precios, nada caros, de determinados restaurantes madrileños, de los llamados restaurantes económicos, a los que concurren muy diversas personas" (The newspaper *Pueblo* has reported on the inexpensive prices of certain Madrid restaurants, amongst the so-called economical restaurants, which are frequented by very diverse clientele; Issue 162, 11). *Alimentación nacional* also outlines a number of measures taken by various state organizations to regulate food consumption in the public sphere. As important as censoring press references to luxury food was the prohibition of "la ostentación en escaparates de artículos alimenticios de tal profusión que puede constituir alarde de abundancia" (the ostentation in shop windows of foodstuffs of such profusion that they seem to boast of abundance; Issue 11, 10). Both the descriptions of Spain's modest food culture and the affordable restaurants mentioned in this official publication, as well as the measures taken to prohibit the public display of luxury foods, are suggestive of official attempts to cover up the abundance of food to which some sectors of society had access.

The newspaper *ABC* offers further corroboration of this trend. In the immediate post-war period there are no detailed descriptions of food in it, even when mention is made of official banquets. For example, an article from 1942 titled "Contestación del Caudillo al discurso del alcalde" (The leader's reply to the mayor's speech) describes the event, giving the names of attendees and a description of Franco's speech, yet there is only a very perfunctory reference to the "comida oficial" (official meal) and no description of any of the food or wine served (8). There are also articles describing the end-of-year festivities in Madrid in 1940. Once again, none of them describe the food served at the "cenas o/y bailes de Año Nuevo" (New Year dinners and/or dances; *ABC*, "Las fiestas" 25). The only reference to food eaten is to the twelve grapes: "en los teatros se comieron las clásicas uvas" (the classic grapes were eaten in theatres; *ABC*, "Las fiestas" 25).[7] This reference can be seen more as a reminder of a New Year's Eve ritual that unifies the nation than a description of culinary abundance, which officials worried would generate a great deal of discontent given that most suffered deprivation.

Another example of the tendency in official food discourse to downplay luxury or culinary abundance can be found in the official Sección Femenina publication *Medina*, which was published between 1940 and 1945. In this women's magazine only one or two pages per issue are dedicated to cooking. Compared to the many pages dedicated to women's fashion, this absence is noteworthy for the way it upholds the official tendency to conceal just how much food some Spaniards had. Myriad photos of well-dressed women and advertising for expensive clothes and beauty products certainly indicates that Spain still had a well-heeled upper middle class during the immediate post-war years. In times of devastating starvation, adverts for food or luxury recipes would have enraged the all-but starving population, so this publication – in line with official discourse – upholds the public erasure of culinary abundance, while still making a nod to the country's elite.

Medina offers readers advice on table settings in some of its issues, but the accompanying pictures of the pristine tables set with expensive-looking crockery are missing any food. Implicit here is that knowing how to set a table is a valuable skill to learn, even in times of hunger. Although this section of advice was clearly directed at Spanish housewives who continued to throw dinner parties in post-war Spain, the periodical creates the impression that there is no food to be served: this article does not depict guests eating at the table or in fact show any pictures of food, again maintaining the official cover-up of how much food some households actually had.

Another way in which this publication attempts to downplay culinary abundance is by creating the impression that there is little need for furniture related to eating. In one article readers are instructed to turn unwanted dining tables into bedroom dressers, producing in readers a sense that dining tables are redundant in post-war Spain. The intent here is to decentre food from the publication's household management or domestic advice. Indeed, parts of the house or furniture in the house typically associated with eating became entirely disconnected from food. In the context of post-war Spain, women's magazines such as *Medina* engage very little with food, providing domestic advice that ignores the kitchen's primary function. They can therefore be seen as upholding official discourse in the way they disassociate household management from cooking or eating.

No Place at the Table for Hunger

Depictions of hunger were also censored. So transgressive was any mention of hunger at this time that scholars argue that it is only foreign accounts – not subject to censorship – that honestly depicted deprivation and starvation. In addition to British diplomatic reports of post-war Spain's foodscapes, other foreign visitors penned poignant descriptions of suffering. These include Gerald Brenan, who wrote that "much of the country was in a state of famine, which the press would not mention and to which the possessing classes closed their eyes" (71). The censoring of or refusal to acknowledge the extent of the deprivation rendered transgressive not just any mention of hunger, but the hungry body itself.

The hungry body was, according to Tatjana Pavlović, considered transgressive in post-war Spain because, as she explains, it "contrasted with that of [Franco]. While most of his nation was starving, Franco's well-known austerity was rapidly diminishing and Franco's body was quickly expanding" (46). By virtue of its divergence from Franco's expanding girth, the hungry body exposed the inequities of Spain's post-war foodscape. In its own right, the hungry body was also transgressive for the way it revealed the failings of autarky, providing evidence of just how deprived most Spaniards were.

An example of the exclusion of the hungry body from public discourse at this time can be found in a *No-Do* documentary from 1945. Showcasing some of the most important stories and images for "los años de hambre," the documentary contains a vignette about the "redemption" of a child delinquent caught stealing an apple. From his clothes and unkempt appearance, one would assume that this child resorts to stealing food because he is from one of the many desolate, war-torn families with so little to feed their children. The child, however, does not appear malnourished or underfed; his corpulent body is suggestive of an excess rather than a lack of food. This vignette is an example of the tendency in official or pro-official food discourse to highlight how well fed Spanish children were, for even in the context of child delinquency, children are depicted as well nourished and almost radiant in their good health.

Images and descriptions of well-fed children are present, too, in some of the issues of *Alimentación nacional*. One article, titled "El régimen alimenticio de los campamentos del Frente de Juventudes," depicts children happily drinking bowls of chocolate with bread: "El cuartelero plato de alumno se llena pronto de chocolate y pan, que los pequeños se encargan de hacer desaparecer, siempre entre risas" (The student's camp plate was quickly filled with chocolate and bread, which the little ones take responsibility for making disappear, always laughing; Issue 10, 13). The food at the camp is, according to the article, "variada y suficiente en riqueza católica" (varied and ample in Catholic wealth), creating the impression that it is the generosity of the church, one of the main pillars of the regime, that shelters Spain's youth from the devastating food shortages caused by the Republicans. Moreover, the image of children eating chocolate brings to mind Spain's imperial grandeur, since it was as part of the Colombian exchange that cocoa beans were introduced into the European foodscape. The bowls of chocolate, therefore, do not just represent the "generosity" of the church, but can also be read as a reminder of the belief, inherent to Francoism, in "Spain of imperial grandeur and Catholic tradition, the Spain of Isabel and Ferdinand" (Valis 7).

While official discourse creates the impression that Spain's children will be cared for by the state and well fed by the fruits of autarky, other sources paint a bleaker picture. According to one scholar, the initial Rockefeller report on the food situation, carried out in 1940, wrote of unprecedented levels of hunger and starvation, especially amongst the young:

> The school could feed less than 30 of the 700 children who needed meals, and desperate mothers would come daily to beg for food for their children because there was none at home ... The children who were eligible for publicly supplied meals ... were receiving no more than 400 calories a day. (Brydan 151)

In spite of the reality painted here and of similar reports of droves of starving children, *Alimentación nacional* not only chooses to ignore this suffering, but uses its own account of the provision of publicly supplied meals to create the impression that Spain's children want for nothing thanks to the benevolent state. According to the aforementioned Rockefeller report, even children who had access to such meals were receiving very few calories. Official discourse, by way of contrast, writes of children happily drinking bowls of chocolate.

The effect of this discourse is twofold. First, it upholds the false impression that Spain's children are not starving. Second, this depiction of the church feeding Spain's children can be seen as an attempt in official discourse to remind readers of the authority of the state in matters relating to food. In his discussion of food and power in the case of Israel, Nir Avieli writes that for some governments "control over food is a means of exercising power" (225). The depictions in *Alimentación nacional* of government- or church-supplied meals remind readers of the power of the state to feed its citizens, especially those of Catholic faith. Also implicit in such an image is a directive to readers to remain true to Catholicism. Alejandro Pérez-Olivares writes that "la dictadura optó por la administración del abastecimiento desde la amenaza del castigo" (the dictatorship elected to manage supply under the threat of punishment; 168). This rings true here, as readers are instructed in the uptake of Catholicism if they wish to receive food.

Pro-official Cookbooks in Times of Hunger

The tendency in official discourse to downplay not just hunger but also culinary abundance had an impact on cookbooks after the war. Post-war cookbooks that uphold official food discourse are of interest for the way they attempt to manage the conflicting tensions inherent to Spain's foodscape. One of the authors considered here, José Sarrau, upheld official discourse in the way he sought to produce readers and citizens who, like the state, did not explicitly acknowledge or feel hunger. If Sarrau is successful in upholding this aspect of official discourse, less convincing is his attempt to erase any mention of culinary abundance. Indeed, there are many slippages in his food discourse, the result of his attempt to write a useful cookbook for his readers – Spain's elite – while also trying to create the impression that all Spaniards had access to the same moderate amounts of food. Sarrau's role as cookbook author sees him pen a text that in fact – and most likely inadvertently – reveals just how much food some Spaniards had in post-war Spain. His inadvertent disruption of official discourse is particularly significant given his official connections with the Sección Femenina, as discussed in the next chapter.

Sarrau was well known for his role (both before and after the civil war) as director of Madrid's Academia de Gastrónomos (Academy of gastronomes), a Cordon Bleu school. The little that has been written about Sarrau focuses on his gastronomic academy. For instance, in his book *Libro de cocina de la República* (Book of Republican cooking), the journalist Isabelo Herrero mentions Sarrau primarily in relation to the academy: "en Madrid existió una importante Academia Gastronómica, dirigida por el gastrónomo José Sarrau y que impartía cursos a los que asistían señoras, señoritas y profesionales. Tenía sus aulas y fogones en la calle de Rocoletos número 14" (in Madrid there was an important gastronomic academy, directed by the gastronome José Sarrau, and which offered courses attended by married and single women, and professionals. Its classrooms and stoves were located at 14 Rocoletos Street; 17). According to Herrero, Sarrau concerned himself with "las gentes ilustradas" (enlightened people) and held out great hope for putting his Spanish cooking academy on par with the more established ones in Europe and the Americas. Yet when describing Sarrau's pre-war food activity, scholar and food historian Francisco Abad Alegría writes that his academy "enseñaba mucha cocina francesa y arte de servir la mesa, y algún punto de la cocina clásica española" (taught much French cuisine and the art of serving the table, and some classic Spanish cuisine; Abad Alegría et al. 40).

Martínez Llopis also makes a brief reference to Sarrau in *Historia de la gastronomía española* (A history of Spanish gastronomy), but only to describe his *Nuestra cocina* (Our cuisine) – the cookbook examined in this chapter – as "una obra muy voluminosa, dedicada al ama de casa, que contiene un nutrido repertorio de recetas de cocina internacional y muchas de la española" (a voluminous work, dedicated to the housewife, which contains a large repertoire of international recipes and many Spanish recipes; 434). Also mentioning Sarrau is María del Carmen Simón Palmer in her exhaustive *Bibliografía de la gastronomía y la alimentación en España*, where she lists all his titles with information such as number of editions, number of pages, publisher, and the size of each book in centimetres.

Because there are so few references to Sarrau in existing scholarship, thorough bibliographical research of his cookbooks is called for if we are to better understand the significance of his codification of Spanish cuisine. That codification is especially noteworthy given that it emerges at a time when most of the citizenry was living in a state of misery. The size of Sarrau's 1946 second edition of *Nuestra cocina* is, for instance, worth comment: twelve hundred pages long, it contains 104 images (8 in colour), 252 menus, and over a thousand recipes. Not just generous in size in its own right, this second edition contains nearly twice the number of pages as the original 1935 edition. In researching cookbooks, Elizabeth Driver argues, differences between editions are likely to be an important source of information for the food historian ("Cookbooks"). Certainly, the differences here point to broader socio-economic circumstances. We know that the standard of living in post-war Spain was much lower for most of the citizenry than it had been in 1935. Indeed, not until the 1960s would most housewives once again boast of "hornos de gas, frigoríficos, aspiradores eléctricos y otros electrodomésticos" (gas ovens, refrigerators, electric vacuum cleaners, and other household appliances; Herrero, jacket copy), and have access to the same amount and variety of foodstuffs as in 1935.

That Sarrau makes the post-war re-edition so much bigger than the 1935 publication inadvertently reveals that while most Spaniards wanted for the most basic of foodstuffs at this time, others, like the readers of his cookbooks, had ready access to supplies, including luxury foodstuffs. Although officials emphasized the universality of food shortages and rationing, social historians of the post-war years maintain that the deprivation and misery of "los años del hambre" did not extend to well-connected officials, civil servants, and their families. In publishing a cookbook in 1946 that was very expensive to purchase (two hundred pesetas) and that required ingredients most families would have been unable to access, Sarrau must have had Spain's affluent elite (including many of the students of his academy) in mind. Certainly, the "reader reviews" – published in the opening pages – are a good measure of the exclusivity of this text. Highly complimentary of *Nuestra cocina* is, for instance, Consuelo Duque de Estrada, who writes: "Creo que entre todos los libros publicados merece el primer lugar, no sólo por lo fino y selecto de sus recetas, sino por lo detalladas y preciosas que están" (I believe that of all the published books, this deserves first place, not only because of the quality and selectness of its recipes, but because they are so detailed and beautiful; 13). Since, as established above, media references to banquets or feasts were ruled out by official discourse, it is noteworthy that *Nuestra cocina* was not censored given that it reveals that some readers/citizens felt a need for such a luxury cookbook.

The following recipe indicates that Sarrau expected his readers would still be entertaining in post-war Spain. Providing ten serves, this recipe forms part of the *merienda* (afternoon tea) section of the cookbook and in no way speaks of deprivation:

> Chantilly Con Fresas (Helado) Receta num 66 – Presentación – Al servir el helado se saca el molde del cajón, se baña al chorro de agua fría y se desmoldea en fuente sobre servilleta, adornando los costados con bonitos claveles naturales; se sirve acompañado de servicio de pastas finas.
>
> Ingredientes – Para diez personas Claras de huevo 4 piezas; Azucar 100 gramos; Nata fresca ½ litro; Agua ½ decilitro; Anis 1 copa de las de licor; Fresas pequeñas 250 gramos.
>
> Preparación – Las claras se baten a punto de merengue, según costumbre, y una vez montadas, se incorpora el jarabe formado de antemano. La nata se bate muy fría, incorporando a mitad de montar, 100 gramos de azúcar, y una vez montada y frío el merengue se mezclan ambos preparados y las fresas, maceradas estas de antemano con la copa de anís; se vierte en uno o dos moldes a biscuit, se cubren las dos tapas con papel blanco y se ponen en un cajón sobre una capa de hielo y otra de sal gorda de seis a ocho kilos de hielo y dos de sal gorda y se deja en un sitito fresco tres horas.
>
> (Chantilly With Strawberries (Ice-cream) Recipe no. 66 – Presentation – When serving the ice cream, take the mould out of the box, place under running cold water, and remove from the mould onto a napkin, decorating the sides with pretty fresh carnations. Serve accompanied with pastry forks.
>
> Ingredients – for ten people – 4 egg whites; 100 grams of sugar; ½ litre of fresh cream; ½ decilitre water; 1 shot glass of anise; 250 grams small strawberries.
>
> Preparation – beat the egg whites until almost meringue, according to custom, and once whipped add the pre-prepared syrup. Beat the cream

while very cold; add 100 grams of sugar at the halfway point. Once the meringue is stiff and cold, combine both mixtures and the strawberries, which should be macerated beforehand with the cup of anise. Pour into one or two biscuit moulds. Cover with white paper and put into a box on a layer of ice (6–8 kilos) and another of coarse salt (2 kilos). Leave in a cool place for three hours.)

Although reader reviews of *Nuestra cocina* as well the intricate and luxurious meal plans that Sarrau provides betray the unevenness of food shortages in post-war Spain, Sarrau does attempt to codify his cuisine as suited to the everyday Spanish housewife. In a one-page advertisement in the *ABC* in 1948, *Nuestra cocina* is described as "el libro de hogar de la mujer española" (the household book for Spanish women; 7). The only reference to food deprivation in post-war Spain is in the description of the cookbook as "un libro completo en las actuales circunstancias" (a complete book for the present circumstances), reinforcing the official tendency to homogenize experiences of the post-war foodscape. The national press in general is instrumental in determining the reach that Sarrau's construction of Spanish cuisine in *Nuestra cocina* would have had amongst the Spanish citizenry. Certainly, the notion implicit in all of the advertisements is that Sarrau's cookbook is for the entire citizenry, not just an elite few. While the cost of his cookery would have been prohibitive for the majority, newspapers were much more affordable and had a much greater circulation. Thus, the series of advertisements for Sarrau's cookbook that ran in the *ABC* likely played an important role in determining how Spaniards came to view their food culture at this time.

While Sarrau's *Nuestra cocina* primarily calls for foodstuffs that would have been unfamiliar to most Spanish households, he does at times – mirroring the tone of these advertisements – try to transcend class in his presentation of the recipes. For instance, towards the end of the cookbook in a section called "muy interesante" (very interesting), Sarrau explains how with *Nuestra cocina* "se puede hacer cuanto place, lo mismo un plato sencillo que un plato montado" (you can do as much as you like, whether it be a simple dish or an elaborate one; 1143). He then provides a concrete example with his recipe for "el cocido llamado a la Madrileña o a la Española" (the stew described as Madrid-style or Spanish-style). Sarrau codifies this dish as truly national – that is, belonging to the masses rather than to an elite few – in his description of how it can be made from differing amounts and types of ingredients: "El cocido ... puede llevar el máximo de ingredientes, según se dice en la receta, pero también puede llevar el mínimo, que se compone de garbanzos, una verdura, patata, algo de carne" (the stew ... can contain the full number of ingredients, following the recipe exactly, but it can also be made with only a few, being chickpeas, a vegetable, potato, and some meat; 144). Even here, though, there are telling indications: while on the one hand Sarrau's recipe for *cocido* upholds the official message that in post-war Spain all Spaniards were more or less eating the same dishes, it betrays, most likely unwittingly, that food supply during these years was very uneven. There are a number of slippages like this throughout *Nuestra cocina*, speaking to the multifaceted nature of Sarrau's food discourse. These slippages reveal the tension produced as Sarrau upholds official discourse – which often distorted the reality of post-war Spain's foodscape – while also penning a cookbook that would be useful in times of deprivation.

Another example of this tension can be found in Sarrau's introductory "Meditaciones Gastronómicas" (Gastronomic reflections), where at the outset he boasts of Spain's gastronomic grandeur at the same time as he laments the nutritional problems facing most of the country. Joining a line of pre-eminent male Spanish intellectuals and gastronomes, most notably Mariano Pardo de Figueroa (Dr Thebussem) and Post-Thebussem – who had written about Spain's shifting gastronomic fortunes – Sarrau describes Spain as "uno de los países en que peor se ha comido, en el siglo pasado, aunque en otros tiempos fue la madre de la Humanidad; pero hoy vuelve a ocupar el lugar que le corresponde" (one of the countries with the worst diet, in the last century, despite previously being the mother of humanity; but today it is returning to its rightful place; 15). This creates the impression that war-torn Spain is poised and ready to return to its position at the epicentre of world gastronomy. Conversely, however, Sarrau's gastronomic mediations reveal a concern with the nutritional problems facing his country: "En España tenemos planteados, en todos sus múltiples y variados aspectos, el problema de alcanzar una alimentación sana y perfecta. Es uno de los grandes y urgentes problemas" (In Spain we have raised, in all of its multiple and varied aspects, the issue of achieving a healthy and perfect diet. It is a significant and urgent problem; 16). As a solution to this "urgent problem" of nutrition, Sarrau lists all the vitamins, the major food groups, and physiological functions, bringing to mind the genre of bellic cookbooks. Any parallels between Spain's wartime and post-war cookbooks are noteworthy for what they reveal about similarities in food shortages and deprivation. Although Sarrau never directly acknowledges these similarities, implicitly – and perhaps without meaning to – he provides yet another example of the way his culinary discourse speaks to the reality of deprivation.

Prologues and dedicatories are similarly important to situating a text (Driver, "Cookbooks" 258; Parkhurst Ferguson 133). These paratextual elements help here to produce a particular narrative about Sarrau's cookbook. It should come as little surprise (on account of Sarrau's alignment with the Sección Femenina) that he dedicates *Nuestra cocina* to his daughter: "A mi hija Pilar, en prueba de mi paternal afecto" (to my daughter Pilar, as evidence of my paternal affection; x). This dedication to his daughter makes clear his own role in upholding the values of the Francoist state. For not only does he teach Spanish women much about Spanish cooking with his tome of one thousand recipes, but he also, according to the dedication, has transmitted to his daughter the traditional gender roles prescribed by the regime.

The role of women is important as well to Juana Salas de Jiménez, who pens the prologue to Sarrau's book. Her writing on gender is conservative and she upholds the official dictate of the era that women dedicate themselves solely to the care of their families. Also reflective of official discourse are her comments on food shortages and autarky which uphold, too, official discourse on post-war Spain's deprivation. Euphemisms abound, as seen for instance in her opening consideration of the commercial fate of this edition "sin estar todavía España nadando en la abundancia de productos alimenticios" (with Spain still not swimming in an abundance of foodstuffs; 7). Rendered invisible in official discourse, hunger is also absent in the prologue, as Salas de Jiménez talks about a "lack of abundance" rather than extreme deprivation. Autarky is another topic implicitly touched on in this section: "España," Salas de Jiménez writes, "es rica; su producción agrícola, ganadera y avícola, que está muy encima de otras naciones, nos permite esperar que la normalidad vendrá antes que en otros países que sostuvieron guerras" (Spain is rich; our agricultural, livestock, and poultry production is much higher than that of other nations, which allows us to expect that normality will return more quickly than in other countries that have experienced war; 7). Salas de Jiménez's reference to the superiority of Spanish agriculture, farming, and olive production can be seen as reflective of the official justification for autarky that Spain wanted for nothing.

Salas de Jiménez's prologue also upholds official discourse in the way she distances Sarrau's cookbook from Ignacio Doménech's transgressive ones, which speak with brutal honesty of deprivation. An important feature of Doménech's cookbooks was the notion of replacement ingredients, as he both documented and provided his readers with solutions to the scarcities of post-war Spain. His food discourse can be seen as disruptive of official discourse: in calling for replacement ingredients, he makes clear the gravity of post-war Spain's food shortages. Salas de Jiménez assures her readers that Sarrau's cookbook is nothing like these "libritos que nos ofrecen recetas para guisar sin aceite" (little books which offer us recipes for cooking without oil; 48). In her condemnation of cookbooks like Doménech's (referred to here in the diminutive, as "libritos") that explicitly acknowledge food shortages, Salas de Jiménez produces or privileges subjects that, like the state, do not speak of deprivation.

While never writing explicitly of hunger and food shortages, Salas de Jiménez does implicitly acknowledge that post-war Spain's foodscape is not what it was in her hope that "este libro de Sarrau será consultado como siempre lo ha sido, y volveremos a saborear los ricos manjares de la variada y rica cocina española" (Sarrau's book will be consulted as it always has been, and we will once again savor the rich delicacies of Spain's rich and varied cuisine; 8). Until such time as the Spanish citizenry can once again enjoy the variety and richness of Spanish cuisine, it is, according to Salas de Jiménez, the responsibility of the Spanish housewife to make life as agreeable as possible. Of interest here is the way Salas de Jiménez shifts the responsibility for "solving" the problem of food shortages from the state to the individual, and in particular to women. We know that the regime's autarkic political economy was responsible for food shortages, yet in food texts that uphold official discourse, there is no mention of the state's role in causing such misery. Instead, moral fortitude, strength of character, and culinary creativity are called for if the housewife is to make the most of what food is available.

Not only does such instruction to Spanish housewives downplay enormously the deprivation faced by most of the population, it also genders sacrifice in times of hunger as female. Bravery, generosity, and abnegation are required of Spanish women by the Francoist state, a point that brings to mind present-day scholarship on food shortages. Indeed, as a number of scholars have argued, given women's familial responsibility for the provision of food and for making a little food go a long way, women live the reality of food shortages much more directly than men.[8] Also making the experience of hunger a predominantly female one is the fact that "men traditionally receive the highest food allocation" during times of rationing (Shepler 47). The New Spain's rationing system, which ran from 14 May 1939 until 1952, covered the entire national territory, and the "rationing affected every food product and many other basic items" (del Arco Blanco, "Hunger" 460). The self-sacrifice required of Spanish women as everyone waited for the return of normality can be thought about in terms of how women have traditionally been more affected by rationing than men or children. Implicit in Salas de Jiménez's call to Spanish women to be self-sacrificing is the belief that women will be the first to go without in times of deprivation.

Although Salas de Jiménez does place the responsibility for dealing with food shortages with Spanish women, she never speaks of hunger per se. This stands in stark contrast to the final two cookbooks we will look at, penned by Doménech.

Providing an Account of Hunger in Cookbooks

Hailing from Catalonia, Ignacio Doménech wrote a number of cookbooks in Spanish as well as a bestseller in Catalan. If both Doménech's affiliation with Catalonia and his promotion of Catalan cuisine represent an important point of difference from the dominant official discourse, so too did his preference for European culinary modernity. Of this aspect of his culinary persona, Simón Palmer writes that "simboliza la modernidad en la cocina española … de formación europea, comprende la importanica de transmitir los conocimientos profesionales" (it symbolizes modernity in Spanish cooking … with European training, he understands the importance of communicating his professional knowledge; 4). After working for some years as a chef and food writer in Barcelona, Doménech went to Europe, where he studied under Escoffier, "quien le reclamaba entre la brigada de cocineros para intervenir en los banquetes de mayor compromiso" (who demanded he join the team of chefs working on the most important banquets; Sella Montserrat in Doménech, *Cocina de recursos* (Resourceful cooking, 17). He worked, too, "a las órdenes de Escoffier en El Savoy londinense, durante la época de los esplendores culinarios de la cocina francesa" (under the orders of Escoffier in the Savoy in London, during the height of French cuisine's splendour; Abad Alegría et al. 103). Back in Madrid after his time in Paris and London, he took on "el papel de jefe de cocina de la embajada británica en Madrid" (the role of head chef in the British embassy in Madrid; Abad Alegría et al. 103). Most of Doménech's cookbooks, not to mention the culinary periodicals he founded for food professionals – *La cocina elegante* (Elegant cooking, 1904–5) and *El gorro blanco* (The white hat, 1906–45) – show a clear preference for French haute cuisine. Spanish cuisine could only benefit, according to Doménech's culinary discourse, from being elevated to the dizzy heights of that of neighbouring France. Such a cosmopolitan and pro-European viewpoint represents a major contrast with the official Francoist tendency to "build Spain against Europe" (Humlebaek 82).

This discussion of the general subversiveness of Doménech's culinary discourse provides us with important context for analysis of the challenge to official views posed by his *Claudina sabe guisar: Platos fáciles* (Claudina knows how to cook: Simple dishes) and *Cocina de recursos* (Resourceful cooking). *Claudina sabe guisar* seems to have all but disappeared from histories of Spanish gastronomy. A number of official sources, such as the Generalitat and Catalonia's Biblioteca Nacional, contain no reference to it in their listings of Doménech's culinary oeuvre. Nor is the book listed in Joan Sella Montserrat's introductory chapter to the most recent edition of *Cocina de recursos* (2011). It is, however, included in Simón Palmer's *Bibliografía de la gastronomía y alimentación en España,* where she includes the year of publication as 1939 with interrogation marks. Spain's Biblioteca Nacional lists this book too, but with 1940 as the publication date. Given that there is no mention of wartime conflict in this cookbook, it was most likely published after the end of the civil war, but either publication date is possible, in 1940 – as indicated by the BNE – or in 1939, after the cessation of conflict.

Claudina sabe guisar has perhaps not made it onto official and scholarly listings for Doménech because of the text's apparent insignificance. A mere ninety pages, it had much less visibility in the national press than his other cookbooks (it was promoted only once in the *ABC* in 1943, compared to the multitude of advertisements for his others) and was much smaller and more rudimentary in appearance. Economical to purchase according to the 1943 advertisement in the *ABC, Claudina sabe guisar* cost 2.75 pesetas, a scant fraction of the cost of Sarrau's massive tome, which just some three years later would be sold for 200 pesetas. We can infer from ads for the eight other cookbooks on the same *ABC* page that *Claudina sabe guisar* was amongst the cheapest of the cookbooks to appear during these years, costing, for instance, four times less than Doménech's *Cocina de recursos*, published more or less contemporaneously.

As food historian Driver ("Cookbooks") informs us, much can be made of the changes between a cookbook's different editions. In the case of Sarrau, it was remarkable that his post-war edition of *Nuestra cocina* was so much more grandiose than the first, published during the prosperous years of the Second Republic. Although there is no prior edition of *Claudina sabe guisar* to which we can turn, Doménech wrote a very similar type of cookbook some twenty years earlier: *Marichu: La mejor cocinera española* (1919). This similarly took the name of a Spanish woman, and also featured a picture of a woman surrounded by her cooking utensils on the front cover. But there are some important differences between the two cookbooks, indicative of the drastic decline in post-war Spain's standard of living. As well as consisting of nearly three times as many pages as the post-war *Claudina sabe guisar*, *Marichu* is reflective of the increasing affluence and optimism of the time, and its cover features an elegantly dressed *señora* alongside her modern oven and array of succulent, expensive dishes.

Published some years into twentieth-century Spain's long-awaited period of economic growth (1913–35), *Marichu* is written for a nation at the dawn of modernization. Conversely, *Claudina sabe guisar* speaks (at least implicitly) of deprivation and food shortages. The image of the woman on the front cover of the latter could not be more rudimentary: dressed in a simple brown dress and dull grey headscarf, she stands at a table with nothing but a rolling pin, a cookbook, and a bowl of eggs. The simplicity of the text is reinforced at the outset, with Doménech explaining to his readers that "en las páginas de *CSG* [*Claudina sabe guisar*] se ha reunido el contenido más sencillo" (the simplest material has been gathered in the pages of *CSG*; 2). The recipes themselves further corroborate the self-professed simplicity of the cookbook, such as those for the most basic of sandwiches, made from just "requesón machacado o miel" (cottage cheese or honey; 8). Though Doménech never mentions directly how little food most people had, it is nevertheless clear that he is writing at a time when most of his readers would have lacked anything but the most basic of foodstuffs. In further recipes for single-ingredient sandwiches, Doménech writes of the delicious "bocadillos" that can be made from as little as bread, wine, sugar, olive oil and salt: "Con estos cinco ingredientes, y por raro que parezca a algunos lectores, pueden hacerse unos sabrosos bocadillos típicos de nuestras regiones" (With these five ingredients, as strange as it might seem to some readers, you can make various delicious sandwiches, which are typical to our regions; 10). Present-day accounts of post-war Spain's foodscape certainly point to the prevalence of this particular recipe, with one stating that during times of rationing and deprivation, "pan untado con aceite, ajo y sal otras veces con vino y azúcar, eran comida que nos daban a los chavales" (bread smeared with oil, garlic, and salt, or else with wine and sugar, was what we fed the kids; Unjubilado n.p.).

The rest of the cookbook continues more or less in this vein, with Doménech making allowances for the horrendous food shortages and deprivation of these years. Providing, for instance, a recipe for *sopa de cebolla* (onion soup; 16), he explains that the soup should be made from broth and onions but goes on to write that if one doesn't have enough ingredients to make the broth (typically made from a variety of vegetables and different types of animal protein), water can be used instead.

Given that in addition to broth the recipe calls for a measly "media cebolla de las grandes ... para 4 personas" ("half a large onion ... for 4 people"), for the reader who was forced to replace broth with water this dish would have been not only tasteless but also not at all nutritious. Also telling of scarcity is the chapter titled "Los platos para las festividades de cada mes" (Dishes for each month's festivities). In the main, these recipes do not speak of abundance in the same way as Doménech's pre-war books. January's festive recipe is, for instance, *crepes con mermelada de frutas* (crepes with fruit jam) made from flour, sugar, eggs, and milk with just "una ligera capa de mermelada" (a light spread of jam; 17). Diminutives and instructions calling for moderate or prudent amounts of different ingredients point to the fact that most of Doménech's readers would have been facing a daily struggle to access the majority of foodstuffs.

Both *Claudina sabe guisar* and *Cocina de recursos* were written from Barcelona, where Doménech lived from the 1920s on. Although the whole of Spain suffered from food shortages and rationing during the civil war and post-war period, this distress was often much worse in Republican areas, which, according to Almodóvar, "padec[ieron] hasta lo indecible los rigores de la desnutrición y el espectro del hambre" (suffered unspeakable depths of malnutrition and the spectre of hunger; 121). Foodstuffs considered inedible before the war, such as horse or donkey meat and sunflower seeds, quickly became a staple in Spanish households, especially in the republican areas. During the civil war, food shortages in Catalonia were exacerbated, too, by the growing number of refugees (Graham, "Against the State" 511). This only worsened after the war, with some million and a half immigrants moving to Barcelona from other parts of Spain (Eaude 193). The trauma of the conflict was then compounded by the dictatorship, which brought to Catalonia (as to other regions) "terror, social control and food shortages" (Dowling 40). The hardship was worst for the peasantry and working class, who were unable to leave and did not have the resources to access foodstuffs. The Franco years also saw the loss of many of Catalonia's French-style restaurants, for only the rich were able to frequent them (Eaude 249).

While *Claudina sabe guisar* is a post-war cookbook, *Cocina de recursos* is ostensibly a wartime cookbook. Although not published until 1941, it narrates the devastating impact of the civil war on Spanish food culture and provides recipes that teach readers the necessary accommodations to wartime penury. Unlike the other cookbooks looked at in this chapter – including *Claudina sabe guisar* – *Cocina de recursos* has been taken seriously by scholars, who have been more alive to its importance. Inés Butrón writes, for instance:

> Uno de los mejores gastrónomos y cocineros de la época, el catalán Ignasi Doménech, escribió en 1938 un recetario, *Cocina de recursos (Deseo mi cocina)*, cuyas preparaciones son el fiel reflejo de una situación caótica en la que la falta de casi todas las materias primas básicas llevaban a este amante de la buena mesa a imaginar platos imposibles. (38)
>
> (One of the best gastronomes and cooks of the epoch, the Catalan Ignasi Doménech, wrote a cookbook in 1938, *Cocina de recursos: Deseo mi cocina*, with recipes that faithfully reflect the chaotic situation in which almost all basic raw ingredients were missing, leading this lover of good food to imagine impossible dishes.)

In his introduction to the 2011 edition of this cookbook, Sella Montserrat describes it as belonging to "al género de literatura gastronómica bélica" (the genre of bellic gastronomic literature; 9). María Moreno has also written insightfully about *Cocina de recursos*, compellingly arguing that it should be considered a post-war as well as a wartime cookbook:

> Lo que resulta curioso es que, a pesar de que el libro menciona en repetidas ocasiones que se refiere exclusivamente a los años de la Guerra, el lector avisado se da cuenta muy pronto de que esto no es del todo cierto … Resulta evidente que *Cocina de recursos* no habla solo del pasado, sino también del presente de la posguerra. (*De la página* 40)
>
> (What is curious is that, despite the book's repeatedly mentioning that it is exclusively focused on the war years, the savvy reader promptly realizes that this is not at all true … It is obvious that *Cocina de recursos* is not only speaking about the past, but also of the post-war present.)

Moreno argues that Doménech probably framed *Cocina de recursos* as an exclusively wartime cookbook because he was too afraid of censorship to make explicit that his cookbook was also relevant to post-war Spain. Food shortages did not disappear at the end of the civil war; the period known as "los años del hambre" lasted until 1952. It is, according to Moreno, the "frecuentes saltos de la voz narradora del pasado al presente y la aparente inconsistencia temporal" (frequent jumps in the narrator's voice from the past to the present and the obvious temporal inconsistency; *De la página* 41) that indicate Doménech was documenting or discussing the deprivation not just of wartime Spain but also of the post-war years. Inspection of the original 1941 copy of *Cocina de recursos* held at the Biblioteca Nacional shows that this cookbook was subject to censorship. Nevertheless, because Doménech framed the text as a wartime cookbook, it is probable that censors did not read it carefully enough to see just how disruptive he was of the official tendency to ignore hunger or the hungry body. The shifting narrative voice allows an implicit challenge to a regime that at its outset was totalitarian and merciless. The subtitle of the cookbook is *Deseo mi comida* (I want my food), so although Doménech tells the readers that he is writing of the hunger he experienced during the civil war, from his subtitle we can infer that he is talking, too, about present-day conditions.

The included recipes make clear that Spaniards are faced with severe food shortages, and many of the dishes he suggests come with replacement ingredients or without the main ingredient, such as the recipe for *Calamares fritos sin calamares* (fried calamari without calamari). Another such recipe is:

> Tortilla sin huevo Tomar unas patatas, cebollas, judias, calabacín, pimientos y alcachofas. Trocear. Poner en un recipiente, frotado el fondo con ajo, 1 cucharada de perejil picado, un poco de pimentón, 1 cucharada de bicarbanato, 6 cucharadas soperas de harina, sal, 10 o 12 cucharadas soperas de agua, 1 cucharada pequeña de aceite. Dejar reposar la mezcla 15 minutos, batir todo y hacer la tortilla.
>
> (Tortilla without egg. Take some potatoes, onions, beans, zucchini, peppers, and artichokes. Slice. Place in a bowl, with the bottom rubbed in garlic, 1 teaspoon of sliced parsley, a little chilli, 1 teaspoon of bicarbonate, 6 tablespoons of flour, salt, 10 or 12 tablespoons of water, 1 teaspoon of oil. Rest the mixture for 15 minutes, beat everything, and make the tortilla.)

These recipes make visible the ingredients or foodstuffs that are missing from most households, as they challenge the official tendency to downplay the country's food deprivation.

In contrast to the dominant tendency of disregarding or downplaying deprivation, Doménech documents hunger in painstaking detail, not just textually but also in the cookbook's illustrations. Unlike the dominant image of domestic bliss conjured up in so many cookbooks, the image on the cover of the original edition of *Cocina de recursos* features an unhappy family. A mother, father, and small boy sit around a dining table looking away from each other and making grimaces. Obviously, they are all hungry, yet none of them are depicted eating the unappealing, broth-like rice dish in the middle of the table. Also featured in the picture is a cat, obviously hungry and appearing to be on the lookout for any morsel of food that may fall its way. Because Doménech's cookbook is not exclusively documenting the hunger of wartime Spain, this image can be seen as also a reflection of the harsh reality of post-war Spain.

The hungry body was, as noted above, considered transgressive because it called into question the merits of autarky, with official discourse producing readers and citizens who did not use words such as "hunger" or "deprivation." By contrast, Doménech's cookbooks sought to produce readers who thought about and spoke of hunger. The image used on the front cover of *Cocina de recursos* transmits the suffering of wartime/post-war Spain, while textually he conveys, too, the all-consuming thoughts about food in times of hunger. Of himself and his fellow countrymen, he writes that it is impossible to escape thoughts of food:

> Observo en todas horas las conversaciones más variadas para resolver el problema de comer nada más que regularmente. En las fábricas, talleres, oficinas, en todas partes, todos los días, semanas y meses que no se puede soñar más que en comida. Cuando me acuesto y cuando me levanto, de día y de noche, ocupan mi imaginación detalles recordatorios impregnados de un realismo impresionante de la Buena mesa … Percibo también en el olor de apetitosos asados, de magnificas frituras y tortillas. ¡Oh qué importancia insuperable tienen para mí aunque sean unos modestos huevos fritos, unas patatas fritas, bien dorados como en otros tiempos, un buen trozo de pularda asada, teniendo en cuenta está época tan desagradable, habría motivos para considerarse el más feliz de los morales! Nada, queridos lectores, la boca se me hace agua, ilusiones, ya que de pronto, despierto, para darme cuenta de la tristísima realidad que nos rodea, ya que todo lo anterior no responde a la verdad del momento, y sigo, naturalmente, deseando mi comida, por modesta que sea. ¡Nada! ¡Ha sido una pesadilla! (45–6)
>
> (At all hours, I hear the most varied conversations about how to resolve the problem of regularly eating nothing. In factories, workshops, offices, everywhere, every day, week and month we can't dream of anything but food. When I go to bed and when I get up, morning and night, my mind is full of the most detailed memories, imbued with an impressive realism, of the Good Table. I also smell the scent of delicious appetizers, magnificent fritters, and tortillas. Oh how incredibly important they are to me, even if they are only modest fried egs, fried potatoes, well browned as in

previous days, a good slice of roasted poultry, bearing in mind that in this unpleasant moment, one would have cause to consider oneself as happy as a clam! Nothing, dear readers, my mouth starts to water, illusions, given that all of a sudden I wake up, only to realize the sad reality that surrounds us, where nothing of what I've just described is presently true, and I still, of course, want my food, as modest as it is. Nothing! It was a nightmare!)

If in his pre-war cookbooks Doménech uses such discursive spaces to reinforce his authority in relation to his readers, many of whom were aspiring chefs, in *Cocina de recursos* there is no such difference between author and reader. Instead, Doménech forges a sense of comradeship as all suffer together the pangs of hunger. Moreover, the tone of his prologue is familiar and evokes one family member speaking to another. Even in the body of the cookbook, when Doménech goes on to teach his readers how to adapt to wartime or post-war penury, he never establishes a paternalistic or hierarchical dynamic.

It would seem that for Doménech the key to his wartime and post-war culinary discourse is to escape hunger through fantasies about food, even if he also provides instruction for how to best to accommodate to food shortages and deprivation. It is worth noting how different his culinary discourse, in positioning hunger in this way, is from official and pro-Franco discourse. Doménech's cookbook challenges official rhetoric not only by making hunger fully visible, but also by constructing it as a highly undesirable state. For even in the rare instances when official discourse did acknowledge food shortages, euphemisms were plentiful and Spaniards were asked to remain stoic for the good of the nation as the country returned to normality. Contrast this with Doménech, who writes of his obsessive thinking about food in its absence, allowing his readers to also feel the full effects of deprivation. He is nostalgic for the good food of his past and invites his readers to join him in this flight of fantasy rather than pretend, as official discourse would have them do, that hunger is at most a minor inconvenience that a bit of willpower or strength of character can overcome.

Doménech's *Claudina sabe guisar* similarly stands at odds with official discourse by speaking implicitly to the reality of post-war Spain's impoverished foodscape. The official tendency, as we know, was to downplay shortages and speak of a slightly worsened national diet. We also know that Spain would not return to its pre-war levels of sophistication until the 1960s, and it is this decline in the country's standard of living that Doménech's all-but-forgotten cookbook captures so clearly. Indeed, the basic style of cooking presented in the pamphlet-like

Claudina sabe guisar reflects a reality that was all-but-absent from official discourse. In providing instructions for how to make dishes out of such simple combinations as bread, water, and sugar, or half an onion cooked in water, Doménech sought to produce a cookbook that was useful in times of deprivation. Moreover, like *Cocina de recursos*, this text produces readers and citizens who can acknowledge the extent of hunger and scarcity, rather than turning a blind eye, as official discourse insisted upon. Doménech's food discourse challenges the Francoist biopolitics by encouraging his readers to not simply be stoic in the face of food shortages; instead, he allows his readers to join him in an experience of the all-consuming nature of hunger.

Francoist Food Discourse: Autarky, Hunger, and Culinary Patriotism

Food discourse was integral to the experience of the political economy of autarky as it related to notions of food culture, culinary patriotism, hunger, and the uneven experience of food shortages in post-war Spain. Official food discourse sought to produce readers and/or citizens who upheld the principles of autarky. Texts about food or descriptions of food in the press asked Spaniards not just to consume local foodstuffs but to believe in Spain's capacity to keep its citizenry strong and healthy via recourse to just the fruits of autarky. Such official discourse also produced readers and citizens who upheld the notion of Spain's cultural isolation, a further key component of autarky. In relation to food culture, this cultural closure resulted in a fervent culinary patriotism, which I identify as a trademark feature of the food culture of the early Franco regime.

Other food discourse disrupted official notions of autarky and produced subjectivities with differing ideas about Spanish food culture, or the state of post-war Spain's foodscape. The most significant example was food texts that allowed readers and citizens to speak of and feel the true impact of hunger and the food shortages. The Marquesa de Parabere's history of gastronomy is also importantly subversive in its attempt to produce readers or gastronomes with a much less patriotic understanding of Spanish food culture. In asking her readers to be less fervent in their culinary patriotism, the Marquesa advocates an openness to French culture and cuisine. This openness would have stood in stark contrast with the official desire for not just economic but also cultural isolation.

2 Beyond the Kitchen: Food Texts, Gender, and Compliance in Franco Spain

Franco's National Catholicism depended on nothing less than women's exclusive dedication to domesticity and family life. Food discourse was central to upholding this gender divide at the heart of Francoist biopolitics, as it was in part through official domestic cookbooks and educational cookery manuals that women learnt what was expected of them as wives and mothers. Yet there are also, as we will see, various examples where food texts contest this ideology. Some scholarship has looked at the role of the Sección Femenina's (SF) cookbooks in maintaining this gender divide, but I delve a little deeper in this chapter, asking how the SF food texts produce not just highly gendered subjectivities but also compliant ones. I investigate what it is about the form and genre of these food texts – rather than just their content – that makes them so prescriptive about not just gender roles but specifically female subservience to the state and to men.

Writing Women Back Into the Kitchen

It is only when we treat the SF cookbooks as part of a broader narrative about food that we are able to appreciate that they were unique not just in content but in form. Because the SF all but dominated the market for women's cookbooks during the Franco regime, those texts not commissioned by this organization have received little scholarly attention. But a comparison of official and non-official women's food texts reveals broader points of continuity and difference. This is pivotal if we are to appreciate the extent to which some of the non-official cookbooks provided alternatives to the world imposed by the SF.

The ultra-conservative view of gender relations at the heart of Franco's ideology meant that as soon as the Nationalists were victorious, Spanish women lost all the gains they had won during the short-lived

Second Republic. Participation in the public sphere, particularly the workplace, was seen as the antithesis of the ideal female pursuit, and women were precluded from "holding high positions at the state level, furthering their academic education, or having the power to choose how they lived their lives" (Castillo 179).[1] Spanish women were defined first and foremost by their roles as wives and mothers and, according to one scholar's estimate, around thirty laws were passed "para estimular la natalidad y desuadir el trabajo femenino" (in order to stimulate the birthrate and discourage women from working; Barrachina 71) These included

> la promulgación del *Fuero del Trabajo* (9 de Marzo de 1938) que compromete al Estado para "librar a la mujer casada del taller de la fábrica" (II, I), y la promulgación del *Fuero de los Españoles* (17 de julio de 1945) que atribuye a la familia "derechos y deberes anteriores y superiores a toda ley humana positiva" (II, 22). (Barrachina 71)

> (the promulgation of the Work Law (9 March 1938) that committed the state to "liberating working women from the factory workshop" (II, I), and the promulgation of the Spanish Law (17 July 1945) that attributed to the family "rights and responsibilities before and above any positive human law" (II, 22).)

Such legislative changes were just one of the ways in which Francoist officials would attempt to confine women to home-life and domesticity. State education and official discourse were also important in helping the regime to implement its policy of the *perfecta casada* (perfect housewife) and *ángel del hogar* (angel of the home) that was based on archaic nineteenth-century gender dictates. Women were subject to hyper-vigilance: "none of the previous Spanish political regimes had controlled the women in society in such a severe manner" (Carbayo-Abengózar, "Shaping Women" 81). Through official discourse, including that looked at here, women were disciplined into upholding a new image of Spanish femininity that was meant to be specific to Spain. As Mercedes Carbayo-Abengózar explains, "the image of a new women for a new Spain was a contradictory image in itself in the sense that it was supposed to be new but was in fact based on 'old,' traditional, exclusive, religious and national-patriotic values" (82).

The Franco regime delegated to the SF responsibility for the social and cultural indoctrination of women into such notions. This organization's conservative attitude towards women aligned well with the mix of Falangism and Catholicism at the heart of National Catholicism.

Throughout her tenure as national spokesperson for the SF, Pilar Primo de Rivera consistently promoted women's obligation to form families and to not put themselves in competition with men (see Enders). As the mediator between the state and Spanish women, "la Sección Femenina fue la única organización que se ocupó seriamente de la promoción y formación de la mujer española (esposa y madre, ante todo) tras la Guerra" (The Women's Section was the only organization that was seriously concerned with the advancement and training of the Spanish woman (wife and mother, before anything else) after the war; Abad Alegría et al. 35).

Education was key to the SF's approach. Although women were encouraged to study, knowledge was cast as being of value to them solely in their roles as mothers and wives. The Secondary Education Act of 20 September 1938 "made the study of socio-political training, music, needlework, cooking, domestic economy and physical education compulsory for girls" (Perdiguero Gil and Castejón Bolea 162). Through the SF's compulsory six-month social service program, Spanish women between the ages of seventeen and thirty-five were taught cooking, sewing, and other domestic duties. Appropriate reading material was also an important element of the SF's indoctrination of Spanish women. Libraries were set up across the country (see del Rincón García 77). Cookbooks and other household management texts were a significant part of this reading material, instructing women about what was expected of them in their prescribed gender roles: subordination to men, exclusive dedication to domesticity, and a commitment to the main pillars of Francoist ideology and biopolitics. In addition, women were taught about the importance of culinary modernity and were encouraged to see the role of *ama de casa* (housewife) as a profession of sorts.[2]

A number of scholars have written of the SF's important and sometimes contradictory role in training Spanish women in domesticity and subordination to men (see, for example, Graham, *Interrogating Francoism;* Kebadze). The SF, writes Iglesias, was among the institutions that "formed the backbone for the instruction of the new generations ... Through them, individuals were corrected, guided, and submitted to strict discipline and correct behaviour" (162). Yet there has been much more of a focus on the Falange or the figure of the Caudillo himself. Thus there is, according to some, a "carencia de estudios sobre la Sección Femenina" (scarcity of research about the Women's Section; see, for example, Durón Muniz 7). This chapter addresses this gap by providing a detailed account of the SF's use of food discourse to train Spanish women not just in domesticity, but also in compliance beyond the kitchen. Moreover, showing how the SF used food discourse to discipline Spanish women into certain ways of being contributes to our understanding of Francoist biopolitics. What is less clear is the role played by the SF's food discourse in disciplining and correcting female behaviour.

Some of the more recent scholarship on the SF has looked to its food discourse or cooking classes as a mode of control (see Dunai, *Cooking for the Patria*; Perdiguero Gil and Castejón Bolea). According to Dunai, for instance, the SF made clear to Spanish women that they

> should enjoy several hours in the kitchen each day as they sacrificed for their family [and that it was the duty] of Spanish women to ensure that the family observes the food ideology of the Catholic Church by preparing meals that met fasting requirements or followed holiday rituals. (*Cooking for the Patria* 8)

Observations of a general nature about the SF's role in relation to gender and food preparation are not new. Lacking, however, from scholarship on this topic is a detailed analysis of the discursive strategies employed in these official cookbooks not just to produce highly gendered subjectivities but to reinforce the authority of the state. Close attention to the format and style of SF food texts reveals the strategies that made them an effective mechanism of control.

The compliance required of Spanish women goes beyond the kitchen: it affects relationships with both their husbands and the state. Subordination to men was central to the SF's gender ideology; Spanish women were taught "to let themselves be guided by the stronger will and wisdom of men" (Enders 675). Pilar Primo de Rivera also abided by this dictum in having all her decisions "approved of by the Secretary General of the Movimiento" (Enders 676). Ironically, she sought approval from her country's male leaders for her management of the SF, even with regard to domesticity – which was cast as the domain of women. In a similar vein, Spanish wives required "la aprobación de sus maridos" (their husband's approval) for much of what they did within the household realm (Ofer, "*Teresa*" 131). Official food discourse can be seen as preparing Spanish women for this subordination when it teaches them not just how prepare food, but also how to follow orders in matters relating to the house.

Producing such qualities in women can be thought about, too, in the context of Francoist biopolitics. The Franco regime implemented "un estado de dominación" (a state of domination; Matos-Martín 7) that "buscaba administrar y controlar la vida de todos los españoles – los no exiliados y los no-eliminados – regulando sus costumbres, manipulando sus conciencias, en suma, fabricando sus subjetividades" (sought to manage and control the lives of all Spaniards – those not exiled nor eliminated – regulating their habits, manipulating their consciences, in short, creating their subjectivities; Matos-Martín 2). Obedience was required by the state as Spaniards were instructed in the right and wrong ways to perform their nationality, gender, and class identities. Significantly, obedience was also integral to the Falange's official discourse, seen as central to its mission to promote "the unity of the nation and to facilitate the integration of society" (Enders 676). Because women were tasked with preparing their sons materially and spiritually for public life, whatever they learnt from the SF would be passed on to the next generation. It follows, then, that the compliant and uncritical acceptance of the SF's authority (as mouthpiece of the state) – which women learned through the SF's food discourse – would be passed onto Spain's youth, who would similarly be taught to follow state instruction.

Existing scholarship on the Franco regime – especially that concerned with the notion of biopolitics – argues for the value of studying resistance as well as compliance. In considering resistance, this chapter looks to the creation of alternative worlds that allowed women not just to have a different experience of gender, but also to value their own domestic and past cooking experience, likely passed down to them by their mothers and grandmothers. Because the SF dominated the market for domestic cookbooks and cookery manuals, texts dedicated to the *lectora* (female reader) or *ama de casa* (housewife) without connections with this organization are barely mentioned in scholarship on Spanish gastronomy, and so we know very little about how disruptive some of the discourse produced at this time was of the regime's notions of gender. Here I redress this imbalance by examining five such texts: *La cocina casera* (Home cooking, 1952), *Los dulces caseros* (Homemade desserts, 1950), *Cromos de cocina de Waly* (Pictures from Waly's kitchen, 1955), *Mi recetario de cocina* (My kitchen recipe book, 1957), and *La futura ama de casa* (The future housewife, 1958).

Women's role within the realm of domesticity was transmitted primarily through the SF, but myriad official publications converged to reinforce the notion that women were responsible for all domestic duties, including food shopping and cooking. Although *Alimentación nacional* – analysed in more detail in chapters 1 and 3 for its engagement with autarky and the fascist production of space – does not explicitly deal with gender, it is clear within the context of Spain's post-war foodscape and commitment to self-sufficiency that women are responsible for feeding their families a diet rich in the fruits of autarky. Therefore, although this publication is not concerned with the task of training women in their domestic roles, it certainly reinforces the Francoist notion that women are solely responsible for the uptake of autarkic principles in their homes.

That message is transmitted through the periodical's "Economía doméstica" (Home economics) section. A very minor part of the publication, this section is written with female readers in mind and aims to provide helpful hints about household management in the context of post-war deprivation, as can be seen, for example, in the following:

> Vamos a daros hoy queridas lectoras algunos consejos prácticos de economía casera, especialmente dedicados a la cocina, que, en la actualidad, son de gran importancia, para toda ama de casa, que diariamente, se ve ante el problema de la alimentación familiar. (Issue 9, 21)
>
> (Today, dear readers, we are going to give you some practical home economics advice, particularly about the kitchen, which is presently of great importance for every housewife who is faced daily with the problem of feeding her family.)

In reading such instructions, women understand their obligation to provide food in difficult circumstances. It is significant that women are not addressed directly in any of the other sections of this official publication: they are implicitly excluded from public life. *Alimentación nacional* directs discussion of public matters – such as issues concerning the political economy of autarky or discussion of world food shortages – to male readers. Female readers learn that their role is defined primarily in terms of caregiving, domesticity, and food preparation; masculinity allows male readers access to the public, national sphere.

To summarize: publications such as *Alimentación nacional* form part of a broader discourse that instructs both women and men in the uptake of their gender roles, while the SF food texts are highly prescriptive in the details of what was required of women in the private space of the home.

Constructing Subservient Subjectivities through Cookbooks

Though much of what I analyse in this monograph is the "talk of food," what I noticed first about the SF-commissioned cookbooks was their lack of narrative about food culture or domestic instruction. It became apparent to me that it was ultimately in the missing words that I would find the meaning and function of this official discourse. Cookbooks for women have traditionally been replete with narrative or personal anecdotes, as authors strive to forge a personal relationship with readers. Often this speaks to a community of women who are united in their use of a particular cookbook. Implicit in these communities is the fact that the group as a whole shares ownership of the collection of recipes, as each reader/cook offers her own take on a particular dish. Speaking to the closeness of female friendships and relationships between grandmothers, mothers, and daughters, such cookbooks remind us of how recipes have traditionally been passed down from one generation to a next.

In the case of the SF cookbooks/food texts, the important question is why narrative is all but absent in these texts: it is because the SF does not want to invoke such a community of cooks or invite readers to make revisions to the recipes. One of the effects of this absence is to make Spanish women feel that their past cooking experience and knowledge of food culture are irrelevant to what they will learn from the SF. This serves to reinforce the authority of the SF as expert in all matters relating to cookery and household management. As well, the lack of narrative in these food texts makes this official food discourse all the more prescriptive. Cooking is, as noted above, one of the most instructed activities in which we partake, but cookbook authors often use narrative and storytelling to make their cookbooks more about personal relationships and less about instruction. By design, then, the SF's food texts for women do not incorporate the narrative that generally makes cookbooks less prescriptive.

The most notable feature of these official cookbooks, in contrast to other domestic examples, is their absence of prologues or discursive introductions to the different sections, which creates an ultra-authoritative culinary discourse that is devoid of any familiarity between the author and his/her readers. This results in a relationship that upholds official ideology in its production of subject positions that are hyper-aware of hierarchy and unquestioning in their acceptance of instruction. In viewing SF-commissioned cookbooks as hyper-prescriptive I diverge from existing scholarship; Dunai, for example, observes of cookbooks commissioned or written by the SF that the "recipes present advice in a way that gives readers the feeling of making a free decision" (*Cooking for the Patria* 14). It is, I suggest, what the SF cookbooks fail to say that makes the recipes so prescriptive and so much more than just "helpful suggestions" (Dunai, *Cooking for the Patria* 14).

To appreciate just how prescriptive the SF food texts are, it is useful to outline some of the key features of the cookbook genre compared to other types of food writing. Cookbooks, much more so than gastronomic texts, have traditionally been gendered female and viewed as prescriptive or "instructional" (see Elias; Floyd and Forster; Neuhaus; Tomlinson; Vester). Writing about prescriptive recipes of cookery sections found in North American marital manuals between 1920 and 1963, Jessamyn Neuhaus argues that "recipes are by their very nature prescriptive: they demand a certain set of actions, performed in a certain sequence, to produce a certain product" (94). Neuhaus observes, too, how regularly these cookbooks asserted "that an important part of being a married woman was cooking and serving the daily meals" (96–7). Because the SF food texts contain nothing but recipes and instruction, it is possible to situate them within the broader context of highly prescriptive cookbooks, which instruct not just in cooking but also in gender roles and obedience.

The relationship between recipes and instruction is a longstanding one dating back to the medieval period. The function of a recipe in the medieval era was, according to Ruth Carroll, "to give instructions on how to make something, the most widely accepted examples being a dish or a meal" (145). Janet Floyd and Laurel Forster explain that, more generally, "recipes may be linked with the impulse to rule, hierarchise and differentiate" (5). They consider Jack Goody's emphasis on the relationship between the recipe and the list in his discussion of the prescriptive nature of recipes. According to Goody, the list of diners, the seating list, and the menu listing dishes recall the shopping list and the recipe that have enabled the scene of ranking and exclusion to take place (143). John Finn writes that "every recipe incorporates some element of authority and command; recipes in general might even be founded on a series of commands" (504).

A number of scholars and food writers are, in fact, wary of readers or cooks who become overly dependent on highly instructional recipes. In their introduction to *The Recipe Reader*, Floyd and Forster remind us, for instance, of M.F.K. Fisher's likening of a domestic cook's dependence on instruction to a spoilt child who wants to be told (4). Fisher finds vexatious the fact that domestic cooks want to be told exactly what to do in the kitchen. Given the capacity of food discourse to produce different kinds of cooks/readers, Fisher's irritation should perhaps be directed at the books rather than the cooks. For it is the instructional cookbooks that have produced the dependent cooks in the first instance, and if there is to be more autonomy in cooking, then cookbooks must invite readers and cooks to revise recipes, bringing their own expertise and experience to the table.

Finn considers the relationship between ultra-prescriptive recipes and submissive cooks in terms of politics, writing that highly instructional recipes that are based on the "cook's submission to the terms and commands of the recipe" result in a particular "form of political obligation" (503). As Finn sees it, recipes often make – explicitly or otherwise – the promise of a perfect dish, which tastes just right or is authentic. This "promise" depends, he writes, on the reader's/cook's submission to the author of the cookbook, in that dishes must be prepared exactly as dictated. As part of his description of the political implications of such subservience, Finn writes that "we might thus describe the relationship between the perfect recipe and reader/cook as authoritarian and autocratic (or fascist)" (504). Finn argues, too, that there are parallels between cookbooks and social contracts. While the scale of the exchange is vastly different in the cookbooks and social contracts Finn compares, "the essential trade," he insists – freedom for security – is the same. Finn is wary of the uncritical obedience and servility that the perfect recipe promotes, "which yield docile cooks and complaisant citizens" (514). As he sees it, "perfect recipes ... actively construct ... readers," who lose the ability for "critical thinking and reasoned deliberation, both of which are essential to democratic governance" (514).[3]

Finn considers the implications of following recipes or cookbooks uncritically within the context of democracy, but his view of recipes as political instruments or forms of political obligation is also relevant during times of dictatorial rule. Authoritarian governance relies on a compliant citizenry, so it follows that the subservience required in exchange for the "perfect recipe" will be central to the longevity of any authoritarian regime. The SF food discourse under scrutiny here can be seen, therefore, as producing the ideal subject for dictatorial rule because it produces not just cooks, but also citizens who follow instructions and are ultra-aware of hierarchy.

Cookery Instruction and the Authority of the Sección Femenina

The first text under scrutiny here is *Medina*. Through this publication, Spanish women were taught to think of their role in terms of domesticity. Indeed, apart from just one section dedicated to broader issues under the umbrella term "la actualidad nacional" (current national affairs), *Medina* consists primarily of "typically" female reading material. Brimming with advice on household management, fashion, and beauty, this publication made clear to women that they were to dedicate themselves not just to running their household, but to keeping themselves well groomed for their husbands. In terms of domesticity, women's role as mothers featured a great deal, as did discussions of cleanliness. As one scholar notes, in *Medina* "there was plenty of advertising regarding the way in which women should maintain the family's cleanliness" (Carbayo-Abengózar, "Shaping Women" 82). In addition to this particular responsibility – most likely also an allegory for spiritual purity – women were charged with safeguarding the physical and spiritual well-being of Spain's future males: "Tus hijos – piensa que tu tarea es difícil: pero si sabes preparar para el mañana hombres de bien, habrás cumplido tu deber con la patria" (Your sons – you might think your task is difficult, but if you know how to prepare good men for the future, you will have fulfilled your patriotic duty; *Medina*, September 1943).

Food discourse featured relatively little in this publication; each issue had just one or two pages dedicated to cooking and recipes. This can, of course, be considered in terms of the official tendency to erase mention of culinary abundance, so as not to cause unrest amongst a starving population. What is of interest is that when recipes are provided there is no accompanying narrative. This is in stark contrast with all other sections in *Medina*, which contain narrative that, although prescriptive, is still friendly or amiable in tone. Conversely, there are no introductions to the recipes, nor is there any discussion of Spanish cuisine. Absent also from these pages are any references to the female readers' prior cooking experience or to the body of cooking knowledge that in most cases they would have learnt informally in a domestic setting.

The most that appears in these cooking sections are perfunctory headings and then the recipes themselves. For example, in one of the issues, the cooking page is headed with the word "cocina" (cooking) on the left and "recetas nutritivas" (nutritious recipes) on the right. The rest of the page includes recipes for dishes such as *sopa de leche de almendras, higado de vaca,* and *extracto de carne* (almond milk soup, beef liver, and meat extract; Issue 95, 41). The lack of narrative notwithstanding, implicit in this mosaic of words and recipes is not just the belief that cooking must be healthy and nutritious, but also directives about what constitutes healthy food. If women learn in publications such as *Medina* that their role is first and foremost to ensure the spiritual and physical well-being of their families – including the next generation of male leaders – then this cooking section can be seen as prescriptive of what is entailed in the provision of healthy food. There is no invitation to female readers to add their own voices to debates about nutrition. Rather, they are provided with a normative list of recipes and foodstuffs that they are expected to simply accept.

Although *Medina* was in print only for just under five years, the blueprint this publication laid down for the provision of recipes affected subsequent SF food discourse. Characteristic of the paradigm it established was a glaring absence of narrative, which is noteworthy given that, as mentioned above, all the other sections of this women's periodical do contain narrative. If narrative detracts from instruction, then the cookery section of this magazine is striking in how prescriptive it is. The cookery sections of magazines like *Medina* can be seen as uniquely potent sites of control.

The next SF food text to be considered was penned by Sarrau, who was discussed in the last chapter. Written in 1942, *Ciencia gastronómica* (Gastronomic science) was the official text "para el profesorado de los Institutos Nacionales Femeninos y de las Escuelas del Hogar de la Sección Femenina" (for the teachers of the National Women's Institutes and the home economics schools of the Women's Section; 2). The importance of this text cannot be underestimated, given that its content determined what members of the SF would teach the women who attended cookery classes as part of the compulsory social service program. The SF sought to "professionalize" the position of housewife, and Sarrau's expertise and training were invaluable to this mission. Sarrau's role as a male consultant was also significant: "by putting men in charge of a number of domestic issues, the SF hoped to mimic the authority granted to men in Franco's male-run dictatorship" (Dunai, *Cooking for the Patria* 63). In Francoist Spain, the family occupied an almost sacred position and Franco positioned himself as the national father. Sarrau himself can be seen as occupying this type of paternal role with his readers.

Ciencia gastronómica was the only one of Sarrau's texts to be published through this official organization, and it was reprinted a total of five times. It is, in keeping with my analysis of the authoritative nature of SF food discourse, devoid of any familiarity between the author and his readers. Sarrau – representative of the SF – is positioned as the expert in matters relating to domesticity and cooking, and the SF's instructors are in turn expected to transmit this sense of male authority to their students. The newness or modernity of the SF's domestic instruction is also apparent here, and only serves to reinforce the authority of the SF, or of Sarrau. Moreover, in emphasizing the superiority of domestic modernity, the SF essentially renders Spanish women's past cooking knowledge obsolete. Rather than drawing on cooking instruction that would have taken place informally in a home setting, Spanish women are encouraged to put aside their past knowledge in favour of the SF's modern domestic instruction.

The formality of *Ciencia gastronómica* can be felt, first and foremost, in the very formal dedicatory to no less than Pilar Primo de Rivera, the leader of the SF. Sarrau's dedication to the head of Spain's women's movement makes it clear from the outset that *Ciencia gastronómica* is prescriptive of state ideology rather than reflective of the author's own personal or commercial agenda. As we know, all cultural products at this time had to pass through censorship, and *Ciencia gastronómica*, as an official text, was subject to an even higher degree of control. Edited by the Sección Femenina de FET y de las JONS prior to going to print, it was endorsed by the "Excmo Sr Ministro de Educación Nacional y del departamento central de escuelas de hogar de la Sección Femenina" (his excellency the minister for national education and the central department of the Women's Section home economics schools; 1). It was promoted extensively by the SF, according to Dunai, who notes that "it is the only book that is part of the Sección Femenina's official archive housed at the Royal Academy of History" (*Cooking for the Patria* 24).

In line with the SF's mission to train Spanish women in domesticity, *Ciencia gastronómica,* as well as containing recipes, also included lists of cooking techniques and other domestic advice. The first section of the book addresses elements within the kitchen and dining area and how to prepare foods in certain styles. It opens with a description of what a dining room should look like: "El comedor ha de ser amplio, de líneas sencillas y decorado claro, con luz, sol, muebles cómodos y fáciles de limpiar" (the dining room should be spacious, with simple lines and a light decor, with light, sun, comfortable and easy-to-clean furniture; 5). Yet Sarrau acknowledges how aspirational such luxury would have been for many households, since "las dificultades de la vida moderna, cada vez más cara, han obligado, en muchos casos, a prescindir de esta habitación" (the difficulties of modern life, ever more apparent, have forced people in many cases to forego this room; 5). This first section also contains lists for cooking utensils (19–22), "terminología empleada en la cocina" (terminology used in the kitchen; 23–4), and "preparados auxiliares" (ancillary preparations; 34–6), as well as descriptions of different cooking methods and major foodstuffs. The second section, which starts on page 63, comprises the recipes themselves, and the final section proffers advice on nutrition and calories.

The Authority of Modernity

As with subsequent SF-commissioned food texts, the emphasis in *Ciencia gastronómica* is on culinary modernity. The newness of this book's culinary system can of course be seen as reflective of the modernity of the SF's broader domestic programs. Kathleen Richmond briefly mentions the newness of these domestic programs, noting that the more frequent message in important SF periodicals "was the importance of domesticity and the projection of SF's educational programs as different, modern and in every way better than anything preceding them"

(23). This modernity was combined with ingredients of traditional Spain, such as domestic virtue, religious piety, and family values, which some scholars have identified as one of the most striking contradictions of the SF (see Enders). Upholding traditional, religious values, the SF's "recipe" for Spanish womanhood spoke directly to Franco's National Catholic identity for New Spain. Yet the SF's curriculum was also very modern and broke with tradition in relation to what it taught Spanish women about food culture and household management.

The way in which the SF-commissioned food texts present culinary knowledge as new or modern makes these texts seem more authoritative because they do not in any way draw on or value the readers' existing culinary knowledge. In cookbooks where readers' past experience is valued or drawn on, recipes are effectively seen as belonging to a community (normally of women) who work together to construct and revise them rather than just to the author of a cookbook. Elizabeth McDougall highlights the collective nature of these sorts of cookbooks, stating that "if the act of reading a recipe invites revision, then past experience is central to its reinterpretation" (117). Kathleen Vester also describes the way in which cooks take on ownership of recipes:

> The recipe becomes a recipe not through the act of being given, but through the act of being taken, executed and eventually embodied. The imperative structure explicitly invites readers to engage with the text instead of passively consuming it. (8)

Vester points out that the authority of the author is often under question: "since recipes are derived from oral tradition, they imply a concept of authorship distinct from written tradition" (8). Recipes have, as noted above, traditionally been passed down from one generation of women to the next in the informal setting of the home. If the oral origins of recipes compromise the authority of the author, then it is noteworthy how SF food texts maintain authority as written food texts. Indeed, in contrast to food texts that highlight – either explicitly or implicitly – what women would have learnt informally from their mothers or grandmothers, the "newness" of *Ciencia gastronómica*'s culinary system makes it clear that this past knowledge and the oral tradition upon which it is based are obsolete. Positioned as an expert in this new culinary system, with its readers rendered as complete novices, the SF makes resoundingly clear that the transfer of knowledge is top-down.

All sections of *Ciencia gastronómica* – from its opening chapter on cooking techniques to the recipes themselves – evince a disconnect with past knowledge. In the description of different cooking terms/techniques, readers are taught, for instance, that there is a "manera de espumar" (a method of skimming), which involves taking off "las impurezas o espumas de un caldo" (the impurities or foam of the soup; 35). In discussing this technique, Sarrau makes no reference to the fact that many readers probably would have seen their mothers or grandmothers execute this step in their preparation of the dish at home. He presents this traditional Spanish *caldo* (soup) – based on an age-old cooking technique readers would have learnt in an informal setting – as new and with no connection to any past knowledge of Spanish cuisine or experience of cooking at home. The effect of this is to clearly emphasize the SF's expertise in domesticity and to encourage readers to see this organization as the ultimate authority in matters relating to household management and modernity.

The *consome* section provides another example of how the recipes do not allow readers to draw on past knowledge. In one very well known non-SF cookbook of the time, by Teodoro Bardají, a *consome* is described as "un caldo elevado a la máxima perfección" (a soup of the highest perfection; 27). In preparing a consome from a cookbook, therefore, readers are encouraged by his invoking of the history of *caldo* to draw on their knowledge and past experience of cooking it. By contrast, Sarrau provides recipes for *consomes* with nondescript qualifiers such as "sencillo" (simple) or "doble" (double). There is nothing in his instructions for *consome* that creates a sense of continuity between this dish and the *caldo* that Spanish women would have most likely learnt to cook at some point in the past. The listing of ingredients in metric units also adds to the modernity or newness of this culinary system, again stressing the SF or Sarrau's role in passing down knowledge to readers of this cookbook. And because, as discussed above, narrative often detracts from the prescriptive nature of recipes, there is tellingly no such discursive element in *Ciencia gastronómica*, leaving only the prescriptive or instructional nature of the recipes. In the recipe Sarrau provides for *caldo* (soup), no story is told about this dish or its place in Spanish gastronomy, but instructions on how to serve it are dictated down to the last detail: "un plato sopero no debe llenarse con más de dos decilitros de caldo" (a soup bowl should never be filled with more than ten decilitres of broth; 70).

As the first SF-commissioned food text, *Ciencia gastronómica* can be seen as a benchmark; it solidified paradigmatic boundaries for subsequent official food texts. Yet it is not nearly as well known as the next text I look at, the bestseller *Manual de cocina*.

Ana María Herrera and *Manual de cocina*: The Invisible Author

The most enduring of the SF's cookbooks – after its initial publication in 1950, it went through a staggering forty editions – *Manual de cocina* (Cooking manual) was written by Ana María Herrera, a member of the SF and a "profesora de cocina en varios centros docentes" (cookery teacher in a number of educational centres; jacket copy). We learn little about Herrera in all but the most recent edition of *Manual de cocina,* published in 2009, on account of the invisibility of the authorial persona in SF-commissioned cookbooks. The fact that prologues do not feature in these official domestic manuals makes it all the more challenging for us to find signs of the author and her authorial persona. In the prologue to the present-day edition of this text, however, Herrera's grandson explains that writing the cookbook "compatibilizaba con [su] profesión de cocina en la Escuela del Hogar del Instituto Lope de Vega de Madrid y en otros centros docentes, ya que era diplomada de la Academia de Gastrónomos de Madrid" (compatible with her cooking work at the Home Econoimcs School of the Lope de Vega Institute in Madrid and in other teaching establishments, given that she was a graduate of the Gastronomic Academy of Madrid; vii). We also learn here that the SF immediately accepted Herrera's proposal to write *Manual de cocina,* and that she went on to write two more cookbooks for the organization: *Cocina regional* (Regional cuisine, 1953) and *Recetario de olla a presión y batidora eléctrica* (Recipes for pressure cookers and mixers, 1958).[4] Having studied under Sarrau in his role as director of Madrid's Academia de Gastrónomos, Herrera no doubt learnt a great deal about food culture and food discourse from her esteemed *profesor*. Moreover, that she taught at the SF's Escuela del Hogar means she would likely have been very familiar with his exemplary *Ciencia gastronómica*. Herrera must have seemed well suited to the task of writing these cookbooks, given both her connections with the SF and the fact that she had studied under Sarrau.

Certainly, it is clear from the outset that Herrera's *Manual de cocina* shares a number of important features with *Ciencia gastronómica*. A focus on domestic modernity, a complete absence of any engaging narrative, and a lack of paratextual elements all indicate that we should view both texts as adhering to a similar model. At roughly eight hundred pages long, however, Herrera's book was nearly four times as long as Sarrau's. Divided into four sections, *Manual de cocina* opens with a chapter containing detailed information about a range of cooking-related issues. From diagrams and accompanying instructions on how to cut poultry and meat, to a list of "utensilios de cocina imprescindibles en una casa" (essential cooking utensils for the home; 756), housewives are offered prescriptive advice on nearly every aspect of food preparation. Following this introductory section are the recipes themselves, categorized by season, from *primavera* (spring) through *invierno* (winter). With thirty two-course meals for each season to choose from, readers are offered a vast array of lunch and dinner options. In the cookbook's third section, the 120 recipes are divided under different headings, such as rice, eggs, and pasta.

Because *Manual de cocina* was a popular and commercial success, scholars of Spanish gastronomy and food history have long appreciated its importance. For instance, in *Gastronomía y nutrición*, José Luis Armendáriz Sanz describes it as a

> completísimo manual de cocina tradicional española en el que encontramos el material necesario para una cocina doméstica... Este libro ha sido durante generaciones el libro de cabecera de las amas de casa españolas y un libro de gran ayuda para los profesionales. Quizá uno de los libros más completos del siglo XX en España, y que seguramente, sea el que en más hogares podemos encontrar. (24)
>
> (most complete manual of traditional Spanish cuisine in which we find everything necessary for domestic cooking ... This book has been, for many generations, the leading book for Spanish housewives and a book of great use for professionals. Perhaps one of the most complete books of the twentieth century in Spain, and without a doubt the most widely found book in Spanish homes.)

Another scholar to have mentioned *Manual de cocina* is Abad Alegría et al., who writes: "La nueva mujer española está así pertrechada con una obra tan bien pensada para su papel tradicional de alma de la familia, que el libro tiene grande e inevitable éxito" (The new Spanish woman is thus equipped with a book so well thought out for her traditional role as heart of the family that this book has inevitably been a great success; 45). Finally, Martínez Llopis is of the opinion that "está escrita con gran sencillez y las recetas son fáciles para realizar por el ama de casa" (it is written with great simplicity and the recipes are easy for the housewife to produce; 423).

Although, as Martínez Llopis notes, the recipes may be relatively easy to make, as very few required complex preparation, adhering to this cookbook in its entirety would have been time consuming to say the least. From instructions on sourcing the best ingredients to detailed information on how to set up a kitchen, the book required readers to dedicate hours on end to perfecting the art of cookery. The implications for women's ability to engage in other (non-domestic) activities are readily apparent, as is the fact that being a mother and wife is defined by the all-consuming tasks of caring and cooking for one's family. As well, uncritically accepting the "recipes" for both food and womanhood promotes an unquestioning obedience to Franco's rigid gender divide, which demanded women's exclusive dedication to domesticity. Thus, the onerous domestic system prescribed in *Manual de cocina* can be seen as an example of how food discourse produces gendered subjectivities, upholding Francoist biopolitics.

Highly prescriptive about food preparation and gender, the SF cookbooks and food texts are all the more instructional because they lack narrative. Parkhurst Ferguson considers the question of narrative and cookbooks is in her most recent book, *Word of Mouth*. Of particular interest is her observation that Irma Rombauer's 1943 *The Joy of Cooking* "makes much of stories and recipes – so much so that at times the instructions get lost in the narrative" (92). Each ingredient in *The Joy of Cooking* is introduced with a story. For instance, before giving recipes using pawpaws, Rombauer explains:

> Pawpaws – also known as Poor Man's Banana or Hosier Banana, the pawpaw is the largest edible fruit native to America. Pawpaws often occur as clusters of up to 9 individual fruits. The ripe fruit is soft and thin skinned. These smoky-tasting native fruits should be picked and eaten after the first frost, or when they fall from the tree. (88)

This narrative is presented alongside the recipes and makes the recipes seem less prescriptive. Stories such as these abound in *The Joy of Cooking*, making the cookbook's recipes function also as elements in a story about food.

Parkhurst Ferguson's observation that the instructional nature of Rombauer's recipes gets a bit lost in all her storytelling is of interest for the contrast with the contemporaneous SF-commissioned cookbooks under scrutiny in this chapter. If the effect of narrative on Rombauer's recipes, according to Parkhurst Ferguson, is to make them seem less prescriptive, it follows that cookbooks with an absence of narrative will convey a heightened sense of authority. One of the defining features, as I argue, of the SF-commissioned cookbooks is a complete absence of those discursive spaces where cookbook authors traditionally develop an authorial persona and establish a sense of familiarity with readers. Instead, here the absence of such elements reinforces the sense of hierarchy between the SF and the readers of its cookbooks.

Consisting of many traditional recipes that would have differing degrees of significance for Herrera, *Manual de cocina* does not at any stage make reference to the personal stories behind these dishes. The majority of the recipes begin directly with an instruction or cooking directive, such as, for instance, the recipe for *el flan*. This opens with a list of ingredients and then goes directly into instruction mode, telling the reader: "en una flanera se ponen cincuenta gramos de azúcar" (to place fifty grams of sugar in a crème caramel mould; 559). This impersonal formality is repeated time after time in Herrera's cookbook, with most of the sections lacking a preamble or general introduction to the topic at hand. The main section of the cookbook – which is the second section detailing "las minutas diarias de comida y cena propias de cada estación" (daily menus and appropriate meals for every season) – begins directly with yet another list. Instead, for instance, of a narrative about the importance of seasonal ingredients to Spain's traditional and primarily local (and at that stage still mainly autarkic) food culture, Herrera simply begins with an impersonal inventory of the "productos propios de esta estación" (products suitable for each season; 43).

The following recipe for Spanish-style croquettes is exemplary of the format all recipes adhere to in *Manual de cocina*:

Croquetas a la Española

Ingredientes y cantidades:

Jamón 50 gramos; carne de cerdo 150 gramos; Caldo concentrado ½ litro; Manteca de cerdo 1 cucharada; Harina 50 gramos; Huevo 1; Cebolla picada; 1 cucharadita sal.

Modo de hacerlo

Se frie o se cuece la carne y se pica muy fina. Se pica también el jamón, en una sartén se pone la manteca, se derrite y se echa la cebolla picada, menudísima, se deja freir un poco y se añade el jamón picado, la carne del cerdo y la harina; se rehoga todo junto y se añade el caldo hirviendo, removiendo rápidamente con el batidor. Se sazona de sal y nuez moscada y una pizca de canela y se deja cocer un cuarto de hora sin dejar de mover. Se retira del fuego y se mezcla un huevo batido, se deja dar un hervor al lado y se vierte en una Fuente. Para moldearlas y freírlas, véase la receta anterior.

(Spanish-style Croquettes

Ingredients and quantities:

50 grams of ham; 150 grams of pork; ½ litre concentrated broth; 1 tablespoon of pork lard; 50 grams of flour; 1 egg; 1 sliced onion; 1 teaspoon of salt.

Method

Fry or cook the meat and chop finely. Chop the ham. Place the lard in a frying pan, allow to melt, then add the finely sliced onion. Fry for a little, then add the sliced ham, the pork, and the flour. Fry everything lightly together, then add the boiling broth, stirring briskly with a whisk. Season with salt, nutmeg, and a pinch of cinnamon. Leave to cook for 15 minutes without stirring. Take off the stove and mix with a beaten egg. Bring to the boil briefly, then pour into a dish. For moulding and frying the croquettes, refer to the previous recipe.)

This recipe is made up of lists: lists of ingredients and quantities, as well as a list of the different steps readers must follow to make the croquettes exactly as Herrera stipulates. Such lists throughout *Manual de cocina* make this cookbook seem all the more instructional for, as Thomasen tells us, "lists can be either descriptive or prescriptive" (10); descriptive lists are value neutral, while prescriptive lists connote a strong sense of normativity. Those in this text are highly normative, functioning to tell Spanish women what they must do to successfully fulfil their role as housewife. By way of example, there is a list at the outset of the cookbook of "Utensilios de cocina" (Cooking utensils; 27). If this list were descriptive, it might describe what utensils were used in some areas of Spain. But the list is highly prescriptive, telling Spanish women exactly which utensils they must have for cooking according to the text's instructions. The listed items are described as "imprescindibles" (essential; 27) and exact measurements are given for a number of them, making clear that the successful execution of the ensuing recipes and effective household management depends on Spanish women doing what this list – along with the myriad subsequent ones – prescribes.

In this cookbook, lists generally stand in for narrative, which renders the prose not just prescriptive but also austere. One of the few recipes that begins with something by way of an introduction is *el cocido* (stew; *Manual* 295). *Cocido* has since the nineteenth century been considered the iconic national dish for its embodiment of the principle of unity in diversity, as it is eaten in some form or another across the whole of the peninsular. While Herrera acknowledges that *cocido* is "el plato más clásico de España" (Spain's quintessential dish), she underplays the importance of the regional variations on it, stating that "en el fondo siempre es el mismo, pues hay varias cosas que son comunes a todas las regiones" (in effect it is always the same, since there are various things that are common to all regions; 295). National unity was central to the regime from the outset, and official food discourse was both reflective and prescriptive of this, but Herrera's single recipe for *cocido* does more than produce readers or cooks that are hyper-aware of national unity. It also replaces traditional recipes for this dish with one that is highly modern in its uniformity.

Another way in which Herrara's cookbook endorses modernity is in its use of the metric system in lists of ingredients, instead of more homely measurement styles, which women would have learnt instinctively from cooking with their mothers and grandmothers. Beyond this, use of the metric system further reinforces her distance from the friendly, maternal figures that we often associate with domestic cookbooks. Herrara's lists of ingredients for "traditional" recipes such as *cocido, gazpacho, croquetas,* and *arroz* (rice) call for precise metric measurements: as Dunai has noted in her observations of SF cookbooks, readers are taught that there is a difference of two grams between "un pellizco de sal [y] un polvillo de sal" (a pinch of salt and a dusting of salt; *Cooking for the Patria* 28). Such precision is one of the most important ways in which Herrera's cookbook renders the old new.

In disconnecting the recipes and cooking techniques not just from her own past, but also from Spain's traditional foodscape, Herrera encourages her readers to do the same. If we think about the way food discourse produces subjectivities, then *Manual de cocina* can be seen to produce female subjects who, while confined to traditional roles, privilege the impersonal modernity of the SF's instruction. That impersonal modernity comes at the expense of the author; that is, this type of culinary discourse can only be upheld in the absence of a strong authorial voice. As Leonardi notes, producers of cookbooks construct an "identifiable authorial persona" (342). Because Herrera does not at any point create a nurturing or caring authorial identity for herself or show any familiarity with readers, we can see her as the embodiment of the SF's impersonal and austere authority in all matters relating to the professionalization of the *ama de casa.*

Sección Femenina Cookery Manuals and the Professional Domestic

The last official text looked at in this chapter, *Manual de cocina para alumnas* (Student cooking manual), is one the many cookery manuals produced by the SF for use in the Bachillerato, Carrera de Comercio y Magisterio (High school diploma in commerce and teaching) as well as by the students who participated in "las escuelas de Hogar de Sección Femenina" (the home economics schools of the Women's Section). These cookery manuals follow the blueprint laid down by *Ciencia gastronómica* and *Manual de cocina.* Immediately apparent is the absence of paratextual elements, such as a prologue or dedicatory, where authors normally establish a relationship with their readers. In the absence of this discursive space, it is once again the SF's authority in the domestic and moral education of Spanish women that gives meaning to the text. Prescriptive of how Spanish women should manage their kitchens and meal preparation, the text makes clear, too, that the only role envisaged for the married Spanish women is that of *ama de casa* (housewife). Meal preparation is therefore of the upmost importance to the Spanish housewife, and the manual opens with the instruction that the good *ama de casa* will spend "la mayor parte del tiempo para la preparación de las comidas, cuidados de la vajilla etc" (most of her time preparing food, looking after the dishes, etc.; 5).

The manual is not just prescriptive about how the Spanish housewife will execute food preparation; it also demands women's exclusive dedication to domesticity. It is in these cookery manuals that we get the strongest sense of how broad a women's education was meant to be, even if, ultimately, this knowledge would be dedicated solely to domestic pursuits. The ideal Spanish woman was, according to one scholar, expected to care for others,

> but at the same time was called upon to invest time and energy in improving herself physically and intellectually. She was evaluated according to her homemaking skills, but also according to her ambitions to influence society at large. (Ofer, *Señoritas in Blue* 588)

It was the professionalization of the position of *ama de casa* through structures such as Servicio Social (social service), Cátedras Ambulantes (travelling classrooms), and Escuelas del Hogar (home-based schools) that allowed the SF to uphold a conservative gender divide while also giving women access to an education of sorts. Although a woman's activity was limited to the domestic sphere, her influence, according to the SF, would be felt through the whole of Spanish society and she would be indispensable to the construction of New Spain.

A strong advocate for formal education for Spanish women, Pilar Primo de Rivera "manifestó durante toda su vida una mezcla de admiración y desconfianza por las mujeres universitarias" (exhibited throughout her life a mix of admiration for and distrust of college women; Alpuente 62). Believing that women should be trained, for instance, in math and science in as much as these subjects were applicable to their domestic duties, Primo de Rivera nevertheless harboured very gendered ideas about education: "En las mujeres el conocimiento analítico no puede perturbar las finas arterias de la feminidad" (Analytical knowledge in women should not disturb the fine veins of femininity; Alpuente 62). Typical Spanish women would practise traditionally masculine disciplines such as reading, science, and nutrition, but it would be, according to Dunai, "when they prepared breakfast, lunch, and dinner for their families" (*Cooking for the Patria* 77). A broad education was therefore supported through the SF, but only as it related to domesticity. On the one hand, the fact that the SF offered women training in a number of different areas would have been liberating for those wishing to access education. Nonetheless, the fact that this extensive and broad education was required of women solely for the purposes of domesticity is yet further confirmation of the SF's mandate that women dedicate themselves only to home life.

Manual de cocina's chapter 5 (La Compra – Ración en peso de cada alimento; Shopping – Portions of each food in weight) provides an excellent example of how Spanish women were expected to draw on a broader education in math and nutrition in the execution of their domestic duties. The housewife was directed to plan the meals for the day "teniendo en cuenta las personas que integran la familia y las personas que integran la familia y las necesidades calóricas de cada uno de ellos, ofreciéndoles una alimentación adecuada" (keeping in mind the people that make up the family and each of their caloric needs, offering each of them sufficient food; 20). According to the manual, the average requirement was seventy-five calories "por kilo de peso" (per kilo of weight; 20). This information is important because the quantity of ingredients bought depended on the specific calorific needs of each family member. The housewife was also expected to be well versed in nutrition, and certain foodstuffs were recommended on the basis of nutritional physiology. Fats and carbohydrates were recommended, for instance, because "dan calor y energía" (they provide warmth and energy; 26). The Spanish housewife's broad knowledge was thereby focused on the food intake and nutritional requirements of her family.

The manual also teaches the history of certain foodstuffs, such as wheat, chocolate, tea, and coffee, at the same time as readers/students are taught how to cook with or serve these ingredients. Certainly, the SF's ideal of a homemaker with a broad education is evident in these sections too. The student learns that chocolate "es la merienda española por excelencia" (is the quintessential Spanish snack; 135), and she is also taught about its history at the height of Spain's imperial grandeur: "El caudillo Hernán Cortés lo apreciaba particularmente por sus cualidades alimenticias, y decía que una taza de la preciosa bebida sostenía las fuerzas de un soldado todo el día" (The military leader Hernán Cortés particularly appreciated it for its nutritional value, and used to say that a cup of this precious drink could maintain the strength of a soldier all day; 39). Reminding readers of Spain's past imperial grandeur upholds official discourse, for "what Franco and his supporters most desired was to obliterate history, and return to an earlier myth of Spain, the Spain of imperial grandeur" (Valis 8). Moreover, this anecdote serves to reinforce to readers that food preparation can have an impact on national fortunes. Hernán Cortés's claim that a cup of chocolate kept the soldiers fighting fit reminded Spanish housewives how important healthy, strong bodies were to the successful construction of the new Spanish state.

The Gendering of Gastronomy: Sección Femenina and La Marquesa de Parabere

Another way in which the SF's food texts uphold official discourse is through the gendering of gastronomy, particularly apparent in its women's magazine, *Teresa*. Published later in the regime, *Teresa* was, according to one scholar, of all the journals published by the SF the one that "functioned as the official mouthpiece of Falangist women between the years 1954–1977" (Ofer, "*Teresa*" 122). In the later years especially, *Teresa* defined a woman's role in terms of both the private and public spaces, providing women advice about cooking as well as fashion, art, literature, film, and theatre, yet still focused primarily on the domestic. Although this publication is directed to female readers, it does have sections on gastronomy, which render gastronomic writing and the art of fine eating as pertaining to the domain of males rather than females. *Teresa*'s cooking sections, however, are dedicated explicitly to female cooks and contain little more than lists of recipes for different occasions, such as "cenas sencillas" (simple dinners) or "la navidad" (Christmas). The comparative lack of narrative in the cookery sections again highlights the prescriptive nature of cookery. Here it is worth noting that because prescriptive food discourse is directed solely at women, ultimately instructional food writing is gendered as exclusively female.

The sections dedicated to gastronomy are, by contrast, written in an amiable tone that highlights male expertise and aplomb within the field. For instance, an article in *Teresa* from 1956 titled "La cocina y la erudición" (Cooking and scholarship) includes a picture of a man seated on an armchair surrounded by books. According to the article, when a man realizes that the key to happiness is good food, "no resulta nada extraño que se dedique a coleccionar libros que traten del arte del preparar las viviendas de la manera más apetitosa" (it is not at all strange that he should turn to collecting books about the art of preparing the home in the most appealing way; Issue 26, 15). In reading about male collections of gastronomic texts – all of which were likely penned by male gastronomes – female readers understand that the writing and thinking about food inherent to the realm of gastronomy is the domain of their male counterparts. The fact that *Teresa* genders gastronomy as male is significant, for it reminds female readers that this aspect of Spanish cuisine is off-limits. When women do partake in the realm of food, it is only as cooks or readers of hyper-prescriptive food texts.

The Marquesa de Parabere, in spite of her disruption of official discourse in other areas, enters the realm of gastronomy with a surprising degree of self-doubt. There were other women at this time in other countries who penned gastronomic-style food writing. Describing the food writing of authors such as Elizabeth Robins, M.F.K. Fisher, and Elizabeth David, Alice McLean lists the key tenets of their food writing as including:

> (1) a focus on dining as an art form and on the aesthetic pleasure of eating, (2) an unconventional form that incorporates personal anecdote, historical reference, and literary allusion, (3) a cosmopolitan sensibility, (4) an emphasis on dining as a social event, (5) a concern with elegance of expression and with writing as an artistic medium nourished by the pleasures, and (6) an undomesticated appetite. (8)

Although the Marquesa authors a history of gastronomy, it focuses much less on the pleasures and aesthetics of gastronomy than do contemporaneous authors. She provides a relatively dry account of world gastronomy in which she writes a great deal about French cuisine, but she does not use the opportunity to carve out a place for herself as an author of a work on gastronomy.

In the introductory note to her *Historia de la gastronomía* (A history of gastronomy), which reads like a friendly note, the Marquesa writes:

> Ni por un momento he pensado hacer un libro científico. No me creo capacitada para ello. La HISTORIA DE LA GASTRONOMIA, pese a su pomposo título, es tan solo un ligero esboso de ella, en el que roza ligeramente algunos temas que he creído fueran interesantes. Ya sé que muchas de las anécdotas que incluyo son harto conocidas, y otras direan que las he "copiado" ... Aparte de que no tengo capacidad y sabiduría para más, yo tan solo he pretendido entretener; ¿lo he logrado? Mis lectores tienen la palabra. (11)
>
> (Not for one moment did I intend to write a scientific book. I don't believe myself capable of it. *A History of Gastronomy*, despite its pompous title, is

only a light outline of it, in which I touch lightly on some topics I found interesting. I know that many of the anecdotes I have included are known, and others will say that I have "copied" them ... Apart from the fact that I am not capable or wise enough for more, I have only hoped to entertain; have I achieved this? My readers will have the last word.)

With a great deal of professional training, experience in food writing, and important personal connections to the world of gastronomy and haute cuisine, the Marquesa may seem to be falsely modest in claiming that she is not capable of writing serious gastronomy.[5] On the other hand, it is likely that in spite of her eloquent and knowledgeable tome, she understands that gastronomy is a male domain and she must therefore make apologies for her entry into the public sphere of gastronomic writing, especially at such a conservative stage of the dictatorship. Just as Spanish women exist only as the readers of cookbooks, the Marquesa positions herself solely as an authority on cooking, failing to properly take up her rightful place as a gastronome.

The authorial persona she creates for herself as a gastronome is also noteworthy, given how authoritative she was as a cookbook author. Indeed, her magnum opus, *La cocina completa* (1933), was rigorous and academic in style, as is obvious from the prologue, where she writes:

> Certifico que cuantas recetas integran esta obra han sido experimentadas por mí ... Mi libro está estructurado según las normas más modernas; primeramente lo he seperado en capítulos, cada cual referente a un manjar o a una de las modalidades del complejo arte de la cocina, y, segundo, le he aplicado el novisimo sistema que reclamo como exclusivamente mió. (9)

> (I certify that many of the recipes included in this book have been made by me ... My book is structured according to the most modern standards; I have first separated it into chapters, each of which refers to one delicacy or one method from the complex culinary arts; and, second, I have applied this brand-new system that I claim is exclusively mine.)

As one scholar notes, the thoroughness and rigour of *La cocina completa* eventually led to its becoming a key reference point in modern Spanish cuisine: "Con el tiempo, la seriedad de sus recetas, todas ensayadas – y su riguroso academicismo, convertieron este libro en vademecum para profesionales y aficionados al noble oficio de las cazuelas" (With time, the seriousness of the recipes, each one tested – and its rigorous scholarship – turned this book into a leading manual for professionals and aficionados of the noble art of cooking; Capel 7).

Breaking the Mould: Non-official Cookbooks

Some of the non-official cookbooks for women follow the SF's paradigm for domestic cookbooks, as is the case, for instance, of a 1955 collection of recipes written by Pablo Arigita Mezquiriz titled *Cromos de cocina de Waly* (Pictures from Waly's kitchen). This series consists of a total of eight *fichas* (files) published monthly for 18.80 pesetas each. *Cromos de cocina de Waly* was Arigita Mezquiriz's first cookbook, and he went on to write three more, all similar in style and format. Of interest about this collection of recipes is that, similar to the SF-commissioned cookbooks, there are none of the extra-textual elements that we so often find in cookbooks. With no dedication, prologue, or introduction, we learn nothing about the author himself, nor the relationship he might imagine having with his readers.

Though there is little textual space for Arigita Mezquiriz to articulate his authorial persona, he does utilize the front page of the first of the *fichas* to direct this collection of recipes at Spanish women, albeit perfunctorily. Using the command form to tell them to be sure to make use of *las fichas Waly* (the Waly files), he warns that marital happiness "depende de su manera de cocinar" (depends on your cooking style; 1). It is not just the lack of narrative or of any friendly authorial persona that renders Arigita Mezquiriz's food discourse similar to that of the SF. Significant, too, is the way in which he genders cookery as female, while making it clear to Spanish women that being able to cook well is a prerequisite for being a good wife.

Other non-official cookbooks are of interest because of the challenge they represent not just to the SF's hegemonic paradigm for domestic literature, but also in some instances to official gender discourse. Two of the three non-SF books looked at below belong to a series titled *La riqueza en la mano* (Wealth in hand), which consists mainly of titles for "el hombre práctico" (the practical man). With around twenty titles for the industrious male reader, including *El pavo* (Turkey), *La huerta familiar* (The family farm), and *El caballo* (The horse), the series also published two cookbooks for female readers: *La cocina casera* (Home cooking, 1952) and *Los dulces caseros* (Homemade desserts, 1959). Given, as we have seen, that the SF's entire domestic and culinary systems reproduced the official directive that women and men were to reside in separate spheres, and that SF cookbooks themselves produced highly gendered subjects and upheld Francoist biopolitics, it is of interest that these women's cookbooks were published as part of a series for the "practical man." That *La Riqueza en la mano* contains both male and female titles questions from the outset the rigidity of this gender divide.

The first cookbook I will examine is *La cocina casera*, written by María Luisa Alonso Duro and published in 1952 by the Librería y Casa Editorial Hernando S.A. Madrid. Alonso Duro penned a number of cookbooks before the civil war as well as writing for the well-regarded weekly magazine *Blanco y Negro*, which "dedicó una sección especial a la cocina, denominada 'Página de cocina' en la que publicaba recetas extraídas de libros" (dedicated a special section to cuisine, named "Cooking Pages," in which it published recipes extracted from books; Acosta). Writing for such an important periodical would have given Alonso Duro a significant national presence as a food writer. Further, because *Blanco y Negro* was officially affiliated with the Catholic Church, Alonso Duro's authorial persona as a food writer or cookbook author would have been viewed in terms of the conservatism of this institution.

Of immediate interest is the presence in *La cocina casera* of a prologue and a strong authorial voice.[6] Alonso Duro makes use of this discursive space to strike up a conversation with her readers conveying closeness and intimacy. Many scholars point in general terms to the tone of "friendliness" in domestic cookbooks. Helen Zoe Veit writes, for instance, that "writers providing domestic information often personified their books as friendly teachers, and many actually called them a friend or companion or guide" (36). Fleitz suggests that "through informal conversations about cooking, women have participated in a practice that has allowed them throughout history to connect with other women and validate their own existence in the domestic sphere" (1). This intimacy with readers can be seen in the role Alonso Duro takes on of an older family friend or relative as she talks about cooking skills not in terms of obligation, national renewal, or the health of the nation, but rather as the way to catch a good man: "Y todas sabemos de aquel solterón recalcitrante que al final cayó con una chica no guapa, pero de reconocida habilidad culinaria. Un rosbif a punto, una cocada deliciosa conquistaron su amor" (And we all know about the recalcitrant bachelor who finally ended up with a girl who isn't pretty, but is renowned for her cooking. A well-done roast beef or a delicious macaroon won his love; 9). Her book's connectedness with readers is an important point of difference from the SF-commissioned cookbooks.

Yet Alonso Duro's comments about how to find a good man do reinforce the belief inherent in many of the women's periodicals of the time that "todos los consejos y la mayoría de los artículos son para que las mujeres acomoden su comportamiento en función de un hipotético varón" (all of the advice and most of the articles are designed to make women adapt their behaviour to the hypothetical man; Muñoz Ruiz

102). Indeed, in telling her readers that most men cannot resist a delicious meal, Alonso Duro reinforces the conservative view – which she likely also expressed in her journalistic food column – that women should shape themselves in accordance with men's desires and wishes.

This text also differs from that of the SF cookery texts in its format. There is, for instance, a much more haphazard approach to the ordering of the different sections, with the book starting off with advice about how to use an *olla express* (pressure cooker), then going on to general cooking terms, a section dedicated to vitamins, and then recipes for different dishes. Another important stylistic difference is that Alonso Duro does not include a separate list of ingredients for each of the recipes. Instead, the ingredients are incorporated into the body of the recipe itself, which is informal in tone. If the prescriptive lists in the SF's food texts function normatively to tell Spanish women exactly what they must do in the domestic sphere, the lack of lists in Alonso Duro's cookbook renders her food discourse much less instructional. Occasionally, measures are given in metric units, but Alonso Duro is often vague in her specifications of cooking times and measurements. Her recipe for *pollos modernistas* (modernist chickens), for instance, starts by saying that the chicken is filled with "un poco de jamón en pedacitos" (some pieces of ham; 171). Just as it is left to the cook to decide how much ham to use, it is also up to her to know when the chicken "casi está en su punto" (is almost done; 171). The recipe also calls for some alcohol, but once again there is a certain amount of leeway, as the reader has the option of choosing between sherry and white wine. The vagueness of Alonso Duro's cooking instructions implies an awareness – and valorization – of readers' past cooking experience.

The authority that Alonso Duro accords to her readers to choose ingredients, cooking times, and measurements is an example of what scholars describe as the "communal" nature of recipes (see McDougall). Unlike the SF recipes, recipes like these, which encourage revision and modifications, can be viewed as "unauthorized" (McDougall 117) because they do not come from any single cook or source of authority. Moreover, in producing readers who make autonomous decisions, unlike the SF, Alonso Duro privileges the home as a site of informal education. Many Spanish women of the era, as we have noted, would have learnt cooking from their mothers or grandmothers in the family kitchen, where they would have come to instinctively know how much of a certain ingredient to use or when a dish was "just right." By encouraging her readers to draw on this embodied knowledge in the execution of these less authoritarian recipes, Alonso Duro can be seen as implicitly supporting a mode of cookery that was not part of the

SF's professionalization of the role of the housewife. And just as Alonso Duro's recipes are much less prescriptive than those written or commissioned by the SF, she is also less rigid in the role she envisages for Spanish women. From love of their husbands, fathers, or sons to simply being "aficionadas a la cocina," there are, according to Alonso Duro's culinary discourse, many reasons why Spanish women might turn their hand to cooking – not just to fulfil their obligations as housewives.

The other title for female readers in this series was *Los dulces caseros* (Homemade desserts), written by Fernando Alburquerque. The recipes themselves adhere more to the model set out in the SF cookbooks than do those of *La cocina casera*, in that they list ingredients in metric units at the beginning of each recipe. Where Alburquerque's cookbook does differ from those of the SF is in the implicit – yet rather bold – challenge it makes to the rigid gender divide upheld by the latter. And Alburquerque is not just less rigid about gendered roles; he is also much more flexible and less prescriptive about the authority of his cookbook. Rather than demanding that readers follow recipes and menu plans rigidly, he writes that they should choose as they wish "los típicos o los preferidos de cada comarca" (the typical or favourite dishes of each region; 15).

While the inclusion of male and female titles in the same series can be seen as implicitly disrupting official discourse on gender difference, Albuquerque's cookbook could not be more explicit in its critique of the official gendering of domesticity as exclusively female. He makes ample use of the prologue to define his domestic system, which includes more than just cuisine. Alburquerque does not write texts that are exclusively "male" or "female" in the two prologues he penned to his cookbook, *Una manera fácil de crear riqueza* (An easy way to produce wealth) and *Crear riqueza donde no la hay* (Creating wealth where there is none). Instead, in the first prologue he introduces the aim of the series, which is to help readers to find "un medio fácil y sencillo de crear riqueza" (an easy or simple way of creating wealth) out of "los animales domésticos o el cultivo mejorado de la tierra" (domestic animals or improved cultivation; 7). His second prologue starts off with a few lines to his male readers, explaining that in this particular volume the topic will be "un tanto ajeno a la mirada principal de estos Manuales" (a little alien to the main focus of these manuals) and that "vamos a hablar y tratar de *los dulces*" (we are going to talk about *desserts*; 11, italics in original). While in the opening lines to his second prologue Alburquerque speaks exclusively to his male readers, it quickly becomes apparent that he does not subscribe to the dominant, official gender divide. Instead, he writes that *la confitería* (confectionery) will be of interest to a wide range of readers, such as "las amas de casa ... los confiteros, cocineros, o, más sencillamente, aficionados a las cosas de la cocina" (housewives ... confectioners, chefs, or, more simply, aficionados of the kitchen; 12). Indeed, knowing how to make cakes and sweets from one's region or town should, according to Alburquerque, be obligatory for "hombres y mujeres, o mujeres y hombres, si ustedes quieren" (men and women, or women and men, if you prefer; 12).

It is not just in relation to *la confitería* that Alburquerque espouses his more modern views on gender. Commenting on what a luxury it is to have a *criada* (servant) or a *cocinero* (cook) at home, he writes: "En los matrimonios jóvenes, sobre todo, marido y mujer se tienen que ingeniar para hacerlo todo en la casa" (In young marriages, especially, husband and wife need to manage to get everything in the house done; 12). In addition to household budgets affecting the domestic load that both husband and wife must take on, Alburquerque talks, too, about how perceptions of gender have changed in Spain as a result of "las costumbres y la vida norteamericanas, como las inglesas [que] se van introduciendo más en nuestra Patria" (the habits and lifestyle of the North Americans, which, much like those of the English, are being increasingly introduced into our homeland; 13). He suggests (perhaps not quite correctly) that nobody would laugh at the sight of an English lord helping his wife with the domestic chores when servants are sick or on holiday. Moreover, Alburquerque writes of the responsibility that guests take for domestic chores in these countries: "Todos sabemos que en Inglaterra y en los Estados Unidos, cuando gentes de la clase media celebran fiestas familiares, los convidados ayudan a la señora de la casa en todos los menesteres domésticos, empezando por los de la cocina" (We all know that in England and in the United States, when middle-class people celebrate amongst family, the guests assist the lady of the house with all the domestic tasks, starting in the kitchen; 13).

Alburquerque makes these observations about the more progressive gender arrangements in Anglo-Saxon countries as early as 1950, a period when Spain was still very much closed off economically and culturally from most of the world. This is of interest because, at that time, "carteles, boletines episcopales, revistas, periódicos y libros orientados a deslegitimar a la República, subrayan la acción destructiva de la modernidad y la adopción de hábitos y modas extranjerizantes" (posters, episcopal newsletters, magazines, newspapers, and books aimed at delegitimizing the republic highlight the destructiveness critiqued by the regime and linked to the disorder and chaos of the Republic, underlying the destructive force of both modernity and the adoption of foreign customs and habits; Alburquerque 22). Not only does this cookbook disrupt Francoist gender biopolitics, it also attempts to produce in readers a greater openness to the very outside influences that the regime believed capable of bringing about Spain's moral and spiritual decline.

All the more significant is that it is not just the gender arrangements that Alburquerque comments on; he writes, too, that the division of domestic labour in these countries is a sign of greater tolerance. Viewing the "treatment" of women as a sign of the state of a nation, as it were, emerged in "armchair" travel writing in the eighteenth and nineteenth century.[7] Depictions of a backward Spain full of oriental-like harems vexed even the most lackluster of Spanish patriots. It is of interest, therefore, that such an anti-patriotic and pro-European/Anglo-Saxon judgment was allowed to go to print at a time when censors scanned all texts for anti-Spanish commentary.[8] We can only assume here, as we did of disruptive cookbooks looked at in the previous chapter, that censors were less alert to the potential of cookbooks for social and political critique because of their association with women and domesticity.

Mi recetario de cocina: Sarrau's Authorial Persona Emerges

Of relevance to a consideration of the differences between state-commissioned and non-official cookbooks is the fact that José Sarrau penned both types. In the 1942 cookbook that he wrote for the SF, Sarrau maintains an ultra-hierarchal and impersonal relationship with his readers, which can be seen as reflective of the paternalistic relationship between the nation's leader and its citizenry. As we have seen, an important aspect of Sarrau's role as representative of the SF is that he, like their other authors, does not use narrative to forge a strong authorial voice, which ultimately heightens the prescriptive nature of his recipes. By way of contrast, in *Mi recetario de cocina* (My kitchen recipe book, 1957), Sarrau is both visible and genial as an author. It is worth tracing the impact this more personable persona had on his cookbooks and recipes.

Also significant is Sarrau's dedicatory in *Mi recetario* to Juana Salas de Jiménez. A member of the Acción Católica (Catholic Action), Salas de Jiménez penned a very enthusiastic prologue to Sarrau's *Nuestra cocina*. The two clearly had a longstanding friendship, and Sarrau writes: "¡Hace tanto tiempo que soñaba con este acto! Dedicar un libro a doña, Juana Salas de Jiménez, ilustre dama española, aragonesa de nacimiento" (I have been dreaming of this for so long! Dedicating a book to Mrs Juana Salas de Jiménez, distinguished Spanish lady, Aragonese of birth; 9). That he signed this dedicatory with the diminutive of his name, "Pepe," reinforces the sense of closeness between the pair. Although the dedicatory is not aimed specifically at Sarrau's readers, it injects *Mi recetario* with a sense of familiarity that is absent from SF publications. Sarrau also exhibits a degree of closeness with his readers, describing them generously as the "excelente mujer del hogar que tanto entusiasmo pone en sus actividades" (excellent housewife who embraces her activities with such enthusiasm; 9). Significantly, he makes use of his prologue to define his role in relation to readers. Rather than position himself as the ultimate authority on food culture, he writes, almost as a friend, that he is there to offer a helpful hand to Spain's housewives, whose expertise he readily acknowledges.

Unlike the SF-commissioned cookbooks whose highly prescriptive and excessively detailed instructions demanded full-time commitment to the home, Sarrau's book describes the ease with which his culinary system can be executed: "a poco que estudies puedes combinar la alimentación diaria de tu marido e hijos" (even if you only study a little, you can combine the daily meals of your husband and children; 10). Spain has always had wonderful housewives, he states, but now, with the advances in technology and "modernization" of household equipment, "la mujer, con mayores facilidades, puede desenvolverse con mayor soltura y éxito" (women, with increased facilities, can manage with greater ease and success; 10). In contrast to the SF-commissioned texts, which presented their culinary system as new and detached from past knowledge, in *Mi recetario* Sarrau values his readers' past experience. Implicit in the description of the excellent housewife above is the assumption that Spain's housewives already know a great deal about food culture; all that is needed is minimal assistance and effort to modernize their practices.

Sarrau's much less prescriptive culinary system is tied to a much less rigid gender divide. Although food preparation itself is gendered female in this cookbook, there are aspects of the culinary discourse that are disruptive of the notion of separate spheres that was so integral to the SF and official Francoist discourse. Particularly telling in this regard is the image on the front cover of two close, happy couples: one pair is sitting on a couch in close conversation while the other (the hosts) is serving food and drinks together. Certainly, in the SF cookbooks or training manuals, the instruction to Spanish women was to take charge of the domestic realm and dutifully serve food and drinks to their husbands, other male family members, and guests. The image of a husband and wife hosting their dinner party together indicates a much greater degree of flexibility regarding gender: it puts forward the notion that men and women can participate in similar activities. If, as

Driver contends, extra-textual material in cookbooks is often as important as the recipes themselves, then the images on the front cover of *Mi recetario* should not go overlooked.

Similar to Alburquerque's *Los dulces caseros* in showing greater flexibility regarding gender, Sarrau's *Mi recetario* alludes to the importance of looking to other cultures for a more progressive paradigm for gender relations. Tying national progress or the state of a nation to relations between the two sexes, Alburquerque described Anglo-Saxon countries as more tolerant and much more accepting of a fairer division of domestic labour. In his prologue, Sarrau discusses the importance of looking to "los países más adelantados del mundo" (the most advanced countries of the world) for the key to "la felicidad conyugal" (marital bliss; 10). Yet his SF-commissioned food text was steadfast in its adherence to the official gender ideology.

La futura ama de casa: Constructing a Modern Spanish Womanhood

Another non-official cookbook of interest is María de la Paz Salcedo de Uriol's *La futura ama de casa* (The future housewife), which contains cookery instruction and other, more general advice. In this volume, first published in 1924 and reprinted for the third time in 1958, Salcedo de Uriol adopts a friendly tone with her readers as she offers them her "pequeña guía de fórmulas culinarias y consejos prácticos" (small guide of culinary recipes and practical advice; 4). As well as offering the warmth of her authorial persona, she directs her readers to draw on their own body of cookery knowledge in suggesting they should take from her cookbook what they find useful and modify it as they see fit: "Libros de cocina hay muchos y muy buenos, pero de nada sirven, y al mismo tiempo, de mucho sí se entresaca, escoge y modifica lo que le convenga a cada uno" (There are many cookbooks, and many are excellent, but they are useless, and at the same time, you can extract a lot if you choose and modify what suits you from each one; 6). The only useful cookbook, she writes, is the one that's followed "según el gusto y necesidad individual" (according to one's individual tastes and needs; 6). Salcedo de Uriol's description of what constitutes a useful cookbook accords a great deal of agency to Spanish women, as she gives them permission to determine how much and what of a cookbook they will incorporate into their domestic routine.

The image on the front cover suggests a much more modern notion of Spanish womanhood than was promoted by the SF. It depicts two women sitting close together on a couch. Both have short hairstyles, and one is wearing trousers and flat shoes while the other is dressed in a skirt. They appear to be getting along very well. That the cover foregrounds their friendship or closeness suggests intimacy is considered more important than domesticity or cookery. Although this cookbook offers women a collection of recipes and advice on matters pertaining to household management, the front cover creates an alternative reality to that imposed by the state: it is women's significant relationships – outside of the institution of marriage – that are most fulfilling. Also representing an important point of difference with the SF is that Salcedo de Uriol encourages her female readers to set up their own library where possible and not just rely on that of their husband. She writes: "toda ama de casa debe tener su biblioteca particular como un pequeño refugio de consultario de entretenimiento y hasta oración" (every housewife should keep her own private library as a little refuge of advice, entertainment, and even prayer; 14). Salcedo de Uriol's text allows Spanish women to think differently about their gender roles, while also critiquing certain styles of cookbooks.

A Broader Narrative of Franco-Era Cookbooks: Obedience and Resistance

This chapter has shed light on a category of cookbook that has been overlooked in histories of Spanish gastronomy. Because of the SF's hegemony in relation to domesticity, scholars have tended to associate domestic cookbooks with that organization, producing a skewed narrative about such texts published in the first two decades of the Franco regime. One result is that domestic cookbooks have been viewed primarily in terms of their reinforcement of the rigid gender divide at the heart of Franco's construction of a National Catholic Spain. While official food texts were prescriptive and reflective of this binary, non-official cookbooks were at times disruptive of official ideology and Francoist gender biopolitics, producing subjectivities that were not nearly as highly gendered as those produced by the SF cookbooks.

The recipes and cooking instructions in non-SF cookbooks were also less prescriptive: narrative and highly visible authorial personas detracted from the intrinsically instructional nature of the genre. By contrast, due to the absence of such features, ultra-hierarchal and highly prescriptive cooking instructions abound in the SF-commissioned volumes. We should keep in mind that training readers in domestic docility has broader implications: uncritical obedience, anathema in a democracy, is key to the longevity of any dictatorship. In this regard, the SF food texts produce not just highly gendered subjectivities, but also ones that in more general terms uphold Francoist biopolitics. To rephrase: food discourse transcends the kitchen. Cookbooks can be a site of resistance, as well as a place where official ideology is upheld; their recipes offer instruction not only for food preparation, but also for gender identity and citizenry.

3 A Recipe for Spain: The Production of a Unified Gastronomic Space and the Gendering of Gastronomy

Under the Franco regime, Spanish unity was an absolute and unquestionable principle. While Franco's quest to forcefully unify his nation has been looked at in regard to much of the cultural production and language policies of the time, little has been written about the role of food discourse in instructing the Spanish people in the uptake of a monolithic national identity. This chapter considers the way in which food discourse partook in the production of a unified gastronomic space, showing how regional cuisines were not only subsumed into the national culinary whole but also co-opted for the purpose of centralist nationalism. A key component of Francoist biopolitics was the creation of a unified body politic, and individual behaviour was disciplined and corrected for the purpose of national unity. Most of the food texts published during the first two decades of the regime uphold this aspect of Francoist biopolitics, yet there are some food writers who encouraged readers to think about nationalism in terms of plurality and diversity.

As one scholar notes in relation to the broader context of European fascism, "theories of generic fascism … speak of ultra-nationalist centralization, or at least cultural homogenization" (Núñez and Umbach 295). The connections between Spanish fascism and national unity have been well documented, with José Antonio Primo de Rivera's exclamation that *patria* (homeland) is total unity evolving during the Franco regime into the mantra "Spain: One, Great and Free." In his unrelenting and fascist-like quest to "forcefully [unify] Spain" (Epps 551), Franco sought absolute cultural homogeneity, and was therefore "determined to stamp out" regional diversity (Meisler 203), particularly in the Basque country and Catalonia. Omar Encarnación describes this as "Franco's efforts to annihilate … unique cultural heritage" (39), while Andrew Dowling highlights the "linguistic and cultural character of the Regime's assault" (490). This included the prohibition of the

Sardana, the national Catalan dance (Dowling 495) as well as of the use of regional languages such as Catalan and Basque "dialects" under the imperative issued to "speak the language of the Empire" (Meisler 203).

Ironically, the regime's wholesale cultural and linguistic homogenization resulted in some aspects of regional culture gaining visibility. A number of scholars have described the ways in which the Franco regime laid claim to regional difference for the purpose of nation building. For instance, in his study of cinema and popular folk culture under Franco, José Colmeiro refers to the "Francoist co-option of Galician folk imagery and traditions as a way of demobilizing political Nationalism" (269). This chapter looks at the way in which regional food culture was stripped of any potential political content and then exploited by the regime for its centralizing agenda. As Carmen Ortiz observes in her discussion of the Franco regime's appropriation of regional culture, there was a centralization of functions at every level of society, from the realm of politics to daily life (487). Scholars have traced the different ways in which the Franco regime co-opted regionalism for the purpose of nationalization in areas such as film, music, and folklore (see Colmeiro; Ortiz), but very little has been written about food discourse.

As part of her survey of the state of Catalan cuisine during the regime, Montserrat Roser i Puig writes that "the regime's enforced tendency towards unity, with its fixation on national (i.e. Spanish) homogeneity, produced gastronomic studies where Catalan cookery and the rest of the highly varied cuisine of Iberia were clearly subsumed into a collective whole" (231). As a general observation about the impact of Franco's ultra-nationalizing policies on regional culinary diversity, this statement is accurate. However, the absence of any sustained analysis of the very food texts that codified Spanish cuisine in this way means that Roser i Puig is not in a position to provide a detailed reading of this phenomenon. My aim here is to provide a thorough analysis of the type of text to which Roser i Puig refers, thereby generating a more nuanced understanding of the discursive strategies employed in food discourse to codify Spanish cuisine as a monolithic entity.

Another scholar who has mentioned the centralizing agenda of official food discourse is Suzanne Dunai, whose dissertation on the SF contains some discussion of this organization's cookbook *Cocina regional* (1963). Dunai's major contribution in this regard is her intelligent definition of the term "a la española," which changed meaning, she explains, with the new Spanish state and came to refer "to a large and standardized Spanish method for preparing a type of food" (*Cooking for the Patria* 120). This culinary descriptor, she writes, assumed "that there was a monolithic Spanish way of doing something, such as cooking a meal or serving a dish" (120). This chapter continues Dunai's discussion with a much more detailed analysis of the use of this term, not just in women's cookbooks but in official food discourse and male-authored gastronomic texts. The notion of Spanishness in food that Dunai refers to in fact dates back to the beginning of the regime and impregnates much of the male-authored gastronomic writing under scrutiny here. Indeed, many of these texts were published well before the SF cookbooks and cooking manuals dedicated to regional cuisines, and so likely influenced rather than emulated the SF's codification of regional cuisines.

Significantly, the term "a la española" was used in some of Franco's earliest menus. An example of one of these from 1939 shows not only a relatively modest menu, but also a desire to use food to bolster national unity:

> RESIDENCIA DE S. E. EL JEFE DEL ESTADO Y GENERALISIMO DE LOS EJERCITOS – MENU – Almuerzo – (Plato único) Sopa al cuarto de hora – Cocido a la Española – POSTRES – Monte nevado – Queso y fruta – I-VI-1939 Año de la Victoria. (Cuarto poder)
>
> (The residence of the CHIEF OF STATE AND SUPREME GENERAL OF THE ARMIES – MENU – Lunch – (Single dish) Quarter-of-an-hour soup – Spanish-style stew – DESSERTS – Custard – Cheese and fruit – 1 July 1989 Year of Victoria. (Fourth power))

This reference to a Spanish-style food culture represents just one of myriad efforts made by the Francoist state and associated food writers to create or impose a unified gastronomic space.

Establishing the Borders of Spanish Food Culture

The eclectic mix of food texts looked at in this chapter serves to establish the boundaries of Spanish gastronomic culture, producing a gastronomic map of Spain that upholds or imposes national unity. This discourse helps to normalize a right way to think about Spanish gastronomy and national unity. This chapter's analysis of the ways in which such food texts uphold the regime's imposition of national unification draws on theorizations of space and considers how space is produced. According to scholars, new social orders or political regimes require new types of space. This is, they argue, particularly the case for fascist regimes, so it is vital to look to their use of space (see in particular Santiáñez-Tió). An important aim of this chapter is to contribute to this scholarly discussion of fascist space through an analysis of its gastronomic iteration. I contend that food writing upheld fascist or Francoist space through the production of a unified gastronomic space that reimagined the country's culinary borders. Functional culinary zones served to erase culinary regionalism, while Castilian cuisine was positioned not just at the centre of Spain's gastronomic map, but also as the very essence of Spanish cuisine.

This chapter looks not just to gastronomic writing but to various cookbooks, all of which were purportedly concerned with the promotion of regional cuisines. The cookbooks under scrutiny are the SF's cooking manual *La cocina regional*, 1958) and Isabel de Trévis's series of cookbooks titled *La cocina regional: Las mejores y más típicas recetas* (Regional cuisine: The best and most typical recipes, 1959). Because a number of the texts from these years – including the SF-commissioned cookbooks – offer readers collections of regional recipes, at first glance it can seem as though many of the food writers considered here were in fact more concerned with culinary regionalism than culinary nationalism. Tellingly, traditional histories of Spanish cuisine describe many of the texts looked at in this chapter as regional in their focus. The visibility of the concept of regional cuisines in these food texts led Martínez Llopis, in his exhaustive history of Spanish gastronomy, to not even touch on the ultra-nationalizing agenda of so many of the texts penned during these years. Close reading of these sorts of food texts demonstrates, however, that they not only accord more weight to the category of the nation, but also undermine regional diversity, stripping culinary regionalism of political content.

Like the other chapters in this monograph, this one looks to disruptive food discourse, since food writers often found ways of challenging hegemonic notions of food culture. As we have noted, cooking advice and instructions about food represent a textual space where subjectivities are both produced and contested; it is thus important to investigate the way in which some writers resist the imposition of a monolithic Spanish identity. As early as 1942, Ignacio Doménech penned *Mi plato: Cocina regional española* (My plate: Spanish regional cuisine), which – like his other subversive food texts – offers an alternative to official discourse. Much later on in the regime, Isabel de Trévis upholds official discourse in some regards while also pointing to the importance of codifying regional cuisines as separate entities rather than just smaller pieces of the incomparably greater national whole. Such food writers challenge Francoist biopolitics in the way their food discourse creates an alternative space. If space functions to discipline people into certain ways of being, then disruptive food discourse creates a space that allows or encourages Spaniards to experience themselves as belonging to their region of origin, of which Spain has many, some with their own historic identity and language.

The Gendering of Gastronomy and Food Discourse

In my consideration of the nexus between food discourse and national unity, I also examine the gendering of gastronomy. As I discuss below, male writers turned their hand to the topic of Spanish gastronomy because it was relevant to the national sphere of public life. Writing about Spanish cuisine, or discursively creating an entity that can be recognized as Spanish cuisine, is a phenomenon that dates back to the nineteenth century, when male Spanish writers and intellectuals started to look to its impoverished state in the context of nation building.[1] Rebecca Ingram, for instance, insightfully defines Spanish gastronomic texts from the late-nineteenth century onward as "textual entries in the ongoing debate about what it means to eat in Spain and what is Spanish about the food people eat" (*Spain on the Table* 15). According to Ingram, these texts formed

> a "debating forum" about what might constitute the Spanish culinary nation ... and how food production, food distribution, economic factors, and the homogenizing expectations generated by the processes of nationalization and modernization affect what people eat. (15)

Since its inception, this nationalist project was – with the exception of Emilia Pardo Bazán[2] – gendered male on account of its connections to the public sphere and the politics of nation building. During the final years of the Primo de Rivera dictatorship and the first two decades of the Franco regime, male gastronomic writers continued to define the borders of Spain's culinary culture.

As well as producing a gastronomic space that subsumed regional cuisines into the nation's culinary centre, these writers were also prescriptive about gender. In defining the limits of Spanish gastronomy, Franco Spain's male gastronomes contributed significantly to the gendering of Spanish food writing. The male writers looked at here uphold the traditional gendering of cookery as female and gastronomy as male. And when women did write cookbooks about Spain's regional cuisines that incorporated gastronomic-like discussion of Spain's national food culture – texts that we could label "gastronomical in nature" – they were all but replicas of male-authored gastronomic texts.

The gastronomy that these male writers penned was, unlike French gastronomy, not concerned with refining the aesthetic pleasure of eating. Writing about the development of gastronomy, Stephen Mennell observes that virtually everything dates back to French gastronomy, which worked to "promote an aesthetic sensibility, to define good taste, and to create a standard of etiquette for the gourmand" (17). Spanish gastronomy, by contrast, was connected to nationalism and politics, as Spanish intellectuals and food writers attempted to codify or define the borders of Spain's food nation.

The Production of a Unified Gastronomic Space

I turn now to the ways in which male-authored gastronomy and official gastronomic maps codified Spain as unified in its culinary offerings. One of my main premises here is that in demarcating the borders of the country's culinary culture, this food writing can be seen as contributing to the production of a fascist or Francoist space. A great deal of scholarship in recent years has looked at the importance of space and geography to fascist and nationalist projects. Indeed, according to Santiáñez-Tió, if we are to "properly understand fascism we need to a proper understanding of how the fascists conceived of, used and produced space" (6). The theoretical underpinnings of space can be traced back to Henri Lefebvre, who wrote that new social relationships call for new spaces and that space is a social product, which in itself is actively produced. Space is not ontologically prior to the cultural and semiotic codes through which its existence is expressed.

In his monograph on Spanish fascism and space, Santiáñez-Tió draws on the work of Lefebvre to show how the new social, political, and economic worldview implied by fascism and early Francoism required "new representations of space, new spaces of representations, and, once the fascists were in power, new material spatial practices" (9). Words or writing, according to Santiáñez-Tió, were "fundamental tools for producing space" (31). He notes that it was apparent in Spanish fascist discourse from as early as the 1930s that the fascists saw themselves as charged with the mission of producing a unified Spain:

> In Spain, Primo de Rivera defined the task assigned to his generation as one of "building a new politics" ... upon the fatherland's unity, or, as he put it elsewhere, of carrying out "the building of the harmonious, whole Spain" ... [This national unity was dependent on] the total subordination of the regions to the state. (29)

Given that writing was pivotal to this project, it follows that food writing was impregnated, too, by a fascist notion of space, and many authors were in fact producing the very gastronomic spaces that they claimed to be describing.

Also of significance in this analysis of how food texts reimagined Spain's national food culture is Jacobo García Álvarez's discussion of the fate of Spain's different regions during the regime. Adopting the term "un regionalismo sin regiones" (a regionalism without regions), García Álvarez describes the process whereby regional discourses were "neutralizado en sus componentes ideológicos, hasta bien avanzada la década de 1950" (neutralized of ideological content, until well into the 1950s; 356). "Frente a los regionalismos políticos e historicistas" (Faced with political and historicist regionalisms), the regime took part in the administrative division of regions, known as "neoregionalismo" (neo-regionalism) or "regionalismo funcional" (functional regionalism; 359). Socio-economic, administrative, and political factors were positioned as central to this new form of regionalism, which was described as "eminentemente técnico, funcional y económico" (above all technical, functional, and economic; 358). The redrawing of the national territory for the purposes of more efficient administration is an excellent example of how Francoist officials reimagined or produced a different kind of space for their new political order. Official food writing also took part in this "regionalismo funcional" in the way it classified Spanish cuisine according to new zones that were eminently functional while at the same time emptying culinary regionalism of any historical or political content.

Also integral to the fascist/Francoist production of a unified national space was the discipline of geography. As a number of scholars have shown, geography was central to national unification and was taught extensively in Spanish schools and universities from the outset of the regime (García Álvarez and Garrido López). Through the teaching of geography, students were indoctrinated in "la exaltación de la unidad de la patria y la condena de los regionalismos y nacionalismos egoístas y separadores" (the exaltation of national unity and the condemnation of selfish and separatist regionalisms and nationalisms; García Álvarez 358). Geographical teaching and research focused on the diversity of regional and local landscapes, yet always with a focus on national unification. While, for instance, the country's regionally diverse flora was studied, it was classified according to several arbitrary zones rather than according to Spain's multiple regions. Lessons about the Spanish language also upheld the notion of national unity. Described as "la expresión de la unidad de la patria" (the expression of national unity; Capel), *Castellano* was codified as a language uniting all of the country's citizenry. Unsurprisingly, linguistic difference was underplayed, with Spain's diverse other languages being described as "modalidades lingüísticas" (linguistic modalities), while geography texts waxed lyrical about *Castellano*'s "belleza, fuerza expansiva e inmortalidad" (beauty, expansive strength, and immortality; Capel). As these examples demonstrate, all descriptions of Spain's natural and human elements reinforced the notion of national unity.[3]

Food texts can be seen as taking part in this production of a unified national territory through their imagining of a cohesive gastronomic space. These texts either include drawn maps or discursively codify gastronomic maps for the Franco regime's New Spain. Here we should note that maps do not merely represent or symbolize the world. Rather, they "produce the borders, grammar, contents, and meaning of a particular space as well as the places enclosed in it" (Santiáñez-Tió 68). Often appearing abstract and scientific, maps are frequently viewed as equivalent to a photograph of the space they represent. Yet they can be highly subjective, codifying the very space that they claim to be represent. Given the ability of maps to produce and give meaning to space, it comes as little surprise that Francoist food discourse is so focused on gastronomic map making.

Of interest in the first instance are images or discursive descriptions of Spain's gastronomic map drawn from the official publication *Alimentación nacional*. My first example comes from the patriotic orange campaign *¡Consumid más naranjas!* (Eat more oranges!), discussed in chapter 1, which aimed to increase the consumption of Spanish oranges. As well as a number of different articles arguing for greater orange consumption, *Alimentación nacional* includes a map of Spain dotted with people from across the country pictured eating oranges. Depicting Spanishness as dependent on the patriotic consumption of this fruit, this image also reinforces the belief inherent to Francoist ideology of Spain's gastronomic food culture as homogeneous. Regional difference does not feature on this map, which codifies Spaniards as unified in their consumption of local produce in support of the national economy.

Another example of how Spanish food culture was produced as monolithic can be found in the descriptions in *Alimentación nacional* of the *Mapa nacional de abastecimentos* (National provisions map), also published in the post-war period. According to *Alimentación nacional*, this official map provides readers with a way to get to know Spain as well as the national economy: "Conocer España, conocer la economía española es lo que propuso el Mapa Nacional de Abastecimientos"

(Knowing Spain, knowing the Spanish economy, is what is promoted by the National Provisions Map; Issue 22, 6). Purportedly providing important information about post-war Spain's foodscape, the *Mapa nacional de abastecimientos* in fact produces a new way of viewing the national foodscape, reimagining Spain's national territory for the purposes of food supply and food rationing. It ignores regional difference and creates new administrative zones, which privilege functional regionalism over Spain's long history of cultural and political regionalism. This map also makes evident that official or government food supply is dependent on such a practical or administrative division of Spain's national territory, in a sense training readers to view such administrative divisions as necessary for the effective management of state-led food provision.

Also codifying Spanish gastronomy as a unified entity is the official gastronomic map that was produced for the 1945 Feria Oficial e Internacional de Muestras (Official and International Exhibition Show) in Barcelona. Dating back to the late-nineteenth century, the Feria de Barcelona is an organization that holds numerous trade shows bringing together leading companies from different economic sectors. In addition to showcasing Spanish industry for the purposes of trade and commerce, during the Franco regime this trade show was seen as a way to honour the nation. The *Mapa gastronómico de España* produced for the 1945 event not only makes evident the richness and diversity of Spanish cuisine, but also codifies Spain's food culture as a cohesive entity. Importantly, in its codification of Spanish cuisine as "un mosaico de platos regionales" (a mosaic of regional dishes; 1), this official map highlights the importance of Spain's national food culture, placing Castile at the centre of the country's foodscape.

Including an entry for all of Spain's regional cuisines, the *Mapa gastronómico* provides a list of different dishes eaten in each region. Regional denominators of place are used for such dishes, such as "a la gallega" (Galician style), "a la catalana" (Catalan style), and "a la valenciana" (Valencian style). The visibility given to regional cuisines – as well as the use of regional descriptors – could mistakenly be taken as a promotion of Spain's regional cuisine. However, it is clear from the multiple entries for Madrid – which also include celebratory menus – that Castile has a privileged place in Spain's gastronomic map. The use, moreover, of the terms "a la española" (Spanish style) and "nacional" (national) to describe the dishes typical of Spain's capital makes evident that the food of the country's political centre should be seen not just as typical of that region but also as representative of the food nation. In sum, in its codification of Spanish cuisine, this map makes clear both that Castile sits at the centre of Spanish cuisine and that Spain's national culinary whole is much more significant than any regional part.[4]

Uniformity is also a feature of gastronomic maps that attempted to produce a paradigm for Spanish cuisine that adhered, to differing degrees, to the notion of unity and diversity. (Significantly, this had also been a defining feature of Spanish culinary nationalism at the time of nation building and the Primo de Rivera regime.) A gastronomic poster-sized map of the Iberian Peninsula published in Madrid in 1959 by the publisher Iberoamericana S.A. offers an identical entry for each region. Each one lists an iconic dish and shows people dressed in the typical clothes of the region, alongside an image of the dish. Regional denominators are used, and the map on the one hand gives visibility to Spain's richly diverse foodscape. Yet the uniformity of the different entries gives the impression that Spain's regional cuisines are equal in their contribution to Spanish gastronomy, when in reality areas such as Catalonia and the Basque country had a unique culinary identity quite separate from Spanish cuisine. It is also significant that the larger and incomparably greater culinary whole of this gastronomic map is the outline of the Iberian Peninsula, which stands in for the very notion of Spanish cuisine. Indeed, in looking at this map, viewers and readers are reminded of the very small contribution that each regional cuisine makes to the nation's much greater gastronomic map.

Although this map purportedly promotes regional culinary diversity, it does so in the service of Spanish culinary nationalism. Scholars of Franco Spain have shown the way in which regional culture was given visibility while simultaneously being co-opted for the purpose of the broader nationalist project (see Colmeiro and Ortiz). This gastronomic map is one example of the way in which Spanish food culture or food discourse took part in this process. Importantly, this gastronomic map alludes also to Spain's imperial grandeur, in that it contains the image of a boat sailing towards Latin America with a victorious, fist-waving captain at its helm. The key message of the Franco regime – "Una, Grande y Libre" (One, Great and Free) – expressed the concept of Spain as indivisible, imperial, and free of foreign influence. In representing Spanish gastronomy as unified, with allusions to imperial grandeur, this map can be seen as making the promise inherent to Francoist ideology that national culinary unity would somehow restore imperial greatness.

The way in which these gastronomic maps produced a unified culinary culture for Spain is an important feature as well of a number of gastronomic texts published contemporaneously. Such commonalities between official food writing, maps, and gastronomic texts buttresses the strategy of viewing food discourse as one cohesive entity, rather than keeping different genres of food writing separate. The synergies between the myriad types of food texts under scrutiny here point, I believe, to the relevance or impact of the food discourse under scrutiny, because the ideas were not present in just one text type, but belong to a broader body of discourse that was present in many different facets of life and genres of texts.

The Male Gastronome and National Unity: Erasing Regional Difference

Like the official food writing just discussed, the male-authored gastronomic texts to which I turn now are prescriptive – rather than just descriptive – of national unity. The first food text considered here, though titled *Mapa gastronómico* (Gastronomic map), does not contain any visual gastronomic maps of the Iberian Peninsula per se. Nevertheless, the book discursively produces a gastronomic map of Spain, or a way for readers to understand their national food culture. Published in 1953 and written by Luis de Fontefrías, *Mapa gastronómico* was number 33 in a series of texts published under the umbrella heading "Temas Españoles" (Spanish themes). Its front cover has an illustration of a road winding into the distance, a dinner table, and, importantly, a post with signs marked "paella," "gazpacho," "cocido," and "fabada" pointing in different directions. Similar to the other visual maps just discussed, this publication creates the impression of Spanish cuisine as the sum of its regional parts. Certainly, these iconic dishes from different parts of Spain are meant to be seen as parts of the national culinary whole, with the winding road suggestive of a journey of discovery through gastronomic Spain.

In the text itself, the travel motif continues with the first chapter, titled "Los caminos del comer" (The routes of eating; 3). Explicitly mentioning the process of map making, de Fontefrías writes of his role in the production of a gastronomic map:

> Ahora, armados de buen apetito, lo primero, y también de cuchara, tenedor y cuchillo – a veces también se podrá echar mano de los dedos – , vamos a establecer, como si fuéramos unos señores ingenieros de esos que todo lo saben, un mapa. (3)
>
> (Now, armed with a good appetite first and foremost, and also a knife, fork and spoon – sometimes you can also use your fingers – we are going to establish, as if we were those sorts of engineer types who know everything, a map.)

While his map will be devoid of physical features such as mountain, rivers, and sea, there will be different flavours – strong and subtle – as well as aromas of dishes such as "un arroz a punto o de un bacalao a la vizcaina" (a well-cooked rice or a Biscay cod; 3). Although in the opening pages de Fontefrías creates the impression of an impending journey through Spain's gastronomic territory, he puts this journey on hold for most of this perfunctory text, stipulating that before he takes his readers on a culinary tour of the Iberian Peninsula, it is important to provide them with general information about food culture, "un poquito de las mesas y los cocineros, de cómo se debe y no se debe comer" (a little about the tables and the cooks, about how you should and should not eat; 4).

In spite, therefore, of his promise to produce a gastronomic map for his readers, most of de Fontefrías's text deals with issues that do not seem directly related to his country's foodscape. Of interest, however, in this more general discussion is the way he attempts to remind his readers of what is universal about food culture, rather than focus on the diversity of Spain's regional cuisines. If food culture can both unite and divide groups of people, then it significant that in his textual attempt to establish the boundaries of Spanish gastronomy, de Fontefrías writes about those aspects of food culture that are universal. In the very few pages that he actually dedicates to food as material object, he also emphasizes aspects of Spanish food culture that can be seen as unifying rather than divisive. The first dish he writes about is *el cocido madrileño* (Madrid stew), which he presents as a national dish of sorts for the way it transcends class, given that it can be made from the simplest to the most luxurious of ingredients.

Another aspect of de Fontefrías's food writing that can be seen as unifying is his discussion of *sopa de ajo* (garlic soup). The significance of this dish is that it represents a model for Spanish gastronomy, which, while based on "unified diversity" (L. Anderson, "Unity and Diversity" 400), ultimately accords more status to Madrid. Originating from Madrid, *sopa de ajo* travelled to the country's peripheries, where it took on or assumed different regional flavors or ingredients.[5] If Castile was seen in Franco Spain not just as the administrative centre of the country, but also as the essence of the nation itself, then *sopa de ajo* is an apt culinary symbol for Castile's special status: the dish is, at its core, a Castilian dish. While regional ingredients have added a small amount of local flavour, they have not changed the essence of the dish.

The title of de Fontefrías's text, *Mapa gastronómico,* suggests that he self-consciously takes part in the demarcation of culinary borders for Franco's New Spain. Moreover, his references to map making suggest he is more than aware of the ways in which his text is formative rather than descriptive of his country's culinary landscape. While it would seem from the front cover and promise of a journey through Spain's regional foodscape that de Fontefrías's "map" will give visibility to regional food cultures, his text in fact erases all such diversity. Placing Castile at the centre of Spain's gastronomic map – in both a literal and figurative sense – de Fontefrías seeks to unify Spaniards through not just by adopting *sopa de ajo* as a national dish, but also by writing in much more detail at the outset about aspects of food culture that can be considered universal.

Another food writer to erase regional culinary difference in spite of the promise of a gastronomic text dedicated to Spain's regional foodscapes is Bosch Bierge, who penned *Cocina regional española* (Spanish regional cuisine). This text was published in 1940 as part of the series "Biblioteca Gastronómica y Hogar" (Home economics and gastronomic library). As in the case of de Fontefrías, little has been written about Bosch Bierge, and there are no entries for his cookbook in either Martínez Llopis's extensive history of Spanish gastronomy or Simón Palmer's exhaustive bibliography of Spanish food texts. We do know, however, that he was the editor of the monthly periodical *Menaje* (Housework), a domestic magazine for women published out of Barcelona. Most of the magazine contains recipes, but it also instructs women in the art of domesticity and is pro-Franco in its adherence to official gender ideology. One of the 1943 editions of this magazine also reprinted some of the content of *Cocina regional española*. At the height of post-war devastation, Bosch Bierge's codification of Spain's regional cuisines may not have been highly visible to many – which might explain why this cookbook is omitted from the aforementioned historical and biographical studies. Nevertheless, some three years later, his gastronomic map would have likely had a much greater circulation as part of his magazine.

As we saw in chapter 1, Bosch Bierge believed it was his patriotic mission to defend Spanish cuisine against the attack of its French neighbour. It is not surprising that this culinary patriotism goes hand in hand with the culinary nationalism I discuss in this chapter, given that the focus on national unity in fascism or early Francoism went hand in hand with Spain's isolation from foreign influence. As I mention above, knowledge of Spain's regional cuisines should, according to Bosch Bierge, be ample ammunition in the fight against the hegemony of French cuisine. Although he wrote about the importance of Spain's regional cuisines in maintaining the purity of the nation's culinary borders, it is clear from his descriptions of Spain's regional foodscape that he is not writing about regional cuisines as separate and richly diverse entities, but rather as smaller, insignificant parts of the greater national whole.

Importantly, Bosch Bierge's *Cocina regional española* does contain a gastronomic map, which reduces Spanish gastronomic diversity to a paltry four areas: "cocina castellana, levantina, norteña [y] andaluza" (Castilian, Levantine, Northern, and Andalusian; 4). He codifies Spanish gastronomy in such a way for practical reasons, he claims, or "mejor comprensión de los sitios donde rigen las cocinas o maneras de cocinar que publicamos en este tomo" (a better understanding of the places where the cuisines or cooking methods that are published in this tome rule; 4). This functional division of Spain's regional cuisines is reflective of the neo-regionalism described earlier. It is also a further example of how food writers imagined a new national gastronomic space, one that was highly reductive in its treatment of culinary regionalism.

Bosch Bierge's gastronomic map positions the notion of unity as integral to Spanish food culture, with the aforementioned division of regional cuisines occurring under the umbrella term "la unidad divisible de España" (the divisible unity of Spain; 4). His codification of Spain's gastronomic map assumes unity as the starting point that, like official discourse, demands adherence to the indisputable unification of the state. Spain's gastronomic territory is, as Bosch Bierge sees it, by its very nature inherently unified. His task is therefore to superimpose a map of four different zones or modalities onto an already unified territory. While his writing claims to be primarily descriptive, he in fact produces a new map of Spanish cuisine, impregnated with a fascist or Francoist notion of a unified national space. This gastronomic map is highly normative in that it instructs readers in how to view Spanish food culture according to the Francoist logic of functional regionalism.

As part of his production of this gastronomic map or zoning of Spain's four food modalities, Bosch Bierge speaks of unity and diversity. "La cocina levantina" (Levantine cuisine), for instance, is described as consisting of the cuisines of Catalonia, Valencia, Aragón, Murcia, and the Balearic Islands. On the one hand, he recognizes the inherent diversity of a cuisine that spans several autonomous regions, writing that "en todo ese conglomerado de frutos y productos de la región levantina se asienta una cocina regional variada como pocas" (this assortment of fruits and produce of the Levantine region forms the basis of a regional cuisine more varied than most; 15). On the other hand, he then attempts to unify the small parts that make up the whole that is "la cocina levantina" through broad-brush statements about how the cuisine of this area has evolved in relation to the specificities of the climate: "Y como pocas formáis una alimentación del pueblo sana y fuerte, como respondiendo al clima moderado que no requiere ni el excesivo vigor de los alimentos de una región fría ni los propios de regiones casi tropicales" (And you have developed, like few others, a healthy and strong popular diet, in response to a moderate climate that requires neither the excessive vigour of food from cold regions, nor those of an almost tropical region; 15).

From the end of the nineteenth century on, Catalans in particular pointed to their unique culture and the long history of migration to the area as key factors in the evolution of their distinct cuisine. Bosch Bierge all but obliterates this unique culinary identity by positing the climate as the overriding factor in the development of its cuisine. Indeed, a belief in environmental determinism arises frequently in his explanations, as he refers to the physical environment as a key factor in character or human behaviour: the fisherman of Catalonia, he writes, is a "hombre bravo como la 'Costa brava,' en que vives, en que luchas y en que mueres, aferrado a tus sanas costumbres de trabajador infatigable, y hasta cuando bailas lo haces abriendo los brazos para envolver a tus hermanos en un inmenso abrazo de paz" (man as brave as the "Brave Coast" in which you live, in which you fight and die, clinging to the healthy habits of an indefatigable worker, and even when you dance you do so opening your arms to wrap your brothers in an enormous hug of peace; 14). According to this cookbook, cuisine and character are the product of the environment, which encourages readers to see regional differences in Spain as the result of a geographically diverse national territory rather than as connected in any way to unique heritage and language. And by disavowing regional difference and divorcing identity from any connection to linguistic or cultural heritage, Bosch Bierge empties regionalism of any possible political content.

Bosch Bierge's description of Spain's gastronomic map is also of interest for its codification of Castilian cuisine, which speaks to official discourse. According to fascist ideology, Castile was given a special status as more than a region. It was, beyond a geographic territory, the embodiment of eternal values such as austerity and strength. Highly complimentary of Castilian cuisine, Bosch Bierge writes how "en esta Castilla los manjares son como los hombres, austeros, fuertes, sin arrumacos de floreos ni nombres rebuscados, pero con un contenido substancioso y viril" (in Castile the delicacies are like the men: austere, strong, without floral adornments nor affected names, but with a virile and substantial filling; 6). The gendering of Castilian cuisine as masculine accords this part of Spain a status that sets it apart from the other regions that feature in Bosch Bierge's writing. Bosch Bierge's gastronomic writing renders both the cuisine and men of Castile as superior in their embodiment of of hyper-masculine traits such as strength and virility, thereby setting the seat of Spain's power apart from the country's other regions.

By contrast, Bosch Bierge codifies a number of other regions as inherently feminine. Writing about the Levante zone, he describes Valencia as "tierra de flores y bellas mujeres, eres la más privilegiada de todas; tu huerta ha traspasado los límites de la fama y tu fruta de oro endulza los labios de todo el mundo" (a land of flowers and beautiful women, you are the most privileged of all; your garden surpasses the limits of your fame and your golden fruit sweetens everyone's lips; 15). Valencia is gendered feminine for its abundance of flowers and beautiful women, while Valencian oranges are feminized in the way in which they are positioned as objects of desire. Indeed, in his description of Valencia's oranges as "fruto de oro [que] endulza los labios de todo el mundo" (golden fruit [that] sweetens everyone's lips; 15), Bosch Bierge invokes a tradition of food imagery whereby attractive women and appetizing food become interchangeable, for women are often depicted as sweet objects to be consumed, "a view rooted in cultural stereotypes whereby women have a natural tendency to be sweet" (Crespo-Fernández 156). The sweetness of Bosh Bierge's oranges can be seen, therefore, as further corroboration not just of the feminization of Valencia's foodscape but also of the links between this delectable fruit and Valencia's women.

Guía gastronómica de España: The Eradication of Regional Diversity and the Exclusion of Women

Linking sweetness with femininity is also a feature of the food writing of the next male gastronome we will look at. Although published nearly two decades after Bosch Bierge's *Cocina regional española*, Luis Antonio de Vega's *Guía gastronómica de España* (A gastronomic guide to Spain, 1957) is ultra-conservative in the view it promotes of both women's role in gastronomy and the homogenization of Spanish food culture. Published by the national publishing house Editorial Nacional, de Vega's relatively late gastronomic guide is ultra-nationalizing in its eradication of Spain's culinary diversity.[6] As we will see, *Guía gastronómica*, while supposedly celebrating Spain's richly diverse foodscape, in fact eradicates much of this diversity. In his discursive codification of what he describes as the "España gastronómica" (gastronomic Spain), de Vega "imagines" a taste community with very little diversity indeed.

Importantly, de Vega's codification of Spanish gastronomy also reflects his ultra-conservative views on Spain's linguistic diversity. It was in his earlier role as *jefe de redacción* (editor-in-chief) of the weekly publication *Domino* (Dominion), edited in San Sebastian, that de Vega made it clear how pro-Castilian he was. A language, he insisted, is only spoken in an independent nation, and if this language is spoken in a region it can only ever be a dialect (Sánchez Erauskin 74). Seemingly unaware of the richness of linguistic diversity, de Vega – himself Basque – goes on to say that with the extinction of the Basque language, nothing would be lost; "por el contrario las provincias vascongadas ganarían mucho con un idioma claro y glorioso como el español" (on the contrary, the Vascongada provinces would benefit greatly from a language as clear and glorious as Spanish; Sánchez Erauskin 74). Some years later, in 1962, in the face of public criticism from his fellow Basques, de Vega attempted to soften this comment slightly, conceding that the extinction of the Basque language would represent a loss to humanity because Basque is, in fact, the most poetic of the world's languages (Sánchez Erauskin 74).

De Vega's comments demonstrate that he was in fact opposed to linguistic diversity and that his preference was for all Spaniards to speak a shared national language. If other "languages" were to be spoken in Spain, they would always be inferior or secondary to the national language. Conversely, the taste community he imagines for his country erases gastronomic diversity. Spain, he writes in the introduction to his gastronomic guide, "se divide en cuatro regiones o cinco ... Las regiones son: La Septentrional o de las Salsas; Central o de los Asados: Meridional o de los Fritos, y la Levantina, donde no se come" (is divided into four or five regions ... The regions are: The northern, or sauces; central, or roasts; southern, or fried foods; and the Levantine, where they don't eat; 11). Instead, therefore, of finding discursive and graphic ways of unifying Spain's regionally diverse foodscape, de Vega's gastronomic map (and description of it) simply erases this diversity. Commenting on some of Spain's earliest gastronomic maps, Rebecca Ingram has described the way in which maps symbolize cultural and social order rather than depict reality ("Mapping and Mocking"). De Vega's gastronomic map – in line with the symbolic function of maps – imposes a much more unified order onto Spain than earlier twentieth-century maps, which, according to Ingram, located and catalogued Spain's culinary diversity.[7]

In reducing Spain's gastronomic map to these aforementioned regions, de Vega not only eradicates diversity, but also joins parts of the peninsula that are not in fact administratively unified. The "Zona Norte" or "Zona de las Salsas," according to his description,

> desciende, como hemos dicho, desde los viejos bord'eaux, de Bordeaux; atraviesa la depresión vasca, incluyendo un pedacito de Castilla; las

> Asturias de Laredo, de Santillano y de Oviedo; las Viejas provincias gallegas, lo que significa que le da un pellizco territorial al reino de León, y de Portugal, Oporto inclusivo. (15)
>
> (descends, as we have said, from the old edges of the water, of Bordeaux, crosses the Basque depression, including a little piece of Castile; Asturias of Laredo, Santillano, and Oviedo; the old Galician provinces, which means that it pinches a little territory from the kingdom of Leon, Portugal, and even Porto.)

As well as including parts of the country that are very different in culture and geography, this zone encompasses the territory of neighbouring nations. Losing autonomy as a result of de Vega's gastronomic map are the provinces, which are subsumed into broader and seemingly arbitrary "zones." Many scholars write of the diminishing power of Spain's provincial councils at this time, with one in particular observing that "paralelamente, proliferaron cada vez más una serie de divisiones especiales creadas *ad hoc* sobre áreas territoriales supraprovinciales" (at the same time, there was an increasing proliferation of special divisions created ad hoc around supra-provincial territories; Garrido López 114). De Vega's graphic and discursive codification of Spanish gastronomy therefore speaks to official attempts to curtail the autonomy of the regions.

De Vega's guide was of immediate interest to the public, with one journalist writing, for instance, that it contains no recipes and is thus "un libro interesante para alguien más que para las amas de casa. Un libro para todos" (an interesting book for not just housewives. A book for everyone" (Salcedo). Here again we note that cookbooks are, according to this commentary, gendered female, while gastronomy has a much broader appeal. This particular commentator does not explicitly label gastronomy as exclusively male, but de Vega himself does in the body of his ultra-conservative gastronomic guide. For instance, in a chapter titled "La educación gastronómica de las mujeres" (The gastronomic education of women), he draws a distinction between having a good palate and being able to cook: "La prueba de la cocina no es la prueba del paladar" (The test of cooking is not the test of the palate; 77). Although Spanish women may not possess the palate of a gastronome they are, according to de Vega, excellent cooks: "Uno cierra los ojos ante un mapa de España, avanza un dedo resuelto y alegre, y en cualquier lugar que toque encontrara buenas cocineras" (Close your eyes in front of a map of Spain, point your determined and cheerful finger, and wherever you touch on the map you will find good cooks; 77). His writing discourages women from embracing gustatory pleasures, as he makes clear to them that the palate's education is not central to their identity and social role.

According to de Vega, Spanish women's diminished palates are the result of all the sugar, sweets, and caramels they have been fed since childhood. Like children, he explains, the fairer sex has little sensibility for gastronomic endeavours. Particularly vexatious for de Vega is the supposed fact that even though Spain produces the best fruit in the world, "las mujeres, hasta las de paladar más sabio, pidan de postre, tarta" (women, even those with the most sensible palate, request dessert, cake; 80). There is one exception to this rule, which is Catalonia, where "las mujeres se preocupan del cultivo de su paladar" (women are worried about the cultivation of their palate; 52). "Es una ventaja," he writes, "que las femeninas sepan comer, aunque lo examinemos únicamente desde un aspecto egoísta, para que en la mesa sean buenas compañeras" (It is an advantage that women know how to eat, even if only from a selfish point of view, because they will then be good dining companions; 52). Although he sees advantages to sharing a table with Catalan women, he does warn that "una mujer comedora puede ser, y suele serlo, mandona" (a woman with a good appetite can be, and often is, bossy; 52). So, according to de Vega's codification of gastronomy, Spanish women exist on the margins of gastronomy on account of their infantile penchant for sugary sweets, and when they do take a place in the gastronomic domain, as Catalan women have done, they lose their sweet, agreeable character and take on more masculine characteristics. It is not possible, according to this discourse, for women to hold a place in gastronomy while also properly fulfilling their role as an agreeable wife or companion.

De Vega's gendering of expertise in food writing as male similarly functions to render women as peripheral to gastronomy. As we saw in the last chapter, domestic food preparation is gendered exclusively female in "official" food texts, and de Vega also believes Spain to be teeming with wonderful women cooks. Notwithstanding the fact that women do the lion's share of the cooking, in de Vega's text they are not accorded any authority in relation to food or food writing. As he explains, he looks to male food writers for the final word on matters of taste and food: "Cuando he necesitado comprobar una receta, una fórmula culinaria o ratificar o rectificar una opinión, he acudido a las obras de dos autores insignes, Teodoro Bardají y Casimira" (Whenever I have needed to test a recipe, a culinary formula, or to confirm or correct an opinion, I have consulted the works of these two distinguished authors, Teodoro Bardají and Casimira; 16). Although domestic cooking is gendered female, writing about food – whether it be in the genre of cookbooks or gastronomy – is the domain of men. De Vega's book, as a normative text that defines the limits of Spanish food culture, produces male readers who understand their agency in the production of food discourse and good taste. Conversely, female readers are defined exclusively by the cooking they do in a domestic setting.

Like a number of other gastronomic writers considered in these pages, de Vega had an illustrious career outside of gastronomy. A writer of fiction, a newspaper editor, and a foreign correspondent, he turned his hand to gastronomy many years into his prolific and poly-faceted career. Although he took up food writing or gastronomy later – almost as an afterthought – he assumes a great deal of authority in this domain. The ease with which he assumed that role, in spite of his complete lack of expertise or experience in the area of food culture, presents an important point of contrast with the only female author of gastronomy who published between 1939 and 1959, the Marquesa de Parabere.

Cookbooks and Regional Ingredients in the National Recipe

The women's cookbooks or cookery manuals I turn to next all contain aspects of gastronomic writing, indicating that Mennell's division between gastronomic texts and cookbooks can be too simplistic. The divide between cookbook writing and gastronomy is not always clear-cut: a number of scholars have identified female-authored texts and cookbooks for women as "gastronomical in nature" (McLean 9).[8] While women do write cookbooks with gastronomic elements, however, the SF domestic cookbooks looked at in the previous chapter are devoid of any gastronomic narrative. In these, consisting almost entirely of normative lists for how to cook and run a house, the SF made clear to women that gastronomy is off-limits to them.

The female-authored cookbooks on regional cuisines that we now turn to do contain aspects of gastronomic-style text in their discussions of Spanish food culture. If male-authored food texts establish men as experts in gastronomy, female-authored food texts uphold this male authority by making evident that it is such male expertise on which they draw. By incorporating aspects of male gastronomy in texts on regional cuisines, the SF in particular uses its food discourse to inculcate female readers into the gender divide at the heart of Francoist ideology. In relation to regional cuisines, women readers come to see their role as producing these cuisines within a domestic setting, while men are deemed suitable to partake in their discursive and public codification.

Some of the most well known of the domestic food texts dedicated to the "promotion" of regional cuisines were the SF's cookery manuals and cookbooks. Published in 1958, the manual *Lecciones de cocina regional* (Regional cookery lessons; Lavedán) was used as part of the SF's domestic training program.[9] As we saw in the last chapter in relation to Sarrau's *Ciencia gastronómica* and Herrera's *Manual de cocina*, nothing less than intricate meal planning and the application of scientific and mathematical training to domesticity were demanded of the SF's professional domestic. Required, too, of the Spanish housewife was knowledge of how regional cuisines formed part of Spain's national food culture. Official discourse thus produced subjectivities that were not only bound to the notion of separate spheres for men and women, but also highly alert to the secondary role played by regions in the national culture of Francoist Spain.

Key to understanding how the SF food texts supported official discourse is the point raised earlier that while the regime attempted to eradicate the cultural heritage and political regionalism of Spain's problematic peripheries, it also invoked regional symbols to mobilize support for the regime's nationalizing politics. A number of scholars have discussed the ways in which ultra-nationalism and local and regional identity politics proved compatible, and even mutually constitutive (see Núñez and Umbach). Therefore, although political regionalism was repressed until at least the mid-1960s, cultural regionalism – which involved the promotion of regional folklore and, in some instances, even languages and dialects – was supported (Núñez and Umbach). The work of organizations of the *Movimiento*, such as *Coros y Danzas* (Choirs and dances; the folkloric group of the SF), are an example of the centralist promotion of regional culture and folklore. Under Franco, political homogenization was considered necessary, yet a number of cultural institutions were set up in different regions to study and "promote" their unique traditions.

Just as the SF promoted regional culture through the work of its folkloric group, it also commissioned, in the 1940s and 1950s, some important food texts "dedicated" to promoting or preserving Spain's regional cuisines. To understand these texts, we need to view their focus on culinary regionalism as, in fact, a central ingredient of culinary nationalism. Because the term "regional" is ubiquitous in so many of them, some of the more traditional scholarship, as I mentioned above, mistakenly takes their focus to be regional. To ignore the way in which culinary regionalism in fact serves culinary nationalism is problematic for two reasons: first, because it fails to take into account the broader Francoist co-option of regional culture for the purposes of nation building; and second, because viewing culinary regionalism as inherently separate from culinary nationalism ignores the fact that national cuisines often emerge as a result of regional cuisines, rather than in spite of them.

The connection between culinary regionalism and culinary nationalism has been touched on by a number of scholars, all writing in different national contexts. Arjun Appadurai has explained in relation to Indian cuisine, for instance, that "the idea of an 'Indian' cuisine has emerged because of, rather than despite, the increasing articulation of regional and ethnic cuisines" (21). Eugenia Afinoguénova reminds us that Parkhurst Ferguson has also written about the importance of regional cuisines to French culinary nationalism. According to the latter, the "culinary map of France's regional cuisines was consistent with the Third Republic's program of promoting the 'pedagogy of national distinctiveness through complementary difference'" (qtd. in Afinoguénova, "An Organic Nation" 749). Nineteenth-century Spanish culinary nationalism was also regional in its focus, in as much as it attempted to find symbols for the unity in diversity of Spain's regionally diverse foodscape (see L. Anderson, "Unity and Diversity"). In the context of Mexico, Steffan Ayora-Díaz insists that we look beyond the apparent focus on regional cuisines of many Mexican cookbooks: "instead of replicating recipes from the regional gastronomic tradition," as suggested by titles, some cookbooks "reestablish the dominance of the nationally homogenizing code of central Mexican cuisine" (154).[10]

It is clear from the opening page of *Lecciones de cocina regional* that this text, purportedly concerned with the promotion of regional recipes, serves primarily to assert the dominance of a monolithic national Spanish cuisine. Although the words *Cocina regional* appear twice in bold at the outset of the first chapter or *lección*, they are immediately followed by a discussion of Spain's national cuisine. Indeed, the opening sentence describes Spain's national food culture as constitutive of its regional cuisines: "Hay una cocina nacional clásica, de abolengo española, formada por la aportación de los diferentes modos de aderezar, guisar, conservar de las diferentes regiones" (There is a classic national cuisine, of Spanish lineage, formed by bringing together the different methods of dressing, stewing, preserving of the different regions; 1). This cookery manual, which is all but a carbon copy of Post-Thebussem's early codification of Spanish cuisine in *Guía del buen comer* (Guide to good eating, 1929), makes clear that regional cuisines are to be classified under the umbrella of Spain's national cuisine. Given that food discourse functions to produce different types of subjectivities, the SF food texts, by inculcating Spanish women in the notion of regional culinary culture as a small part of the much greater national culinary whole, produce citizens who view the region as a category not in its own right but as serving the purpose of the nation.

Spanish women are not just taught to view Spain's regional cuisines or foodstuffs as smaller parts of their national whole. Spain's food history is also codified as a unifying component of the national cuisine. The opening pages of *Lecciones* depict Spanish cuisine as having evolved over the centuries as a result of the cross-cultural culinary encounters that were part and parcel of not just the conquest of Spanish lands, but also Spain's own imperial expansion. This account of Spanish culinary history, as with the portrayal of Spain's national cuisine as the sum of the country's regional cuisines, is taken from male-authored gastronomic texts. The *primera lección* (first lesson) of SF's food text treats Spain's position at the pinnacle of culinary sophistication in the sixteenth century, when most of Europe looked to the Spanish court for culinary innovation and refinement. There is also strong emphasis in these introductory pages on the number of Spanish dishes that have been appropriated by other national cuisines: "muchos platos que actualmente llevan nombres extranjeros tienen origen español: tal se puede decir de la tortilla francesa" (many dishes with foreign names are actually Spanish, such as French omelette) (15). Serving in effect to establish the boundaries of Spanish gastronomy, this text codifies Spanish cuisine as the sum not just of its regional parts, but also of its historical ingredients and unified in its rejection of France's culinary hegemony.

In addition to this patriotic introduction, *Lecciones* contains chapters on the country's regional cuisines, which consist of an introduction to the culinary style of the region followed by a small number of regional recipes. The recipe for *Fruta de sierra* (mountain fruits) is an example of the model that all the recipes follow:

> Práctica: Fruta de sierra (fanfarooma), típico de Lorca. 1 docena de huevos, 1 taza pequeña de anís, ½ litro de aceite. La harina que se admita para hacer masa, la miel necesaria y ralladura de limón. MODO DE HACERLO: Se baten mucho los huevos, se agrega el añis y poco a poco la harina necesaria para hacer la masa. Se hacen unas tortas muy finas, como papel, y se fríen en aceite poco fuerte para que se pasen sin dorarse. Se ponen a escurrir y enriar y se pican. Se pesa la masa frita, y por cada libra de ésta se pesan 12 onzas de miel, que se pone en un perol a que tome punto; se añade ralladura de limón y se mezcla la masa picada, se da una vuelta, y se va colocando a cucharadas entre dos obleas. (18)
>
> (Practical matters: Mountain fruits (*fanfarooma*), typical of Lorca. A dozen eggs, a small cup of anise, ½ litre oil. Enough flour to make the dough,

honey as required, and lemon zest. COOKING METHOD: Beat the eggs thoroughly, add the anise, and slowly add enough flour to make the dough. Make into pancakes as fine as paper and fry gently in oil so that they cook without browning. Drain and slice. Weigh the fried dough and add 12 ounces of honey for every pound, which is placed in a pot until it is set. Add the lemon zest and mix in the sliced dough. Mix once and serve by placing a tablespoon between two wafers.)

That all chapters adhere to the same format creates the impression that all regional cuisines contribute equally to the national whole. But in reality Catalan and Basque cuisines are much more varied than many other regional cuisines, each having its own unique corpus of cookbooks and gastronomic texts. Autochthonous food texts – especially in the case of Catalonia – are often pointed to as evidence of the existence of a national cuisine or national identity that is separate from Spain's.

The treatment of Catalan cuisine in this text is an excellent example of how the broader attempt by officials to detach traditional Catalan culture from the region's unique linguistic and cultural heritage plays out in relation to food culture. In the case of Catalonia, it is not just the way in which regional recipes are downplayed that is significant, but also how Catalan cuisine is in effect co-opted into official food discourse for the purpose of the state's ultra-conservative nation-building project. *Cocina regional* explicitly describes de Nola's fifteenth-century Catalan cookbook *Libre del art de coch* (Cookbook) as "un hecho importantísmo en la historia de la cocina española" (a most important event in the history of Spanish cuisine; 2). Claiming *Libre del art del coch* as pivotal to Spanish cuisine does not just fly in the face of official Catalan discourse on this cookbook, it also stands at odds with scholarly wisdom on its origins. Medieval food historian Melitta Weiss Adamson, in a comment representative of scholarship on this book, describes it as "Catalan" and the recipes as being of "Catalan, Italian, French and Arab origin," adding that as a result of its publication "Catalan cooking became more widely known in Italy" (122).

Although the SF does mention in passing that *Libre del art del coch* was first written in Catalan, and published in Barcelona, it treats the translation of the text from Catalan to Spanish as the pivotal moment in its transition from a relatively obscure text to one that is proof of the superiority of Spanish cuisine: "Es prueba que España Sabia comer y quería comer mejor. Es un testimonio valiosísimo de la originalidad y personalidad de la cocina Española, superior entonces a la francesa" (It is proof that Spain knew how to eat and wanted to eat better. It is a priceless testament to the originality and character of Spanish cuisine, at the time superior to French; 2). In fact, the seminal food text *Libre del art del coch* is an important sign of Catalonia's substantive cultural, culinary, and linguistic difference from Spain, and in the final years of the dictatorship would become an important element in the arsenal of Catalonia's political regionalism. By appropriating *Libre del art del coch* as Spanish and all but ignoring its Catalan genealogy, *Lecciones* not only empties Catalan food culture of any potential political content, but also co-opts this text for the regime's monolithic nationalism.

Another way in which the SF's *Lecciones* upholds official discourse is through its creation of new culinary regions, which are reminiscent of the functional regionalism outlined earlier in this chapter. We have noted how Francoist officials reimagined or produced a different kind of space for their new socio-economic, cultural, and political order; the SF in this text contributed to this process with its functional division of regional cuisines for the purpose of a "practical" chapter breakdown. Through its re-imagining of new culinary zones, the SF makes clear its commitment to the broader Francoist preoccupation with space. And, unsurprisingly, the SF's new culinary zones have a particularly detrimental effect on Catalan culinary regionalism. The cuisines of Spain's eastern seaboard are treated as one and the same, with the SF mixing discussion of different rice dishes, *gazpacho*, alioli, and the best ways to prepare seafood in a way that ignores the great variations of cuisine amongst these coastal regions. In discussing the food traditions of Albacete, Alicante, Catalonia, and Murcia in the same chapter, the SF's *Lecciones* essentially denies Catalan culinary regionalism its unique status, presenting the cuisine of this potentially problematic area as one among many small parts of the broader culinary zone.

While it erases culinary difference through the creation of these culinary zones, the SF also writes about aspects of Spanish food culture that unify the different regional cuisines. An important part of Spain's tradition of gastronomic writing from the nineteenth century onwards was to debate the issue of the country's national dish. In the nineteenth century, Spain's pioneering gastronomes nominated *la olla podrida/el cocido* (the rotten pot/stew) because some variant could be found in all of Spain's different regional foodscapes; SF names *el cocido* (stew) "un punto de contacto" (a point of contact; 3): "el plato clásico nacional, que es el cocido, se hace en todas las regiones. A veces, varía algo el nombre: puchero, olla, cocido; varía también el modo de hacerlo" (a classic national dish, stew is made in every region. Sometimes the name differs: stewpot, pot, stew; the cooking method also varies; 3). Discussion of Spain's national dish occurs in the first few pages of the SF's food text, emphasizing yet again to readers that the national is the overarching and most important category in this text.[11] It is also significant that the SF's suggestion for a national dish is an almost word-for-word copy of Dr Thebussem and the king's chef's pioneering recommendation in the nineteenth century. If gastronomy is the domain of male authors, then in those parts of the SF's *Lecciones* that include gastronomic commentary, the SF appropriately relies on male expertise.

Isabel de Trévis and the Authority of Male Gastronomes

The next food texts I consider were published just one year after the SF's *Lecciones* and are similar not just in their "promotion" of regional cuisines, but also in the authority they accord Spain's male gastronomes. Genoveva Bernard, who used the pen name Isabel de Trévis for her food writing, has received little journalistic or scholarly attention, yet between 1936 and 1974 she penned an impressive number of cookbooks, quite a few of which went through multiple editions. In the early years of the regime, many of her cookbooks were dedicated to single ingredients, such as eggs, meat, or ice cream; she went on to write her series *La cocina regional* (Regional cuisine); and towards the end of her career, she published cookbooks on international cuisine, Italian cuisine, and a collection of Basque recipes. Most of her cookbooks are full of cookery instruction and useful recipes, but when de Trévis does write in a more gastronomic style, she, like the SF, accords authority to Spain's long line of male gastronomic writers.

De Trévis's cookbooks were published as part of the Biblioteca – El Ama de Casa (The Housewife's Library), including the 1959 series *La cocina regional*. Given her close association with the Biblioteca – El Ama de Casa, it comes as little surprise that de Trévis upholds traditional notions of gender not just in the role her cookbooks assign to Spanish women, but also in the authority she accords to male food writers. Made up of eight titles, *La cocina regional* followed in part the blueprint laid down by the SF in its "promotion" of Spain's regional cuisines. It was affordable compared to other tome-like cookbooks published contemporaneously. Each soft-cover installment of around sixty pages is an entity in its own right, but readers have the option of buying all of the titles if they want to own the entire series of cookbooks.

In presenting each regional cookbook as part of this larger entity, de Trévis's construction of Spanish cuisine is immediately recognizable to readers used to conceptualizing Spain's taste community as consisting of its regional parts. Like the SF's *Lecciones*, the series seeks to unify Spain's regional cuisines by having the cookbooks follow the same format and layout. Each cookbook opens with a three-page description of the cuisine or cuisines under consideration, followed by "un sumario alfabético" (an alphabetic summary) of the recipes. The recipes themselves are then divided into identical sections, which are presented in the same order in each cookbook. The effect of this is to present regional culinary diversity as highly unified. Also speaking to this unity of Spanish cuisine is the inclusion in each cookbook of dishes that appear (in some form) in each region, such as *cocido*.

Like the SF's cookery manual, de Trévis defers to Post-Thebussem as an ultimate authority on Spanish cuisine. Opening her installment on Catalan cuisine with a quote from this esteemed gastronome, de Trévis frames her own collection of recipes as reliant on male authority. Yet while de Trévis's series begins with a nod to Post-Thebussem, she leaves out most of what he wrote about Catalan cuisine during the Primo de Rivera dictatorship. As I have shown elsewhere, Post-Thebussem's chapter on Catalonia in his *Guía del buen comer* was subversive in its codification of Catalan food culture as more evolved than Spanish on account of Catalonia's long tradition of autochthonous food texts. According to Post-Thebussem, this history of texts about Catalan cuisine meant the cuisine was easily recognizable to Catalans and foreigners alike as a national cuisine or culinary entity in its own right. While de Trévis does defer to Post-Thebussem – upholding the official gendering of gastronomy as male – her choosing to ignore his dissenting statements about Catalan cuisine renders her cookbooks an example of the official Francoist tendency to diminish regional cultures despite the official "embrace" of cultural regionalism.

Post-Thebussem's disruptive codification of Catalan cuisine is replaced in de Trévis's series with a reminder that the incomparably greater entity is Spanish cuisine. Instead of opening with a comment on the richness or historical embeddedness of Catalonia's food culture, de Trévis begins by waxing lyrical about Spanish cuisine in general: "Qué gran riqueza culinaria tiene nuestra patria" (What an incredible culinary wealth our country has; 8). This discursive move evokes the official practice of giving Spanish names to Catalan cities, towns, and public places (see Skerrett). The imbalance between Spanish and Catalan in this cookbook also reinforces the notion of Catalan cuisine/culture as but a small part of Spanish cuisine/culture: with the exception of nine words in a list of two hundred recipes, the entire text is written in Spanish. The presence of so few words in Catalan speaks to the tokenistic nature of the official embrace of cultural regionalism.

Interestingly, the very few Catalan words that do appear in de Trévis's cookbook are set in boldface. This makes them immediately apparent to readers, but also serves to highlight the sizeable imbalance between

Spanish and Catalan cuisines in this volume. De Trévis's writing makes clear to readers that even in a cookbook on Catalan cuisine, the dominant language will be Spanish. Catalan cuisine and the Catalan language, according to this cookbook's visual cues, are very small parts of the greater whole that is Spanishness. Indeed, just glancing at its list of recipes produces readers who are hyper-aware of the hegemony of Spanish culture. De Trévis's collection of Catalan cuisine differs from the SF's food writing in that she does not position Catalan cuisine as part of an arbitrary or administrative culinary zone, her food writing follows the SF's in producing a national gastronomic territory made up of smaller, less significant, regional parts.

Consider the recipe she provides for *huevos Barcelona* (Barcelona eggs), an exemplar of the format all of the recipes follow: a list of ingredients with several lines of instructions, yet with no information about the history or evolution of the dish:

> Ingredientes: 8 huevos, 100 gramos de cerdo, 50 de jamón, 75 de mantequila, 150 de tomates, 50 de harina, 1 cebolla y 1 taza de caldo. Trinchad la cebolla finamente y rehogadla en una sartén con la mantequilla y el jamón y el lomo, previamente cortados a trozos pequeños. En cuanto tome color dorado, añadidle los tomates, ya mondados, picados y sin semillas, la harina, y la taza de caldo. Todo esto lo sazonaréis a vuestro gusto, y deberá hervir tapeado eso de media hora.
>
> (Ingredients: 8 eggs, 100 grams pork loin, 50 grams ham, 75 grams butter, 150 grams tomatoes; 50 grams flour, 1 onion, and 1 cup of stock. Slice the onion finely and fry it lightly in a frying pan with the butter, the ham, and the pork loin, cut earlier into small pieces. Once browned, add the tomatoes, already peeled, sliced, and seedless, the flour, and the cup of stock. Season to taste. Boil covered for half an hour.)

De Trévis's cookbook on *la cocina norteña* (northern cuisine) is highly complimentary of the three cuisines (Navarra, Vasca, and Santanderina) that are included in this culinary zone: "Quiero deciros con esto que esta cocina norteña que agrupo en este volumen es de muy antiguo abolengo y que los guisos que voy a explicaros los conocieron los abuelos de vuestros abuelos y los tatarabuelos de éstos también" (With this, I want you to know that the northern cuisine I have included in this volume is of very ancient ancestry and that the stews I am going to explain to you were known to the grandparents of your grandparents and their great-great grandparents before them; 7). As well as being a cuisine that is rooted in history, tradition, and family customs, Basque cuisine, she reminds readers, has an international reach the other regional cuisines lack:

> A Vizcaya, sobre todo, le es deudora España de una de esas grandes divulgaciones gastronómicas. Un solo plato del portentoso fogón vasco, el bacalao a la vizcaina, se ha convertido en plato mundial. La receta de este guiso no solo se encuentra en Francia y en Italia; es que ha llegado también, hasta el Japón y la China. (8)
>
> (To Biscay, above all, Spain owes a great debt for one of these great gastronomic disseminations. A single dish from the Basque stove, Basque cod, has become a worldwide dish. The recipe of this stew is not only known in France and Italy; it has even reached the shores of Japan and China.)

Her cookbook subsumes the different regions of Navarra, Vasca, and Santanderina within one small cookbook, but she is at pains to highlight the superiority of Basque cuisine: she makes clear that while Spain is the greater entity, Basque cuisine offers a richness and international influence unparalleled in other parts of the country.

Before the civil war there were many cookbooks dedicated exclusively to Basque cuisine, such as *La cocina de Nicolasa* (Nicolasa's kitchen, 1933) and the Marquesa's *Platos escogidos de la cocina vasca* (Selected dishes of Basque cuisine, 1935). Such texts meant that regional cuisines were easily recognizable as entities in their own right. By contrast, during most of the Franco regime no cookbooks were dedicated exclusively to one regional cuisine; those cuisines, as noted, were presented as parts of a much greater whole. De Trévis's cookbook includes only ten words in Basque, used in the alphabetic list of recipes, and the cuisines of Spain's northern regions occupy a paltry sixty-six pages. She does, however, make comments in the prologues to her cookbooks that indicate she is of the opinion that these three regional cuisines have much more to offer than her cookbooks can in any way reflect. "Con facilidad" (with ease), she explains, "se hubiese podido escribir un volumen para cada una de tales cocinas y habría figurado muy dignamente en esta Biblioteca" (one could have written an entire volume for each of these cuisines and it would have had a rightful place in this library; 8).

From her prologue it is possible to infer that she is worried about the fate of Basque cuisine:

> Y, lo que es peor, están en trance de perderse, de ser olvidadas… porque esas mujeres, maestras del buen guisar, no le dan importancia a su propio mérito culinario y no dejan escritas tales recetas de platos insuperables. (*La cocina regional navarra, vasca y santanderina* [Navarran, Basque, and Santanderino regional cuisine] 9)

> (And, what is worse, they are in the throes of being lost, being forgotten … because these women, mistresses of good cooking, do not place importance on their own cooking skills and do not write down the recipes of these unsurpassable dishes.)

Perhaps de Trévis is putting out a call in her cookbook to Basque women to document a culinary heritage that would be all but obliterated during the Franco regime. Her own series of small cookbooks on regional cuisines is proof that there was still at this point little space for exhaustive culinary texts dedicated to just one regional cuisine. In 1974, de Trévis does herself write a cookbook on Basque cuisine, a tome of some 543 pages. Given how long it would take in Franco Spain for food writing to transcend the paradigmatic SF-style cookbooks wherein regional cuisines were very small parts of the greater national whole, de Trévis may be looking for ways in her prologue of reminding readers that cuisines need books just as much as cooks.

Although much of de Trévis's food writing upholds official discourse, there is a clear sense in her publications that regional cuisines should be codified as separate entities. Her comments about her own food texts being unable to do justice to regional cuisines are reminiscent of Doménech's 1942 cookbook, which will be looked at next. While, therefore, her food writing does reinforce the notion of Spanish cuisine as the much greater and all-encompassing unit, she also shows an awareness of the importance of documenting regional cuisines.

Doménech's Food Discourse and Nationalism

Ignacio Doménech's *Mi plato: Cocina regional española: Nuevo manual de cocina familiar muy interesante para las amas de casa* (My plate: Spanish regional cuisine: Updated family cooking manual for housewives, 1942) was, like Bosch Bierge's *Cocina regional española*, published in the immediate aftermath of the civil war. Doménech was one of the most renowned food writers and culinary professionals of the time, and a number of his cookbooks have been analysed above. He is frequently disruptive of official discourse, most notably of the tendency to downplay or ignore the devastating hunger of post-war Spain. *Mi plato: Cocina regional* was the last food text he wrote, and has undeservedly received much less scholarly attention than many of his earlier gastronomic texts and cookbooks.

Political regionalism was suppressed during most of the regime, yet cultural regionalism was supported, including the promotion, for instance, of folkloric traditions. Many of the other food texts looked at thus far uphold official discourse in conflating regional food culture with folklore, thereby stripping it of any political content. Similarly, Doménech begins his cookbook by asking his readers to treat *Mi plato* as they would a performance of regional songs:

> Les estimaré, que admitan mi manual en cuestión como el que suele asistir a una audición de canciones y melodias genuinamente regionales. Es todo cuanto deseaba comunicarles al presentarles este florilegio de cocina, que he titulado Mi Plato (cocina regional española). (7)
>
> (I will kindly ask of you that you approach my present manual as one would generally attend a concert of truly regional songs and melodies. It is all I wanted to communicate to you by presenting this cooking anthology, which I have titled *My Plate: Spanish regional cuisine*.)

It would seem from this comment that Doménech is aware that his cookbook does not engage with regional cuisines in any sustained or meaningful fashion.

Corroborating this interpretation is the fact that Doménech had already produced a cookbook on Catalan cuisine. Published in 1924, *La Teca: La veritable cuina casolana de Catalunya* (Food: Authentic homestyle Catalan cooking) consists of recipes of great personal significance to its author, recipes that "empezó a recoger en la cocina de sus tíos de Manresa, en las fondas del puerto de Barcelona, en la Fonda de Monistrol, de Puigcerdá, y en las cocinas familiares del Bages, su comarca natal" (he started to collect in the kitchen of his uncles and aunts in Manresa, in the port taverns of Barcelona, in the Tavern of Monistrol, of Puigcerdá, and in family kitchens of Bages, his home region) (Real Academia de la Historia). *La Teca* quickly became an essential cookbook in Catalan homes, and between 1924 and 2010 it went through nineteen editions. It is surprising that the subversiveness of Doménech's culinary discourse has received scant scholarly attention, since, in speaking of Catalan cuisine as a distinct entity, *La Teca* clearly stood at odds with the dominant Francoist view of Spanish cuisine as a monolithic entity.

The images on the front and back covers of Doménech's cookbook do not – unlike those of his cookbooks we looked at in chapter 1 – speak to the food shortages and hunger of the time. A picture of a juicy, succulent roast chicken occupies most of the front cover; the back is taken up by an appetizing image of a brightly coloured, steaming paella. But in the opening pages of his cookbook Doménech makes it clear that he knows the times have changed, that these images fail to capture the reality of the food shortages of the early post-war period. He acknowledges that this is not a time for culinary or gastronomic abundance:

> En las presentes circunstancias… no es propicio, al ofrecer al público, un libro de cocina de gran envergadura, de platos caros, muy bonitos, que ahora no tienen ninguna aplicación práctica. Por cuyas razones, es lógico, que mi nuevo manual de cocina *Mi plato (cocina regional española)*, tenga que presentarse a ustedes más modestamente. (6)
>
> (In present circumstances … it is not appropriate to offer the public a book of great magnitude, of expensive, refined dishes, which would presently have no practical application. For these reasons, it is logical that my new cookbook *My Plate: Regional Spanish Cuisine* has to be presented to you more modestly.)

We can glean from this that Doménech had to come up with a more modest book on regional cuisines than the one he was planning, likely either prior to the outbreak of the conflict or before it became apparent that there was no easy or quick fix to the devastation of post-war Spain. It is probable, therefore, that Doménech's 127-page cookbook on regional cuisines represents just a small section of what he would have published on this topic if circumstances had been different. Also suggesting that Doménech probably did not see his paltry cookbook as doing justice to Spain's regional cuisines is his claim that an extensive cookbook could be written for each: "bien pudiera componerse, para cada región, un libro de 500 páginas" (well could each region merit its own book of 500 pages; 7). Other food writers diminished the importance of regional cuisines by subsuming them into ad-hoc administrative or gastronomic zones; Doménech's comment here reveals that he did not subscribe to such a view. The fact that Doménech was Catalan and had written a highly significant text in Catalan about Catalan cuisine further corroborates that he did not subscribe to the official subsuming of regional cuisines into the national whole.

Despite what we can tease out from the text regarding his subversive views, Doménech did emphasize the "Spanishness" of these cuisines, perhaps due to oppressive censoring of all cultural texts at this time, including food texts. One wonders if he is engaging in self-censorship in this early totalitarian phase of the regime. Whatever may be the case, in his opening pages he does describe *Mi plato* as a "manual de cocina españolísima" (a most Spanish cookbook; 7). Doménech's system for presenting recipes also gives the impression that his cookbook, first and foremost, privileges Spanish cuisine. When there is a series of similar recipes, he opens with an umbrella term, such as *sopa a la española* (Spanish-style soup) or *a la madrileña* (Madrid-style), and then lists regional dishes as if they were smaller parts of a greater Spanish cuisine. Indeed, his separation of recipes into primary and secondary tiers has an impact on the presentation of regional cuisines because regional recipes are presented as variants of a "Spanish" dish. In short, although Doménech clearly sees regional cuisines as separate entities, he also – likely because of rigid censorship at this stage of the regime – codifies them as subordinate variants of the national cuisine, in line with the usual practice at this time.

Many of the food writers we have looked at discuss the issue of Spain's national dish, especially at times of heightened nationalism. As we have seen, a number of intellectuals or journalists with an interest in Spain's "taste community" came to see *el cocido* (stew) or *la olla podrida* (the rotten pot) as a metaphor for Spanish culinary nationalism due to its reflection of unity and diversity. Doménech's cookbook contains recipes for both classic and regional variants of this dish, which he describes as "es el guiso más clásico de España" (Spain's most quintessential dish, 17). Although he provides a number of recipes for *el cocido*, as a food professional and top-end chef he also laments how frequently Spaniards consume this dish, charging that the ubiquitous consumption of *el cocido* is one of the reasons so many wonderful regional dishes have been all but forgotten. While Doménech thus partakes in the requisite discussion of Spain's national dish, he also makes clear that there is much more to Spanish cuisine than this national dish, and that *el cocido* has presence and visibility at the expense of regional cuisines.

Doménech's subversive food writing can be seen as directing his readers' attention away from the country's national dish towards their own wonderfully rich regional food culture. He invites his readers to critique discussions of Spain's national dish that were imposed on the Spanish citizenry in a top-down fashion at different times of nation building and centralization. Just as his criticism of Spain's national dish directs attention towards regional cuisines, so too does his comment, mentioned earlier, about each regional cuisine deserving a cookery tome of five hundred pages. Indeed, while his own cookbook on regional cuisines cannot do justice to all of Spain's richly diverse regional cuisines in the way that he would have liked, he reminds his readers of their own culinary heritage and of a knowledge of regional food culture that would have been passed down informally in different family and social settings. No doubt mindful that even cookbooks were subject to censorship, in this instance Doménech emphasizes time after time the Spanishness of his cookbook. Yet his comments evince, too, an implicit belief in regional cuisines as separate entities that need safeguarding.[12] In a way, Doménech – nearly two decades before de Trévis – instructs his readers in what they need to do in their own homes to protect a regional food heritage that will become all but excluded from food discourse until well into the 1970s.

Regional Cuisines: Minimized and Co-opted

This chapter has shown how cultural regionalism was promoted in official discourse, but in a way that was highly reductive. Moreover, when regional culture was made visible or invoked, it was appropriated for the purposes of the nation or national culture. This aspect of official discourse had an enormous impact on food discourse produced during the first two decades of the regime. In line with official discourse, most of these cookbooks and gastronomic texts diminished or co-opted regional cuisines, while apparently promoting them. Ubiquitous during these years were food texts – or cookbooks – with some form of the word "region" in their titles. Such explicit references to regional cuisines have lead some key historians to mistakenly view these texts as evidence of a resurgence of regional cuisines during the Franco regime.

The gastronomic texts looked at here have received very little scholarly attention. Indeed, only broad-brush statements have been made about such texts, like those by Roser i Puig mentioned at the outset of this chapter. I have revealed the discursive strategies that enabled texts like these to subsume the cuisines of the peripheries into Spain's culinary centre. Such publications were all the more effective as weapons of the state for the ways in which they contributed to the production of a unified space that leaves little room for political regionalism. As normative texts, this food writing does not just establish the boundaries of Spanish culinary culture or gastronomy: it also grants the authority to male authors to write the very texts that define the limits of Spanish gastronomy.

Conclusion

In this book, I have outlined several modes for engaging with Spanish food discourse in the period 1939–59 as a site where identities are both imposed and contested. We have seen examples of the ways in which food discourse was an integral part of the Francoist state's hold on power. Significantly, discourse about food, or the "talk of food," is a place where people learn not just about food, but also about the expectations that apply to them in their roles as national, gendered, and autarkic subjectivities. Foucault's notion of biopolitics has proven particularly fruitful for my analysis of the ways in which food discourse is a means of both exerting and resisting power. Scholars of Franco Spain have argued that the regime's unprecedented cultural and political hegemony must be thought about in terms of a totalitarian biopolitics, which allowed for the control of the population through official organizations (e.g., Iglesias). Writers, politicians, teachers, medical professionals, and historians, they argue, all took part in the production of a discourse that allowed the regime to indoctrinate the population in Francoist ideology. My aim here has been to analyse the ways in which food writers, food professionals, cookbook writers, and official organizations discursively took part in this form of control.

Like scholars of Franco Spain, food studies scholars argue for the importance of viewing food discourse as a site of control. Indeed, the important role of the "talk of food" in producing national, gendered or racialized subjects has attracted the attention of various scholars, who understand that the codification of cuisine is often more instrumental to the spread of politics and nation building than political speeches or other official documents. National sentiment, as many studies have shown, is often generated most intensely in culinary texts, or periodicals containing food advice or descriptions of food. These do not simply tell readers how (or what) to eat, but also how to perform other aspects of their identity.

The notion of culinary resistance – that is, the way food discourse can undermine or bypass cultural, political, and culinary hegemony – has also informed my study. Scholars are beginning to recognize that food discourses do not only aid in producing subjects, "they also offer the opportunity to resist being molded into the categories society prescribes" (Vester 2). Existing scholarship on Franco Spain has pointed to the multiple ways in which the population resisted the regime's control. In terms of cultural production more broadly speaking, a number of studies have shown, for instance, how artists or writers subverted the regime's power through the creation of alternative or non-hegemonic spaces (Cancio Fernández; Wright). Existing scholarship on Franco Spain also provides examples of civic resistance to the regime's corrupt handling of food. This monograph contributes to this scholarship by considering the ways in which food discourse and food writing were important sites of resistance during the regime's first two decades. Because food texts have traditionally been viewed – erroneously, in my view – as apolitical, because of their connections with both domesticity and gastronomy, they were not subject to the same degree of censorship. Accordingly, food writing was at times more able to offer disruptive or resistant textual spaces than other forms of discourse.

Thus, each of the three main sections of this book demonstrates the ways in which food discourse functions not just as a place where identities are imposed, but also where they are contested. As I have shown, in some instances the "talk of food" provided a space where readers could experience a world different from that imposed by the state. Some non-official food discourse was counter-hegemonic in its subversion of the core Francoist values of a unified, gendered, compliant, and autarkic nation. As I have outlined, a number of food writers used food discourse to challenge monolithic nationalism, rigid gender divides, compliance, autarky, and the official downplaying of hunger.

Since a number of the primary texts under analysis here are cookbooks and gastronomic texts, I have, in addition to my primary aim of shedding light on the axis between food discourse, Francoist ideology, and resistance, provided a history of Spanish food writing during the first two decades of the regime. Because food writing has been peripheral in the academy, there is much to document in terms of Spain's corpus of cookbooks and gastronomic texts. Considering both official and non-official cookbooks for women, as well as gastronomic texts, has been important for the conclusions it allowed me to draw about the ways in which these different texts fit together. If the absence of narrative in some cookbooks highlights the prescriptive nature of recipes, other types of cookbooks encourage more autonomy and allow readers to make decisions about what to cook and what recipes to use. This comparative approach has also allowed me to identify the gendering of food writing during the first two decades of the Franco regime. As I have shown above, hyper-instructional food writing was directed solely at women, while more conversational gastronomic writing was penned with male readers in mind. The gendering of different genres of food writing during this period upholds Francoist ideology in the way it demands of women not just their exclusive dedication to domesticity, but also their compliance – in the kitchen and beyond. By contrast, food writing produces male subjects who understand their centrality to Spanish gastronomy, not just as the arbiters of good taste but also for the role they play in determining or producing the very boundaries of Spanish food culture.

Although I argue for the ways in which food discourse operated as part of a broader totalitarian biopolitics, it is beyond the parameters of my project to make any definitive statements about the use of the food texts under scrutiny here.[1] A reception history of these cookbooks and gastronomic texts could perhaps provide such information. Such an approach informs, for instance, Eva Woods and Jo Labanyi's collection of "oral histories of Spaniards' memories of cinema going in the 1940's and 1950s" (Sieburth 12). A focus on reception in the area of food texts could, in the future, use focus groups or interviews to provide more information about how cookbooks and gastronomic texts were used, who bought them, whether people just read them or also cooked from them, and whether they were commonly on display in Spanish homes as a reference point for cooking and food culture.[2] Questions could be asked, too, about how people felt about gender and nationality upon reading domestic cookbooks or food texts purportedly dedicated to the promotion of regional cuisines. Did these texts make readers just think about food differently, or did they also have an impact on other aspects of their identity?

We can also look to present-day Spain and Spanish food culture in order to have some sense of the reach of Francoist food discourse. Of immense interest is the way in which aspects of that food discourse continue to act as a reference point for Spanish food culture or cultural representations of Spanish cuisine. From neo-Francoist restaurants to television shows promoting the idea of a unified Spanish culinary nationalism, the food discourse examined in this monograph is still present in contemporary Spain. Given its continued visibility, it is clear that the "talk of food" that emerged during the Franco regime continues to hold an important place in Spain's cultural, social, and political life.

Particularly revealing about the lingering impact of Francoist food discourse in present-day Spain is the ever-increasing number of restaurants paying homage to the country's fascist past. This trend has attracted the attention of the international and national press, and journalists are critical of it. One article in a Spanish newspaper decries "una ruta por los bares franquistas que incumplen la Ley de la Memoria Histórica" (a route through Francoist bars that breach the Historical Memory Law), arguing that while it is illegal to have any plaques, commemorative medals, or other paraphernalia that pay homage to Franco Spain, there are restaurants in Spain that have been turned into "templos de adulación del franquismo" (temples of adulation to Francoism; *El plural*, "Ruta por los bares"). The most well known of these locales is Casa Pepe, a restaurant in the very small town of Almuradiel in Castile La Mancha, which attracts up to one hundred visitors a day. Visitors can purchase bottles of wine honouring General Franco on their labels, as well as typical foodstuffs such as *jamón* (ham) and olive oil bearing the national flag used during Franco's reign. One English newspaper reports on an interview with the owner of the restaurant, in which he explained his positive memories of Franco: "We support Franco. We are proud to honor him and what he did for our country, because it was a really prosperous period in Spain's history" (Martínez Cantera).

Other such restaurants include Arriba España, where the owners answer the phone with "Arriba España, dígame" (Up with Spain, hello) and serve dishes dedicated to Franco and Primo de Rivera. Food served at such premises frequently bears the descriptor "a la española" (Spanish-style), which, as we have seen, came to refer to the ideal of a monolithic, standard Spanish cuisine. When Spaniards visit these restaurants or read about *comida a la española* (Spanish-style food), they perhaps imagine a sense of national unity that offers continuity with the past and stability in the face of ongoing economic problems and a constitutional crisis in relation to Catalonia. This lingering taste for the food culture of Spain's Francoist past speaks to what Helen Graham describes as a much broader neo-Francoist, ultra-nationalist influence in present-day Spain, as well as a "nostalgia for a past of apparent certainty and security" (*Interrogating Francoism* 205).

While there have been calls from Spain's left for the closure of these neo-Francoist restaurants, they remain open to this day. One such restaurant, which was denounced to Spanish authorities to no avail, is Casa Eladio in Avila, which invokes the Nationalist victory during the Spanish Civil War in its culinary offerings. Describing itself as a "Rincón nacional" (National nook), it serves up dishes with evocative names such as *bacalao grande y libre* (great and free cod), *patatas revolconas amargadas 36* (mashed potatoes of the 1936 bitter defeat), *chuletillas del Valle* (little lamb chops from the Valley), *huevos rotos fusilados* (shot eggs), and *chorizos rojos* (red chorizo sausages; see *El plural*, "IU denuncia"). To understand this phenomenon, we might turn to the work of Julian Casanova, who writes of the unique situation in Spain's post-dictatorship society (compared to the case of Germany) where "it was Spain's antifascist resistance groups which bore the brunt of the violence. Also in Spain, and crucially unlike elsewhere, the vengefulness of 'victorious' social groups could count on full state backing" (205). If the violence against Spain's antifascist groups is ongoing, then Casa Eladio's invocation of the defeat of the Republicans in the civil war can be seen not just as a reminder of past violence, but also as a warning of continued violence.

Another less blatant – yet still potent – example of the impact of Francoist food culture on contemporary Spain can be found in the state-commissioned television series *Un país para comérselo* (A country good enough to eat), which, as I have shown elsewhere, is remarkably centralist in its "promotion" of Spain's regional cuisines (see L. Anderson, "A Recipe for Spain"). Now in its fourth year, this program has achieved both critical and ratings success. It has won a number of national gastronomy and tourism prizes, including the "Premio Nacional de Gastronomía" (National Gastronomy Prize) in 2010, and in its first season attracted more than three million viewers per episode. Each episode of the show is set in a different region of Spain, and its hosts take viewers on a tantalizing gastronomic tour, while also providing information about the most important local monuments, architecture, and historic and tourist sites. Although it purports to celebrate regional diversity, *Un país para comérselo* in fact presents Spanish gastronomy as a singular, unified whole.

It is important to view the representation of Spain's regional cultures and foodways it offers as emanating not just from the country's geographic centre, but also from its political one. It is broadcast by TVE, part of whose mandate is "to promote the territorial cohesion and linguistic and cultural diversity of Spain" (RTVE). On closer inspection of the show's pride in Spanish gastronomy, it becomes clear that *Un país para comérselo* tries to unify Spain's disparate parts by downplaying territorial divisions and presenting Spaniards as first and foremost unified in their cuisine. And if the comments posted on the website at the end of each episode are anything to go by, the show's directors have been nothing but successful in fulfilling TVE's mandate to promote territorial cohesion. About one episode on Barcelona, for instance, one viewer writes: "Me encanta 'Un país para comérselo'! Qué gastronomía tan rica tenemos en esta ESPAÑA nuestra." (I love *A country so good to eat*! What incredibly rich cuisine we have in our shared SPAIN.)

The tendency at the time of Franco's death to represent the Transition (the move from dictatorship to democracy) as a break with the past has often meant that Spain's right underplays or disavows any continuity with Francoism. Yet Bradley Epps, for instance, identifies similarities with the past in conservative groups' views on the Spanish whole and its peripheral parts: Franco's "unitarian conception of the State has rather perversely morphed … into the 'threat' of popularly asserted self-determination by whatever 'part' (say, the Basque Country or Catalonia) of the 'whole' that would dare to see itself as a whole of a different sort, even as a whole apart" (556). This feature of Spanish nationalism is reflected in the fact that *Un país para comérselo* can present itself as the bastion of Spain's regional foodscapes (and has been unanimously received as such), while asserting a centralizing – and often paternalistic – view of the relationship between the Spanish whole and its parts. The example given in the introduction to this book of how the present-day royal family has used food culture to impose a particular notion of Spanishness is not dissimilar to the codification of Spanish cuisine in this centralizing television show. And the way in which both codify national cuisine as the incomparably greater whole in the relationship between Spain's centre and peripheries is similar to the way Francoist food discourse imposes a monolithic culinary identity on the country.[3]

Another issue looked at in relation to Francoist food discourse that has emerged in present-day Spanish cultural production is the gendering of food preparation as exclusively female. Elsewhere, I have analysed the role of culinary nostalgia, and the possibility it allows for a critique of the prevailing gender ideology of the Franco era, in the television series *Cuéntame cómo pasó* (Tell me how it happened) and *El Cuaderno de Mercedes* (Mercedes's cookbook), the show's accompanying cookbook. *Cuéntame* is set in the 1960s and throughout the Transition. Its connection to debates about historical memory in Spain has generated a series of expectations about its political content, which for many of its detractors have not been met; instead, they argue, it offers nothing short of a feast of sentimental nostalgia. Yet the memories of Francoist food culture are not simply escapist or apolitical. They are, in fact, significant for the visibility they give to women's histories and memories, which have often been excluded from male-dominated accounts of Francoism and the Transition.

It is certainly the case that many of *Cuéntame*'s episodes generate nostalgia for the sharing of meals with the extended family at the table now that the demands of modern life increasingly threaten the existence of such customs. In each episode, there is at least one scene in which the Alcantara family shares a meal together around the dining table. Yet sometimes such moments are used to highlight the very gendered nature of life under Franco. One of the family meals that is not such a happy occasion is held on the day of Mercedes and Antonio's twentieth wedding anniversary. In honour of this occasion, the grandmother cooks a special lunch, and the children give a book to each parent. Antonio receives a volume of history; Mercedes receives the cookbook *Manual de cocina* by Ana María Herrera, which served, as I have shown above, to reinforce to Spanish women that their main goals in life were marriage, children, and housework, including the art of cooking.

After receiving this cookbook, Mercedes excuses herself and retreats to her bedroom, where she sits on the bed with head in hands and cries. Although she never mentions the gift as the reason for her sadness, the symbolism of the text is clear. The history volume chosen for Antonio alludes to how potentially open and vast a man's world is; the cookbook represents the limitations of female existence in a world dominated by an ideology that defined women exclusively in terms of their domestic and maternal functions. The fact that, in its critical meditation between past and present, *Cuéntame* points to the rigid gender divide of the Franco regime through reference to one of the most important cookbooks of the time is suggestive of the ongoing impact of Francoist food discourse on Spain's cultural and social worlds. As Spaniards turn to cultural production as a way to work through different aspects of their traumatic past, the official gendering of food preparation as female is remembered for the way it seriously curtailed women's lives. The official women's cookbooks that were instrumental in the control of the female body remain present in the country's collective memory.

As these examples of present-day Spanish food culture and food discourse indicate, the food discourse looked at in this monograph – which I argue represents an important mode of control – continues to be relevant today as Spaniards create social and cultural identities for their post-dictatorship society. The codification of food culture during the regime did not cease to be relevant at the time of the Transition. From food texts producing a monolithic culinary code for Spain, to ones demanding women's servitude to men and exclusive dedication to domesticity, the contours of Francoist food discourse remain present in the Spain of today. Although some Spaniards reject the gendered and monolithic experience of Spanish food culture, for others continuity with the past and the notion of a unified cuisine offers stability in moments of change and constitutional crisis.

The theoretical underpinnings of this book allow us to see discourse as an important instrument of power that teaches people how they are meant to perform their everyday lives and subjectivities. The potency of food discourse can also be seen in claims about its apoliticism; food has long been, and still is, viewed as exempt from politics because of its association with everyday domesticity. Consequently, just as in the Franco regime disruptive food texts escaped censorship, in present-day Spain neo-Francoist restaurants remain open despite their affront to the country's historical memory laws. Despite this, as I mention above, political leaders from many national settings have come to understand that recipes or food discourse are often more influential in swaying popular opinion than political speeches or ratified documents.

That so many exceptions are made when it comes to what people eat and how they represent food culture makes it imperative, I believe, to continue researching and questioning the meaning and impact of food culture and food discourse. For it is only as we continue to uncover the multiple ways in which food discourse so significantly influences public opinion that people will be encouraged to be mindful about their discursive and visual representations of food culture. The rise of extreme nationalism and right-wing governments with authoritarian leanings means that now more than ever it is vital to gain insights into how and why authoritarianism takes hold.[4] Viewing food as connected to culture, ritual, and daily life allows us to better understand the impact of the authoritarian state on individual lives. For if food has the potential to unify people, in most cases it is used to generate nationalist sentiment and further intensify social divisions. Certainly, the restaurants paying homage to Francoism and fascism should be held to account for their aggressive recourse to the hegemonic food culture and food discourse of this period; menus celebrating Spain's fascist monolithic culinary code or the Republican defeat in the civil war can only worsen conflict in present-day Spain.

Food is political and linked to both individual and collective identity; it is also intensely personal in the way it is part of our quotidian life and, unlike other physical expressions of cultural specificity, is literally transformed and becomes part of the substance of the body. This deeply personal nature of food has meant that its political or collective nature is often ignored. In writing about the use of food discourse in authoritarian regimes as a potent political weapon, I have attempted to correct this view of food as somehow too connected to our everydayness to be relevant to the academy. For if food has the potential to function divisively, it can also bring people together. We can only hope, as we become more alert to its power, that food – both as a discursive entity and material object – is used as a force of good.

Notes

Introduction

1 In Paraguay, the dictator Alfredo Stroessner's modernization program had a direct impact on the Indigenous Guaraní peoples' foodways. Expelled from traditional lands or squeezed into increasingly smaller forested areas, Guaraní were forced to accept food and medication from the state in order to survive (Horst 132), thereby threatening their own culinary heritage. What role, however, did state-driven food instruction and food discourse play in the Gauraní's learning to eat differently, namely in a way that upheld modernization?

2 There has been a divide in food studies scholarship whereby one looks at food as material object or alternatively as discourse. The main arguments for looking at food as that which we ingest were made by Sidney Mintz, who in *Tasting Food, Tasting Freedom* decries the artificiality of such culinary constructs as national cuisines. Parkhurst Ferguson, on the other hand, makes compelling arguments for the importance of looking at discourse since it is, she writes, texts about French food that turned French cuisine not only into a national cuisine but one with world domination. I believe it is important that scholarship as a whole traverse this continuum between food as material object and food as discourse without setting up a hierarchy.

3 All translations were done by Dr Meribah Rose.

4 Catholicism was a key component, too, of the regime's vision for Spain. As Suzanne Dunai has shown, official cookbooks for women asserted the importance of religion in the Spanish family through recipes connected to different religious festivals and practices. Dunai's analysis of this feature of official food discourse is comprehensive, and so I do not focus on religion in my analysis of cookbooks commissioned by Sección Femenina (Women's Section). I add here to Dunai's analysis through my focus on the Francoist production of autarkic, gendered, and national subjectivities.

5 In articulating this aim I would like to acknowledge a special issue of the *Bulletin of Spanish Studies* (forthcoming), which I have been lucky enough to co-edit with Rebecca Ingram. Within this journal issue, titled "Transhispanic Food Cultural Studies," she and I delineate the emerging field of Hispanic cultural food studies, inserting Hispanist voices into the arena of food studies and making food central to a praxis of cultural studies in the transhispanic world.

6 In this monograph, I join a long line of scholars who argue that cookbooks should be read in terms of broader historical, cultural, economic, and political circumstances (see Driver, "Cookbooks"; Horandner; Mitchell; Nadeau). In her study of American food in the civil war era, Helen Zoe Veit discusses the importance of "reading cookbooks for history" (27). She writes that "people accustomed to thinking of cookbooks as a source of recipes, and not much else, can be surprised how much information cookbooks can reveal about the daily lives, social practices, class aspirations, and cultural assumptions of people in the past" (27).

7 Franco's preference, as Richards also explains, was for change not to take place; he "preferr[ed] to retain the 'purity' of the barbaric immediate post-war years" (14).

8 "Post-Thebussem" was a pseudonym adopted by Dionisio Pérez Gutiérrez.

9 In a similar fashion, David Williamson writes: "because of the strict censorship in Franco's Spain, the first analytical studies of the war and its causes were written abroad" (313).

10 Feminist scholars, such as Sara Evans, use the phrase "politicized domesticity" to discuss how women have found ways – within the metaphorical or literal space of the home – to contribute to political and wartime efforts, as well as social causes. This notion of politicized domesticity has been discussed in relation to a cookbook that women from the United States wrote as part of a broader effort to support Republican Spain during the civil war (see Moreno). However, as noted, the political potential of cookbooks was evidently overlooked by Spanish censors.

1 Food Discourse and the Production of Autarkic Subjectivities

1 Describing government efforts to increase the consumption of rice in Italy, Helstosky writes: "After its founding in 1928, the National Rice Board (*Ente Nazionale Risi*) worked tirelessly to bring rice to the people: special rice lorries brought free bags of rice and samples of risotto to Italians throughout the nation" (6). Mussolini's food propaganda and attempts to encourage rice consumption are inherently political, for they represent an important attempt to shape consumer behaviour as well as demarcate the borders of Italian cuisine.

2 This model of cookbook can also be traced back to Spain's first dictatorship. During that time, as I have shown elsewhere, the state commissioned the writing of a cookbook dedicated to orange consumption, *Naranjas: El arte de prepararlas y comerlas* (Oranges: The art of preparing and eating them; 1929, by Post-Thebussem), which contained both medical and culinary arguments for greater orange consumption (see L. Anderson, "A Recipe for a Modern Nation").

3 Another cookbook from the 1940s dedicated to rice and nutrition is *El arroz: Los 101 modos de condimentarlo* (101 ways to season rice). The author of this book used the pseudonym "Gedelp" for the nine food texts he penned, some of which dealt with nutrition and obesity. Given his interest in matters of health in his other texts, it is unsurprising that Gedelp begins this book with a discussion of the superior health benefits of rice consumption. He describes rice as "un elemento de primer orden, tanto por su valor nutritivo como por sus cualidades higiénicas, teniendo además la importante ventaja de ser uno de los más económicos" (an ingredient of the highest order, as much for its nutritional value as for its hygienic qualities, not to mention the important advantage of its being one of the most economic; 6).

4 Various cookbooks presenting rice alongside other ingredients were published at this time, such as Ricardo Ferrero's 1954 *La cocina para todos: Arroz y pasta italiana: Múltiples fórmulas para la preparación de platos desde el más sencillo o económico al más complicado y selecto* (Food for everyone: Rice and Italian pasta: Numerous ways to prepare dishes from the most simple or economic to the most elaborate and refined).

5 See chapter 3 of my *Cooking Up the Nation* in particular for a discussion of Muro's 1894 *El practicón: Tratado completo de cocina al alcance de todos y aprovechamiento de sobras* (The practice: A complete treatise on cooking within everyone's reach and the use of leftovers). A bestseller, this cookbook was republished thirty-five times, but Muro received a great deal of criticism for writing a cookbook that was all but a replica of French cuisine rather than representative of Spanish cuisine.

6 Hunger, according to scholars, features extensively in present-day memories of the civil war (see Butrón 38; Moreno, *De la página* 34). As Moreno writes: "Una parte importante del presente interés en la memoria histórica son estos recuerdos del hambre sufrido durante la Guerra Civil y los primeros diez años de la post-guerra" (A significant aspect of the current interest in historical memory are the memories of hunger endured during the civil war and the first ten years of the post-war era; *De la página* 34).

7 It is a Spanish tradition to eat twelve grapes on the stroke of midnight on New Year's Eve.

8 Darra Goldstein's research on hunger and starvation during the siege of Leningrad also points to this gendering of hunger: "Admittedly these

women had a physical advantage over men: their better-insulated bodies enabled them to endure greater privation, at least initially. But something else was at play, which had more to do with nurture than with nature" (1).

2 Beyond the Kitchen: Food Texts, Gender, and Compliance in Franco Spain

1 As Morcillo explains, "so that women could perform well as mothers and deliver healthy citizens for the new state, the government prevented them from entering the labor force" (33).

2 The SF placed an emphasis on modernising cooking and housework generally. In relation to cooking, this was primarily through the introduction of the metric system, as well as an emphasis on the science of nutrition.

3 Of interest also is the gender dimension of Finn's argument, given that he believes the primary consumers of "perfect recipes" to be women; hence his focus on "the popularity and meaning of such recipes in domestic households" (504). Finn believes such recipes to be so popular amongst housewives because they offer "an escape from the necessity and weight of having to make and accept responsibility for decisions" (505). Although aspirant chefs in professional kitchens must also follow instructions, he writes that the "meaning and political significance of the servility is dramatically different" (505).

4 The copyright for *Manual de cocina* has shifted several times: "La primera edición, de la Seccción Femenina, es de 1950. A partir de 1960 son depositarios de los derechos los herederos de la autora, imprimiéndose el manual bajo la firma editorial alemana, incluida en la red de comunicación de la FET y de las JONS" (The first edition, by the Women's Section, is from 1950. From 1960 the author's heirs hold the rights, printing the text under a German publisher included in the communication network of the FET and the JONS; "Prologue").

5 As a result of her family's position, the Marquesa had the opportunity from an early age "conoce[r] los mejores restuarantes" (to become familiar with the best restaurants) in both Spain and France, which is said to have ignited her interest in gastronomy, especially haute cuisine (see Garzón Sáez 26). As a result of frequenting such restaurants, over the years she established friendships with a number of important French and Spanish chefs of the time – including Henri-Paul Pellaprat, head of the Cordon Bleu cookery school in Paris, and Teodoro Bardají – "con los que intercambía conocimientos y sostiene correspondencia" (with whom she shared knowledge and exchanged correspondence; Garzón Sáez 26).

6 Carolyn Nadeau's first chapter to her *Food Matters* provides a fascinating account of the history and evolution of cookery manuals in early modern Spain. She writes that "most begin with a prologue, and conform to some internal organization and accepted structural norms" (3), pointing to the importance of prologues within the Spanish cookbook genre, and thereby underlining the significance of the absent prologue in SF cookbooks.
7 For an analysis of this trend, see Anderson and Benbow.
8 Albuquerque also shows a great deal of openness to other cultures in his descriptions of foreign dishes. About "los 'cakes' & 'puddings' ingleses" ("English 'cakes' and 'puddings'") he writes: "Hablemos ahora de dos dulces ingleses que por su excelencia, por su originalidad y su exquisitez se han hecho universales y han tomado también carta de naturaleza en nuestra Patria" (We will now talk about those English sweets that, thanks to their originality and exquisiteness, have become universal and have also taken up their place in our homeland; 214).

3 A Recipe for Spain

1 Some examples include the epistolary series *La mesa moderna* (The modern table, 1888) by Mariano Pardo de Figueroa (Dr Thebussem) and José de Castro y Serrano, Un Cocinero de su Majestad (His Majesty's chef); Ángel Muro's *Conferencias culinarias* (Culinary conferences; 1890); and Dionisio Pérez's *Guía del buen comer español* (Guide to good Spanish eating, 1929).
2 As I discuss in my *Cooking Up the Nation*, Pardo Bazán was the only female writer of the time to partake in textual debates about Spanish national identity. In her two cookbooks, *La cocina antigua* (Ancient cooking) and *La cocina moderna* (Modern cooking), she articulated boundaries for Spanish cuisine. The tensions in these cookbooks between Spanish traditions and French modernity reflected her approach to literary styles such as realism and naturalism. Her cookbooks, in spite of their association with the domestic realm, were therefore connected to the broader literary and nation-building projects with which she was associated.
3 Geographical research was supported, too, through the activities of the Institute of Geography Juan Sebastián Elcano. In his description of the "patriotic geographers of a unified Spain," Erik Swyngedouw writes that "geography played a pivotal role in creating and sustaining a patriotic vision of a unified Spain" (121).
4 Santiáñez-Tió saw Castile as the embodiment of Spain's essence and as an empire rather than simply another region.
5 The first gastronome to identify this dish as a national one was Post-Thebussem. The original version in Madrid is made, according to him,

from just oil, garlic, bread, and eggs. Yet once incorporated into other regional cuisines, the recipe changes: in Andalusia paprika and butter predominate, while in Segovia cumin seeds are added, and in coastal areas one can expect to find local fish and other seafood.

6 Started during the civil war by a group of intellectual Falangists, Editorial Nacional published some of the earliest pro-Franco propaganda and during the regime continued to "poner al servicio del estado, una literatura cultural y política" (put a cultural and political literature at the service of the state; Brown).

7 According to Ingram, locating and cataloguing the diversity of Spanish cuisine is a feature of Spain's first gastronomic map. However, she believes its creator, Ramón Gómez de la Serna, also makes light of the task on account of the poverty of certain parts of Spain ("Mapping and Mocking" 78).

8 The sharp division between a cookbook and a gastronomic text has, according to Steve Jones and Ben Taylor, gradually disappeared in food writing and food cultures There is, they argue, such a thing as gastronomic cookbooks: cookbooks that give practical instruction and also include the key traits of gastronomic literature, such as first-person narrative and anecdotes, and literary immersion in cultural history and historical texts.

9 Five years later, the SF commissioned the cookbook *Cocina regional española* (Spanish regional cuisine), which was a near replica of the earlier pedagogical food text. Although the publication date of *Cocina regional española* does not fall within the twenty-year span of this study, it is worth noting how similar it is in content to the original manual, especially in terms of the inferior and secondary role accorded to regional cuisines.

10 This discussion of the movement between culinary regionalism and culinary nationalism can, of course, be thought about in much wider terms, that is, with regard to the broader nation-building project. Many historians of nation building, as Afinoguénova tells us, view "region making as an inherent component of centralization" ("An Organic Nation" 748). Afinoguénova writes about this in relation to Spain's Krausista movement, which was concerned with both nation building and regional revival, and considered that "the diversity of regional arts and crafts significantly increased the nation's potential for unification, as more specialized cultural forms would produce more and more individualized regions that would need more robust connections" 753).

11 The pioneering discussions about the suitability of *cocido* as a national dish at the time of nation building in the nineteenth century also emphasized unity in diversity (see L. Anderson, "Unity and Diversity"). Spanish cuisine, according to this paradigm, is united by a common dish, yet the dish is also representative of regional difference.

12 Doménech's foreshadowing of the need to safeguard regional cuisines as separate entities brings to mind Vázquez Montalbán's statement at

the end of the dictatorship about needing to recover Catalan cuisine. Drawing parallels between the fate of the Catalan language and that of Catalan cuisine during the dictatorship, Vázquez Montalbán was highly critical of how little attention Catalans themselves gave to their cuisine, lamenting that the majority did not even realize that gastronomy was among the signs of Catalan identity destroyed during the dictatorship. He showed that Catalan cuisine had almost disappeared, drastically reduced to just a couple of dishes; his effort to revive Catalan food culture was, in his words, archaeological. Aware of the centrality of food culture to Catalan identity, Vázquez Montalbán convinced journalists and politicians to take part in the much-needed revival of Catalan gastronomy.

Conclusion

1 In her fascinating study of offal and the Franco regime, Dunai writes that state efforts to promote the consumption of offal did not affect consumer behaviour: "Although the Franco regime attempted to regulate the consumption of offal, sometimes incentivizing consumption and other times prohibiting it – Spaniards maintained many of their habitual patterns, demonstrating the limitations of the State and the spectrum of consensus and non-conformity that occurred in the food culture of the post-war period" ("Marginalized Meats?" 6).

2 Also writing about the reception method in relation to food texts is Rebekah Pite in her monograph on Doña Petrona and the gendering of Argentine food culture. She writes that informal conversations and formal interviews with present-day Argentines enabled her to compile stories, which are shaped by what "Argentines remember about this icon and the changing role of cooking and consumption in their own lives" (11).

3 These similarities between present-day centralist Spanish food discourse and Francoist food discourse certainly evince the point made by a number of scholars that centralist Spanish nationalism is alive and strong and requires further scholarly attention (see Epps). This is particularly important in an area like food discourse, which is not just ubiquitous but often mistakenly assumed to be apolitical.

4 According to the Human Rights Foundation, the citizens of ninety-three countries suffer at the hands of non-democratic regimes, with four billion people, or 53 percent of the world's population, living under authoritarian regimes. A global catastrophe, the resurgence of authoritarianism means there is once again significant debate about how and why non-democratic regimes take hold.

Works Cited

Abad, Vicente. "Naranjas y autarquía (1936–1960)." *La fruta dorada: La industria española del cítrico 1781–1995*, edited by Generalitat Valenciana, Conselleria de Cultura, Educación y Ciencia, 1996, 181–227.

Abad Alegría, Francisco, et al. *Líneas Maestras de la gastronomía y la culinaria españolas (siglo XX)*. Ediciones Trea, 2009.

ABC. "Contestación del Caudillo al discurso del alcalde." *Edición de la mañana*, 10 January 1942, p. 8.

– "Las fiestas de Navidad– La Nochevieja." *Edición de la mañana*, 2 January 1940, p. 25.

Acosta, Yanet. "Análisis del anuncio del cierre temporal de elBulli." *The Foodie Studies: Plataforma de formación on-line*, www.thefoodiestudies.com/analisis-del-anuncio-del-cierre-temporal-de-elbulli/?lang=en.

Afinoguénova, Eugenia. "An Organic Nation: State-Run Tourism, Regionalism, and Food in Spain, 1905–1931." *Journal of Modern History*, vol. 86, no. 4, 2014, pp. 743–79. doi: 10.1086/678951.

– "De la carta a la papeleta: El 'menú del día' entre la dictadura y la democracia en España, 1964–1981." *Bulletin of Spanish Studies*, forthcoming.

Alares López, Gustavo. "The Millennial of Castile (1943): The Historical Culture of Spanish Fascism." *European Review of History: Revue européenne d'histoire*, vol. 23, no. 4, 2016, pp. 707–23. doi: 10.1080/13507486.2016.1154930.

Albala, Ken. *Food in Early Modern Europe*. Greenwood, 2003.

Alberola, Miguel. "La ruta de la naranja." *El país seminal*, vol. 1, no. 364, 2002, pp. 95–7.

Alburquerque, Fernando. *La riqueza en la mano: Los dulces caseros*. 1st ed., Librería y Casa Editorial Hernando, 1950.

– *La riqueza en la mano: Los dulces caseros*. 2nd ed., Librería y Casa Editorial Hernando, 1959.

Almodóvar, Miguel Ángel. *El hambre en España: Una historia de la alimentación*. Oberon Editorial, 2003.

Alonso Duro, María Luisa. *La cocina casera*. Casa Hernando, 1952.
– "Página de cocina." *Blanco y Negro*. Editorial Católica, 1891–1988.
Alpuente, Moncho. "Tú en rojo ayer." *Mujeres de Azul*, edited by Ángeles González-Sinde et al., Ministerio de Cultura, 2009, pp. 55–110.
Álvarez Rey, Leandro. *Bajo el fuero militar: La dictadura de Primo de Rivera en sus documentos (1923–1930)*. Universidad de Sevilla, 2006.
Anderson, Lara. "A Recipe for a Modern Nation: Miguel Primo de Rivera and Spanish Food Culture." *Revista de Estudios Hispánicos*, vol. 52, no. 1, 2018, pp. 75–99.
– "A Recipe for Spain: *Un país para comérselo*'s Centralizing Promotion and Othering of Regional Cuisines." *Bulletin of Spanish Visual Studies*, vol. 1, no. 2, 2017, pp. 287–302. https://doi-org.ezp.lib.unimelb.edu.au/10.1080/24741604.2017.1338431.
– *Cooking Up the Nation: Spanish Culinary Texts and Culinary Nationalization in the Late-Nineteenth and Early Twentieth Century*. Tamesis, 2013.
– "The Unity and Diversity of *La Olla Podrida*: An Autochthonous Model of Spanish Culinary Nationalism." *Journal of Spanish Cultural Studies*, vol. 14, no. 4, 2013, pp. 400–414. http://dx.doi.org/10.1080/14636204.2013.916027.
Anderson, Lara, and Heather Benbow. "Christoph Meiners' History of the Female Sex (1788–1800): The Orientalisation of Spain and German Nationalism." *History of European Ideas*, vol. 35, no. 4, 2009, pp. 433–40. https://doi-org.ezp.lib.unimelb.edu.au/10.1016/j.histeuroideas.2009.07.001.
Anderson, Lara, and Rebecca Ingram, editors. "Transhispanic Food Cultural Studies: Defining the Subfield," special issue of *Bulletin of Spanish Studies*, 2019, forthcoming.
Anderson, Peter. "Madres, niños y hambre en la Madrid de posguerra." Paper presented at Historia y memoria del hambre bajo el franquismo (1939–1951) Conference, 7–8 June 2018, Granada.
Appadurai, Arjun. "How to Make a National Cuisine: Cookbooks in Contemporary India." *Comparative Studies in Society and History*, vol. 30, no. 1, 1998, pp. 3–24. doi: https://doi-org.ezp.lib.unimelb.edu.au/10.1017/S0010417500015024.
Arigita Mezquiriz, Pablo. *Cromos de cocina Waly*. Ediciones S.S, 1955.
Armendáriz Sanz, José Luis. *Gastronomía y nutrición*. Paraninfo, 2013.
Avieli, Nir. *Food and Power: A Culinary Ethnography of Israel*. University of California Press, 2017.
Ayora-Díaz, Steffan Igor. *Foodscapes, Foodfields, and Identities in the Yucatán*. Berghahn, 2012.
Bardají Mas, Teodoro. *La cocina de ellas*. Binéfar, 1955 (reprinted 2002, La Val de Onsera).
Barrachina, Marie-Aline. "Discurso médico y modelos de género: Pequeña historia de una vuelta atrás." *Mujeres y hombres en la España franquista:*

Sociedad, economía, política, cultura, edited by Gloria Nielfa Cristobál, Universidad Complutense, 2003, pp. 67–94.

Ben-Ami, Shlomo. *Fascism From Above: The Dictatorship of Primo de Rivera in Spain, 1923–1930*. Oxford University Press, 1983.

Bosch Bierge, Gonzalo. *Cocina regional española*. Hogar, 1940.

Brenan, Gerald. *The Face of Spain*. Octagon, 1976 [c. 1956].

Brinker-Gabler, Gisela, and Sidonie Smith, editors. *Writing New Identities: Gender, Nation, and Immigration in Contemporary Europe*. University of Minnesota Press, 1997.

Brown, Alex. "La sede de editora nacional, la literatura al servicio del estado (1939)." *El Madrid de Franco: Una ciudad cautiva (1939–1975)*, 30 June 2014, www.elmadriddefranco.wordpress.com/2014/06/30/la-sede-de-editora-nacional-la-literatura-al-servicio-del-estado-1939/.

Brydan, David. "'Starving Spain': International Humanitarian Responses to Hunger under the Franco Regime." *Proceedings of the Seminario Internacional "Historia y memoria del hambre bajo el franquismo (1939–1951),"* Departamento de historia contemporánea, University of Granada, 2018, pp. 145–59.

Camprubí, Lino. "One Grain, One Nation: Rice Genetics and the Corporate State in Early Francoist Spain (1939–1952)." *Historical Studies in the Natural Sciences*, vol. 40, no. 4, 2010, pp. 499–531. doi: 10.1525/hsns.2010.40.4.499.

Cancio Fernández, Raúl. *BOE, cine y franquismo*. Trant lo Blanch, 2011.

Capel, Horacio. "La geografía española tras la Guerra Civil." *Cuardernos críticos de geografía humana*, www.ub.edu/geocrit/geo1.htm.

Carbayo-Abengózar, Mercedes. "Shaping Women: National Identity through the Use of Language in Franco's Spain." *Nations and Nationalism*, vol. 7, no. 1, 2001, pp. 75–92.

Carr, Raymond. *Spain: A Modern History*. Oxford University Press, 2000.

Carr, Raymond, and Juan Pablo Fusi Aizpurúa. *Spain, Dictatorship to Democracy*. Allen & Unwin, 1981.

Carroll, Ruth. "Recipes for Laces: An Example of a Middle English Discourse Colony." *Discourse Perspectives on English: Medieval to Modern*, edited by Risto Hiltunen and Janne Skaffari, John Benjamins, 2003, pp. 137–66.

Casanova, Julián. "Disremembering Francoism: What Is at Stake in Spain's Memory Wars?" *Interrogating Francoism: History and Dictatorship in Twentieth-Century Spain*, edited by Helen Graham, translated by Linda Palfreeman and Helen Graham, Bloomsbury Academic, 2016, pp. 203–22.

Castillo, José Romera. "La Memoria Histórica de Algunas Mujeres Antifranquistas." *Anales de Literatura Española*, vol. 21, 2009. http://dx.doi.org/10.14198/ALEUA.2009.21.09.

Cayuela Sánchez, Salvador. *Por la grandeza de la patria: La biopolítica en la España de Franco (1939–1975)*. Fondo de Cultura Económica, 2014.

Chuse, Loren. *The Cantaoras: Music, Gender and Identity in Flamenco Song*. Routledge, 2003.

Colmeiro, José. "Peripheral Visions, Global Positions: Remapping Galician Culture." *Bulletin of Hispanic Studies*, vol. 86, no. 2, 2009, pp. 213–30.
Comisaría General de Abastecimientos y Transportes. *Alimentación nacional* (periodical). Comisaría General de Abastecimientos y Transportes, 1941–55.
– "Asuntos varios: Importacion de arroz: Federacion de industrials elaboradores de arroz." Archivo General de Administración. Caja CAT (11)7 63/08213.
Cooperativa Nacional del Arroz. *Libro de cocina: Fórmulas variadas para guisar el arroz*. Cooperativa Nacional, 1947.
Crespo-Fernández, Eliecer. *Sex in Language: Euphemistic and Dysphemistic Metaphors in Internet Forums*. Bloomsbury, 2015.
Cuarto poder. "Los menús de Franco en 1939." *Cuartopoder*, www.cuartopoder.es/espana/2014/03/31/los-menus-de-franco-en-1939/1071/.
Cuéntame cómo pasó. Miguel Ángel Bernardeau and Grupo Ganga Productions. RTVE, 2001–.
de Fontefrías, Luis. *Mapa gastronómico: Temas españoles, no. 33*. Publicaciones Españolas, 1953.
del Arco Blanco, Miguel Ángel. "Hunger and the Consolidation of the Francoist Regime (1939–1951)." *European History Quarterly*, vol. 40, no. 3, 2010, pp. 458–83. doi: https://doi-org.ezp.lib.unimelb.edu.au/10.1177/0265691410369744.
– "'Morir de hambre': Autarquía, escasez y enfermedad en la España del primer franquismo." *Pasado y Memoria: Revista de Historia Contemporánea*, vol. 5, 2006, pp. 241–58.
del Rincón García, María Fernanda. "Mujeres azules de la sección femenina: Formación, libros y bibliotecas para el adoctrinamiento político en España (1939–1945)." *MÉI: Métodos de información*, vol. 1, no. 1, 2010, pp. 59–81.
de Nola, Ruperto. *Libre del art de coch*. Maxtor, 2010.
de Torres y Higinio Paris Equilar, Manuel. *La naranja en la economía española*. Sindicato Nacional de Frutos, 1950.
de Trévis, Isabel. *La cocina regional*. Biblioteca – El Ama de Casa, 1959.
– *La cocina regional navarra, vasca y santanderina*. Biblioteca – El Ama de Casa, 1959.
di Febo, Giuliana. "'Nuevo Estado,' nacionalcatolicismo y género." *Mujeres y Hombres en la España franquista: Sociedad, economía, política, cultura*, edited by Gloria Nielfa Cristóbal, Universidad Complutense, 2003, pp. 19–44.
Doménech, Ignacio. *Claudina sabe guisar: Platos fáciles*. Quintilla & Cardona, 1939.
– *Cocina de recursos (Deseo mi comida)*. Ediciones Trea, 1941.
– *La Teca: La veritable cuina casolana de Catalunya*. Quintilla & Cardona, 1924.
– *Marichu: La mejor cocinera española o todos los platos del día*. Quintilla & Cardona, 1915.
– *Mi plato: Cocina regional: Nuevo manual de cocina familiar muy interesante para las amas de casa*. Quintilla & Cardona, 1942.

Dowling, Andrew. "Accounting for the Turn towards Secession in Catalonia." *International Journal of Iberian Studies*, vol. 27, no. 2, 2014, pp. 219–34. doi: 10.1386/ijis.27.2-3.219_1.

Driver, Elizabeth. "Cookbooks as Primary Sources for Writing History." *Food, Culture & Society*, vol. 12, no. 3, 2009, pp. 257–74. doi: 10.2752/175174409X431987.

Dunai, Suzanne. *Cooking for the Patria: The Sección Femenina and the Politics of Food and Women during the Franco Years.* 2012. University of New Mexico, master's thesis.

– "Marginalized Meats? Contextualizing Offal Consumption in 1940s Spain." Paper presented at Oxford Symposium on Food and Cookery, 2016.

Durón Muniz, Virginia M. *Aproximación a la revista* TERESA *(1954–1975).* 2016. Universidad de Sevilla, master's thesis.

Eaude, Michael. *Catalonia: A Cultural History*. Oxford University Press, 2008.

Elias, Megan J. *Food on the Page: Cookbooks and American Culture.* University of Pennsylvania Press, 2017.

El plural. "IU denuncia a un bar que ofrece 'bacalao grande y libre' o 'huevos rotos fusilados,'" www.elplural.com/sociedad/iu-denuncia-a-un-bar-que-ofrece-bacalao-grande-y-libre-o-huevos-rotos-fusilados_105282102.

– "Ruta por los bares franquistas que incumplen la Ley de Memoria Histórica," www.elplural.com/politica/espana/ruta-por-los-bares-franquistas-que-incumplen-la-ley-de-memoria-historica_98174102.

Encarnación, Omar. *Democracy without Justice in Spain: The Politics of Forgetting.* University of Pennsylvania Press, 2014.

Enders, Victoria L. "Nationalism and Feminism: The Sección Femenina of the Falange." *History of European Ideas*, vol. 15, nos. 4–6, 1992, pp. 673–80. https://doi-org.ezp.lib.unimelb.edu.au/10.1016/0191-6599(92)90077-P.

Epps, Bradley. "To Be (a Part) of a Whole: Constitutional Patriotism and the Paradox of Democracy in the Wake of the Spanish Constitution of 1978." *Revista de Estudios Hispánicos*, vol. 44, 2010, pp. 544–68.

Evans, Sara. *Tidal Wave: How Women Changed America at Century's End.* Free Press, 2003.

Favoretto, Mara, and Lara Anderson. "La Historia impuesta y la ficcionalización de la Historia: Estudio comparativo de dos obras publicadas bajo censura en la España de Franco y la Argentina del Proceso." *Letr@s Hispanas*, vol. 6, no. 2, 2009, n.p.

Ferrer Calbeto, Felipe. *Nacionalismo en lo economico ¿simple autosuficiencia o plena autarquia? Libertad y poder nacionales.* Jefatura Provincial de Propaganda, 1940.

Finn, John E. "The Perfect Recipe: Taste and Tyranny, Cooks and Citizens." *Food, Culture & Society*, vol. 14, no. 4, 2011, pp. 503–24. https://doi-org.ezp.lib.unimelb.edu.au/10.2752/175174411X13088262162677.

Floyd, Janet, and Laurel Forster. "The Recipe in Its Cultural Contexts." *The Recipe Reader: Narratives, Contexts, Traditions*, edited by Janet Floyd and Laurel Forster, University of Nebraska Press, 2010, pp. 1–11.

Foucault, Michel. *The Birth of Biopolitics: Lectures at the Collège de France (1978–1979)*. Edited by Michel Senellart, translated by Graham Burchell, Palgrave Macmillan, 2008.

– "The Subject and Power." *Critical Inquiry*, vol. 8, no. 4, 1982, pp. 777–95.

García Álvarez, Jacobo. *Provincias, regiones y comunidades autónomas: La formación del mapa político de España*. Secretaría General del Senado, Departamento de Publicaciones, 2002.

García Viñolas, Manuel Augusto. *Prisioneros de Guerra*. Departamento Nacional de Cinematografía, 1938, www.youtu.be/EA0WgoKWe3I.

Gardiner, Michael. "Everyday Utopianism: Lefebvre and His Critics." *Cultural Studies*, vol. 18, nos. 2–3, 2004, pp. 228–54. doi: 10.1080/0950238042000203048.

Garrido López, Carlos. "El regionalismo 'funcional' del régimen de Franco." *Revista de Estudios Politicos*, vol. 115, 2002, pp. 111–27.

Garzón Sáez, José. "125 Aniversario de su nacimiento: Nuestra Marquesa de Parabere." *Bilbao*, January 2003, 26–7, www.bilbao.eus/bld/bitstream/handle/123456789/36008/26-27.pdf.

Gedelp. *El arroz: Los 101 modos de condimentarlo*. Ediciones Aspas, 1940.

Generalitat Valenciana, editor. *La fruta dorada: La industria española del cítrico 1781–1995*. Conselleria de Cultura, Educación y Ciencia, 1996.

Gibson, Kristina E., and Sarah E. Dempsey. "Make Good Choices, Kid: Biopolitics of Children's Bodies and School Lunch Reform in Jaimie Oliver's *Food Revolution*." *Children's Geographies*, vol. 13, no. 1, 2014, pp. 44–58. doi: 10.1080/14733285.2013.827875.

Gil, Fátima. "Exemplary Women: The Use of Film and Censorship as a Means of Moral Indoctrination during the Franco Dictatorship in Spain." *Journal of Popular Culture*, vol. 49, no. 4, 2016, pp. 856–74.

Goldstein, Darra. "Women under Siege: Leningrad 1941–1942." *From Betty Crocker to Feminist Food Studies: Critical Perspectives on Women and Food*, edited by Barbara Haber and Arlene Avakian, University of Massachusetts Press, 2005.

Goodman, Michael K., Josée Johnston, and Kate Cairns. "Food, Media and Space: The Mediated Biopolitics of Eating." *Geoforum*, vol. 84, 2017, pp. 161–8.

Graham, Helen. "'Against the State': A Genealogy of the Barcelona May Days (1937)." *European History Quarterly*, vol. 29, no. 4, 1999, pp. 485–90. https://doi-org.ezp.lib.unimelb.edu.au/10.1177/a010099.

– editor. *Interrogating Francoism: History and Dictatorship in Twentieth-Century Spain*. Bloomsbury, 2016.

Großmann, Johannes. "'Baroque Spain' As Metaphor: Hispanidad, Europeanism and Cold War Anti-Communism in Francoist Spain." *Bulletin of Spanish Studies*, vol. 91, no. 5, 2014, pp. 755–71. doi: 10.1080/14753820.2014.909144.

Helstosky, Carol. "Fascist Food Politics: Mussolini's Policy of Alimentary Sovereignty." *Journal of Modern Italian Studies*, vol. 9, no. 1, 2004, pp. 1–26. https://doi-org.ezp.lib.unimelb.edu.au/10.1080/1354571042000179164.

Herrera, A. *Manual de cocina (Recetario de la Sección Femenina)*. Delegación Nacional de la Sección Femenina de FET y de las JONS, 1950.

– *Manual de cocina (Recetario)*. 7th ed. Sección Femenina de FET y de las JONS, 1957.

– *Recetario para olla a presión y batidora eléctrica*. Delegación Nacional de la Sección Femenina de FET y de las JONS, 1961 [1958].

Herrero, Isabelo. *Libro de cocina de la República*. Reino de Cordelia, 2011.

Hiroko, Takeda. "Delicious Food in a Beautiful Country: Nationhood and Nationalism in Discourses on Food in Contemporary Japan." *Studies in Ethnicity and Nationalism*, vol. 8, no. 1, 2008, pp. 5–30.

Hola. "Cocina tradicional española para un banquete histórico." 22 May 2004, www.bodasreales.hola.com/principe-felipe-letizia-ortiz/noticias/20040522768/boda/principe/letizia/menu/.

Holguín, Sandie. "How Did the Spanish Civil War End? … Not So Well." *American Historical Review*, vol. 120, no. 5, 2015, pp. 1767–83.

Horandner, Edith. "The Recipe Book as a Cultural and Socio-historical Document: On the Value of Manuscript Recipe Books as Sources." *Food in Perspective: Proceedings of the Third International Conference on Ethnological Food Research*, edited by A. Fenton and T.M. Owen, John Donald Publishing, 1981.

Horst, René Harder. *The Stroessner Regime and Indigenous Resistance in Paraguay*. University Press of Florida, 2007.

Human Rights Foundation. *Geographic Reports on Authoritarianism Worldwide*, www.hrf.org/research/political-regime-map/. Accessed 18 October 2019.

Humlebaek, Carsten. *Spain: Inventing the Nation*. Bloomsbury, 2015.

Iglesias, Iván. "Performing the Anti-Spanish Body: Jazz and Biopolitics in the Early Franco Regime (1939–1957)." *Jazz and Totalitarianism*, edited by Bruce Johnson, Pedro Cravinho, and Heli Reimann, Routledge, 2017, pp. 157–73.

Imágenes, Revista Cinematográfica. *El Arroz y la Paella. No-Do*, 1 January 1955.

– *La Naranja y su Riqueza. No-Do*, 1 January 1951.

Ingram, Rebecca. "Mapping and Mocking: Spanish Cuisine and Ramón Gómez de la Serna's 'El primer mapa gastronómico de España.'" *Cincinnati Romance Review*, vol. 33, 2012, pp. 78–97.

– *Spain on the Table: Cookbooks, Women, and Modernization, 1905–1933*. 2009. Duke University, PhD dissertation.

Instituto Nacional de Estadística. *Producción de arroz, por provincias: Anuario 1932–1933.* www.ine.es/inebaseweb/pdfDispacher.do?td=94989.
– *Producción de arroz, por provincias: Anuario 1934.* www.ine.es/inebaseweb/pdfDispacher.do?td=102985.
– *Arroz: Anuario 1943.* www.ine.es/inebaseweb/pdfDispacher.do?td=161286.
– *Arroz: Anuario 1944–1945.* www.ine.es/inebaseweb/pdfDispacher.do?td=161705.
– *Arroz: Anuario 1946–1947. www.ine.es/inebaseweb/pdfDispacher.do?td=162818.*
– *Arroz: Anuario 1948.* www.ine.es/inebaseweb/pdfDispacher.do?td=164075.
– *Arroz: Anuario 1950.* www.ine.es/inebaseweb/pdfDispacher.do?td=30234.
– *Arroz: Anuario 1954.* www.ine.es/inebaseweb/pdfDispacher.do?td=103880.

Jiménez Aguilar, Francisco. "Auxilio Social en Granada (1937–1951): Un enfoque biopolítico." *Proceedings of the Seminario Internacional "Historia y memoria del hambre bajo el franquismo (1939–1951),"* Departamento de historia contemporánea, University of Granada, 2018, pp. 174–90.

Jones, Steve, and Ben Taylor. "Food Writing and Food Cultures: The Case of Elizabeth Driver and Jane Grigson." *European Journal of Cultural Studies,* vol. 4, no. 2, 2012, pp. 171–88.

Kebadze, Nino. *Romance and Exemplarity in Post-War Spanish Women's Narratives.* Tamesis, 2009.

La Marquesa de Parabere. *Historia de la gastronomía.* Espasa-Calpe, 1943.
– *La cocina completa.* Espasa, 1933.

Laudo, Xavier, and Conrad Vilanou. "Educational Discourse in Spain during the Early Franco Regime (1936–1943): Toward a Genealogy of Doctrine and Concepts." *Paedagogica Historica,* vol. 51, no. 4, 2015, pp. 434–54. http://dx.doi.org/10.1080/00309230.2015.1046889.

Lavedán, A. *Lecciones de la cocina regional: Escuela de Magisterio.* Sección Femenina de FET y de la JONS, 1958.

Lefebvre, Henri. *Critique of Everyday Life.* Translated by John Moore, Verso, 1991.

León, Alberto. *La cocina clásica española.* Editorial Estudio, 1930.

Leonardi, Susan J. "Recipes for Reading: Summer Pasta, Lobster à la Riseholme, and Key Lime Pie." *PMLA,* vol. 104, no. 3, 1989, pp. 340–7. doi: 10.2307/462443

Linz, Juan. *Totalitarian and Authoritarian Regimes.* Rienner, 2000.

Mahamud, Kira. "Emotional Indoctrination through Sentimental Narrative in Spanish Primary Education Textbooks during the Franco Dictatorship (1939–1959)." *History of Education,* vol. 45, no. 5, 2016, pp. 653–78. http://dx.doi.org/10.1080/0046760X.2015.1101168.

Martínez Cantera, Ángel. "This Restaurant Is Nostalgic for Fascist Spain: Do You Miss General Franco? Then Head to Casa Pepe." *Vice,* 14 August 2014, www.vice.com/en_uk/article/7bapdy/casa-pepe-restaurant-franco-dictatorship-nostaligia-375.

Martínez Llopis, Manuel. *Historia de la gastronomía española*. La Val de Onsera, 1995.

Matos-Martín, Eduardo. "Thinking Biopolitics: Reflections on Franco's Dictatorship through Contemporary Fiction." 2010. University of Michigan, PhD dissertation.

Mayes, C. *The Biopolitics of Lifestyle: Foucault, Ethics and Healthy Choices*. Routledge, 2016.

McDougall, Elizabeth J. "Voices, Stories, and Recipes in Selected Canadian Community Cookbooks." *Recipes for Reading: Community Cookbooks, Stories, Histories*, edited by Anne L. Bower, University of Massachusetts Press, 1997, pp. 105–17.

McLean, Alice L. *Aesthetic Pleasure in 20th Century Women's Food Writing: The Innovative Appetites of M.F.K. Fisher, Alice B Toklas, and Elizabeth David*. Routledge, 2012.

Medina, F. Xavier. *Food Culture in Spain*. Greenwood, 2005.

Meisler, Stanley. "Spain's New Democracy." *Foreign Affairs*, vol. 56, no. 1, 1977, pp. 190–208.

Mennell, Stephen. *All Manners of Food: Eating and Taste in England and France from the Middle Ages to the Present*. 2nd ed., University of Illinois Press, 1996.

Merino, Raquel, and Rosa Rabadán. "Censored Translations in Franco's Spain: The TRACE Project – Theatre and Fiction (English-Spanish)." *TTR: Traduction, Terminologie, Rédaction*, vol. 15, no. 2, 2002, pp. 125–52.

Mintz, Sidney. *Tasting Food, Tasting Freedom: Excursions into Eating, Power, and the Past*. Beacon, 1997.

Mitchell, Janet. "Cookbooks as a Social and Historical Document: A Scottish Case Study." *Food Service Technology*, vol. 1, no. 1, 2008, pp. 13–23.

Muñoz Ruiz, María del Carmen. "Las revistas para mujeres durante el franquismo: Difusión de modelos de comportamiento femenino." *Mujeres y hombres en la España franquista: Sociedad, economía, política, cultura*, edited by Gloria Nielfa Cristobál, Universidad Complutense, 2003, pp. 95–116.

Morcillo, Aurora. *True Catholic Womanhood: Gender Ideology in Franco's Spain*. Northern Illinois University Press, 2000.

Moreno, María Paz. *De la página al plato: El libro de cocina en España*. Ediciones Trea, 2012.

Muro, Ángel. *Conferencias culinarias*. Imprenta de Fortanet, 1890.

Lebesco, Kathleen, and Peter Naccarato, editors. *The Bloomsbury Handbook of Food and Popular Culture*. Bloomsbury Academic, 2018.

Nadeau, Carolyn. *Food Matters: Alonso Quijano's Diet and the Discourse of Food in Early Modern Spain*. University of Toronto Press, 2016.

Negre, Javier G. "Catering de Mallorca y cava catalán en la proclamación real." *El Mundo*, 18 June 2014, www.elmundo.es/loc/2014/06/18/53a06b792 68e3e705a8b4585.html.

Neuhaus, Jessamyn. *Manly Meals and Mom's Home Cooking: Cookbooks and Gender in Modern America*. Johns Hopkins University Press, 2003.

Núñez, Xosé-Manoel, and Maiken Umbach. "Hijacked Heimats: National Appropriations of Local and Regional Identities in Germany and Spain, 1930–1945." *European Review of History*, vol. 15, no. 3, 2008, pp. 295–316. https://doi-org.ezp.lib.unimelb.edu.au/10.1080/13507480802082615.

Núñez Puente, Sonia. "The Romance Novel and Popular Culture during the Early Franco Regime in Spain: Towards the Construction of Other Discourses of Femininity." *Journal of Gender Studies*, vol. 17, no. 3, 2008, pp. 225–36. doi: 10.1080/09589230802204258.

Ofer, Inbal. *Señoritas in Blue: The Making of a Female Political Elite in Franco's Spain– The National Leadership of the Sección Femenina de La Falange (1936–1977)*. Sussex Academic, 2009.

– "*Teresa*, ¿revista para todas las mujeres? Género, clase y espacios de la vida cotidiana en el discurso de la Sección Femenina (1960–1970)." *Historia y política: Ideas, procesos y movimientos sociales*, vol. 37, 2017, pp. 121–46.

Ortiz, Carmen. "The Uses of Folklore by the Franco Regime." *Journal of American Folklore*, vol. 112, no. 446, 1999, pp. 479–96. http://search.proquest.com.ezp.lib.unimelb.edu.au/docview/198449968?accountid=12372.

Pardo Bazán, Emilia. *La cocina española antigua y moderna*. Edited and introduced by Mariana Domecq, R & B, 1996.

Parkhurst Ferguson, Priscilla. *Accounting for Taste: The Triumph of French Cuisine*. University of Chicago Press, 2004.

– *Word of Mouth: What We Talk about When We Talk about Food*. University of California Press, 2014.

Pavlović, Tatjana. *Despotic Bodies and Transgressive Bodies: Spanish Culture from Francisco Franco to Jesús Franco*. State University of New York Press, 2003.

Perdiguero Gil, Enrique, and Ramón Castejón Bolea. "Popularising Right Food and Feeding Practices in Spain (1847–1950): The Handbooks of Domestic Economy." *Dynamis*, vol. 30, 2010, pp. 141–65.

Pérez, A. Graciana, et al. *Consumo de Alimentos en España en el period 1940–1988: Una estimacion a partir de hojas de balance alimentario*. UAM Ediciones, 1996.

Pérez-Olivares, Alejandro. "Madrid, capital del hambre: (Des)orden público y control de los recursos en la posquerra franquista (1939–1948)." *Proceedings of the Seminario Internacional "Historia y memoria del hambre bajo el franquismo (1939–1951),"* Departamento de historia contemporánea, University of Granada, 2018, pp. 160–73.

Pinto, Derrin. "Indoctrinating the Youth of Post-War Spain: A Discourse Analysis of a Fascist Civics Textbook." *Discourse & Society*, vol. 15, no. 5, 2004, pp. 649–67. doi: 10.1177/0957926504045036.

– "Education and Etiquette: Behaviour Formation in Fascist Spain." *Analysing Fascist Discourse: European Fascism in Talk and Text*, edited by Ruth Wodak and John Richardson, New York, 2013, pp. 122–45.

Pite, Rebekah E. *Creating a Common Table in Twentieth-Century Argentina: Dona Petrona, Women, and Food.* University of North Carolina Press, 2013.

Podesan, Asunta. *El Arroz: Como base de alimentación.* Vicente Cortell, 1959.

Post-Thebussem [Dionisio Pérez Gutiérrez]. *Guía del buen comer español: Inventario y loa de la cocina clásica de España y de sus regiones.* Suces. de Rivadeneyra, 1929.

– *Naranjas: El arte de prepararlas y comerlas.* Unión Nacional de Exportación Agrícola, 1930.

Preston, Paul. *The Spanish Civil War: Reaction, Revolution, and Revenge.* W.W. Norton, 2007.

Real Academia de la Historia. *Ignacio Doménech y Puigcercós,*www.dbe.rah.es/biografias/97242/ignacio-domenech-y-puigcercos.

Richards, Michael. *A Time of Silence.* Cambridge University Press, 1998.

Richmond, Kathleen. *Women and Spanish Fascism: The Women's Section of the Falange, 1934–1959.* Routledge, 2003.

Rodríguez-Roda, Francisco Ramón. Una cosecha de arroz: Ilustraciones especiales de Genaro Lahuerta y Pedro de Valencia. FSAAE, 1940.

Rombauer, Irma S. *The Joy of Cooking.* Bobbs-Merrill, 1931.

Roser i Puig, Montserrat. "What's Cooking in Catalonia?" *A Companion to Catalan Culture,* edited by Dominic Keown, Tamesis, 2011, pp. 229–52.

RTVE. *Funciones encomendades a la Corporación RTVE,* www.rtve.es/rtve/20160926/funciones-encomendadas-corporacion-rtve/1413065.shtml.

Salcedo, Ernesto. *Entrevista del periodista Ernesto Salcedo a Luís Antonio de Vega en 1957,* www.apiciusysuslibros.blogspot.com/2010/05/entrevista-del-periodista-ernesto.html.

Salcedo de Uriol, María de la Paz. *La futura ama de casa.* Libería y Editorial Rivadenevra, 1924 (repr. 1958).

Sánchez Erauskin, Javier. *El nudo corredizo: Euskal Herria bajo el primer franquismo.* Editorial Txalaparta, 1994.

Sandoval Amorós, José. *Comed naranjas: La naranja, alimento, la naranja, medicamiento.* Reus, 1953.

Santiáñez-Tió, Nil. *Topographies of Fascism: Habitus, Space, and Writing in Twentieth-Century Spain.* University of Toronto Press, 2013.

Saraiva, Tiago. *Fascist Pigs: Technoscientific Organisms and the History of Fascism.* MIT Press, 2016.

Sarrau, José. *Ciencia gastronómica: Libro de texto para el profesorado de los Institutos Nacionales Femeninos y de las escuelas del Hogar de la Sección Femenina.* 1st ed., Delegación Nacional de la Sección Femenina de FET y de las JONS, 1942.

– *Mi recetario de cocina.* Ediciones Sarrau, 1957.

– *Nuestra cocina al uso de familias.* Peña, 1946.

Shepler, Susan. "The Real and Symbolic Importance of Food in War: Hunger Pains and Big Men's Bellies in Sierra Leone." *Africa Today*, vol. 58, no. 2, 2011, pp. 43–56.

Sieburth, Stephanie. *Survival Songs: Conchita Piquer's Coplas & Franco's Regime of Terror*. University of Toronto Press, 2014.

Siegel, Nancy. "Cooking Up American Politics." *Gastronomica: The Journal of Critical Food Studies*, vol. 8, no. 3, 2008, pp. 53–61. doi:10.1525/gfc.2008.8.3.53.

Simón Palmer, María del Carmen. *Bibliografía de la gastronomía y alimentación en España*. Ediciones Trea, 2003.

Sinova, Justino. *La censura durante el franquismo*. De Bolsillo, 2006.

Skerrett, Delaney Michael. "Language & Authoritarianism in the 20th Century: The Cases of Estonia and Catalonia." *Eesti Rakenduslingvistika Ühingu Aastaraamat*, vol. 6, no. 6, 2010, pp. 261–76. doi: 10.5128/ERYa6.16.

Spang, Rebecca. *The Invention of the Restaurant: Paris and Modern Gastronomic Culture*. Harvard University Press, 2000.

Swyngedouw, Erik. *Liquid Power: Contested Hydro-Modernities in Twentieth-Century Spain*. MIT Press, 2015.

Thebussem, Dr. *La mesa moderna: Cartas sobre el comedor y la cocina cambiadas entre el doctor Thebussem y un cocinero de S.M.* Librerías de Fernando FE, 1888.

Thomasen, Einar, editor. *Canon and Canonicity: The Formation and Use of Scripture*. Museum Tusculanum Press, 2009.

Tomlinson, Graham. "Thought for Food: A Study of Written Instructions." *Symbolic Interaction*, vol. 9, no. 2, 1986, pp. 201–16.

Tortella, Gabriel, and Stefan Houpt. "Autarky to the European Union: Nationalist Economic Policies in 20th Century Spain." *Economic Change and the National Question in Twentieth-Century Europe*, edited by Alice Teichova et al., Cambridge University Press, 2000, pp. 127–49.

Unjubilado. *Manjares de la posguerra*, www.unjubilado.info/2006/08/29/posguerra-ii/.

Un país para comérselo. TVE and Grupo Ganga Producciones. TVE, 2010–13.

Valis, Noël. *The Culture of Cursilería: Bad Taste, Kitsch, and Class in Modern Spain*. Duke University Press, 2003.

Vázquez Montalbán, Manuel. *Contra los gourmets*. Barcelona: Mondadori, 2000.

Veit, Helen Zoe. *Food in the Civil War Era: The North*. Michigan State University Press, 2015.

Vester, Katharina. *A Taste of Power: Food and American Identities*. University of California Press, 2015.

Weiss Adamson, Melitta. *Food in Medieval Times*. Greenwood, 2004.

Williamson, David G. *The Age of Dictators: A Study of the European Dictatorships, 1918–53*. Routledge, 2007.

Wodak, Ruth, and John Richardson, editors. *Analysing Fascist Discourse: European Fascism in Talk and Text*. Routledge, 2013.

Wright, Eleanor. *The Poetry of Protest under Franco*. Tamesis, 1986.

Index

TORONTO IBERIC

1 Anthony J. Cascardi, *Cervantes, Literature, and the Discourse of Politics*
2 Jessica A. Boon, *The Mystical Science of the Soul: Medieval Cognition in Bernardino de Laredo's Recollection Method*
3 Susan Byrne, *Law and History in Cervantes'* Don Quixote
4 Mary E. Barnard and Frederick A. de Armas (eds), *Objects of Culture in the Literature of Imperial Spain*
5 Nil Santiáñez, *Topographies of Fascism: Habitus, Space, and Writing in Twentieth-Century Spain*
6 Nelson Orringer, *Lorca in Tune with Falla: Literary and Musical Interludes*
7 Ana M. Gómez-Bravo, *Textual Agency: Writing Culture and Social Networks in Fifteenth-Century Spain*
8 Javier Irigoyen-García, *The Spanish Arcadia: Sheep Herding, Pastoral Discourse, and Ethnicity in Early Modern Spain*
9 Stephanie Sieburth, *Survival Songs: Conchita Piquer's Coplas and Franco's Regime of Terror*
10 Christine Arkinstall, *Spanish Female Writers and the Freethinking Press, 1879–1926*
11 Margaret Boyle, *Unruly Women: Performance, Penitence, and Punishment in Early Modern Spain*
12 Evelina Gužauskytć, *Christopher Columbus's Naming in the diarios of the Four Voyages (1492–1504): A Discourse of Negotiation*
13 Mary E. Barnard, *Garcilaso de la Vega and the Material Culture of Renaissance Europe*
14 William Viestenz, *By the Grace of God: Francoist Spain and the Sacred Roots of Political Imagination*
15 Michael Scham, Lector Ludens: *The Representation of Games and Play in Cervantes*
16 Stephen Rupp, *Heroic Forms: Cervantes and the Literature of War*
17 Enrique Fernandez, *Anxieties of Interiority and Dissection in Early Modern Spain*

18 Susan Byrne, *Ficino in Spain*
19 Patricia M. Keller, *Ghostly Landscapes: Film, Photography, and the Aesthetics of Haunting in Contemporary Spanish Culture*
20 Carolyn A. Nadeau, *Food Matters: Alonso Quijano's Diet and the Discourse of Food in Early Modern Spain*
21 Cristian Berco, *From Body to Community: Venereal Disease and Society in Baroque Spain*
22 Elizabeth R. Wright, *The Epic of Juan Latino: Dilemmas of Race and Religion in Renaissance Spain*
23 Ryan D. Giles, *Inscribed Power: Amulets and Magic in Early Spanish Literature*
24 Jorge Pérez, *Confessional Cinema: Religion, Film, and Modernity in Spain's Development Years, 1960–1975*
25 Joan Ramon Resina, *Josep Pla: Seeing the World in the Form of Articles*
26 Javier Irigoyen-García, *"Moors Dressed as Moors": Clothing, Social Distinction, and Ethnicity in Early Modern Iberia*
27 Jean Dangler, *Edging toward Iberia*
28 Ryan D. Giles and Steven Wagschal (eds), *Beyond Sight: Engaging the Senses in Iberian Literatures and Cultures, 1200–1750*
29 Silvia Bermúdez, *Rocking the Boat: Migration and Race in Contemporary Spanish Music*
30 Hilaire Kallendorf, *Ambiguous Antidotes: Virtue as Vaccine for Vice in Early Modern Spain*
31 Leslie Harkema, *Spanish Modernism and the Poetics of Youth: From Miguel de Unamuno to La Joven Literatura*
32 Benjamin Fraser, *Cognitive Disability Aesthetics: Visual Culture, Disability Representations, and the (In)Visibility of Cognitive Difference*
33 Robert Patrick Newcomb, *Iberianism and Crisis: Spain and Portugal at the Turn of the Twentieth Century*
34 Sara J. Brenneis, *Spaniards in Mauthausen: Representations of a Nazi Concentration Camp, 1940–2015*
35 Silvia Bermúdez and Roberta Johnson (eds), *A New History of Iberian Feminisms*
36 Steven Wagschal, *Minding Animals in the Old and New Worlds: A Cognitive Historical Analysis*
37 Heather Bamford, *Cultures of the Fragment: Uses of the Iberian Manuscript, 1100–1600*
38 Enrique García Santo-Tomás (ed), *Science on Stage in Early Modern Spain*
39 Marina Brownlee (ed), *Cervantes' Persiles and the Travails of Romance*
40 Sarah Thomas, *Inhabiting the In-Between: Childhood and Cinema in Spain's Long Transition*

41 David A. Wacks, *Medieval Iberian Crusade Fiction and the Mediterranean World*
42 Rosilie Hernández, *Immaculate Conceptions: The Power of the Religious Imagination in Early Modern Spain*
43 Mary Coffey and Margot Versteeg (eds), *Imagined Truths: Realism in Modern Spanish Literature and Culture*
44 Diana Aramburu, *Resisting Invisibility: Detecting the Female Body in Spanish Crime Fiction*
45 Samuel Amago and Matthew J. Marr (eds), *Consequential Art: Comics Culture in Contemporary Spain*
46 Richard P. Kinkade, *Dawn of a Dynasty: The Life and Times of Infante Manuel of Castile*
47 Jill Robbins, *Poetry and Crisis: Cultural Politics and Citizenship in the Wake of the Madrid Bombings*
48 Ana María Laguna and John Beusterien (eds), *Goodbye Eros: Recasting Forms and Norms of Love in the Age of Cervantes*
49 Sara J. Brenneis and Gina Herrmann (eds), *Spain, World War II, and the Holocaust: History and Representation*
50 Francisco Fernández de Alba, *Sex, Drugs, and Fashion in 1970s Madrid*
51 Daniel Aguirre-Oteiza, *This Ghostly Poetry: Reading Spanish Republican Exiles between Literary History and Poetic Memory*
52 Lara Anderson, *Control and Resistance: Food Discourse in Franco Spain*